PROVINCIAL POLICY LABORATORIES

Policy Diffusion and Transfer in Canada's Federal System

Edited by Brendan Boyd and Andrea Olive

Canada's federal system, composed of ten provincial governments and three territories, all with varying economies and political cultures, is often blamed for the country's failure to develop coordinated policy responses to key issues. But in other federal and multi-level governance systems, the ability of multiple governments to test a variety of policy responses has been lauded as an effective way to build local and national policy.

Despite high-profile examples of policy diffusion in Canada, there has been surprisingly little academic study of policy learning and diffusion among provinces. Featuring cutting-edge research, *Provincial Policy Laboratories* explores the cross-jurisdictional movement of policies among governments in Canada's federal system. The book comprises case studies from a range of emerging policy areas, including parentage rights, hydraulic fracturing regulations, species at risk legislation, sales and aviation taxation, and marijuana regulation. Throughout, the contributors aim to increase knowledge about this understudied aspect of Canadian federalism and contribute to the practice of intergovernmental policymaking across the country.

BRENDAN BOYD is an assistant professor in the Department of Anthropology, Economics, and Political Science at MacEwan University.

ANDREA OLIVE is chair and associate professor in the Department of Political Science and associate professor in the Department of Geography, Geomatics, and Environment at the University of Toronto Mississauga.

T0339283

Provincial Policy Laboratories

*Policy Diffusion and Transfer in
Canada's Federal System*

EDITED BY BRENDAN BOYD
AND ANDREA OLIVE

UNIVERSITY OF TORONTO PRESS
Toronto Buffalo London

© University of Toronto Press 2021
Toronto Buffalo London
utorontopress.com

ISBN 978-1-4875-3910-8 (cloth)
ISBN 978-1-4875-2639-9 (paper)
ISBN 978-1-4875-3912-2 (EPUB)
ISBN 978-1-4875-3911-5 (PDF)

Library and Archives Canada Cataloguing in Publication

Title: Provincial policy laboratories : policy diffusion and transfer in Canada's
federal system / edited by Brendan Boyd and Andrea Olive.
Names: Boyd, Brendan, editor. | Olive, Andrea, 1980– editor.
Description: Includes bibliographical references and index.
Identifiers: Canadiana (print) 20210156082 | Canadiana (ebook) 20210156120 |
ISBN 9781487539108 (cloth) | ISBN 9781487526399 (paper) |
ISBN 9781487539122 (EPUB) | ISBN 9781487539115 (PDF)
Subjects: LCSH: Provincial governments – Canada. | LCSH: Canadian provinces –
Social policy. | LCSH: Canadian provinces – Economic policy.
Classification: LCC JL198 .P745 2021 | DDC 352.130971 – dc23

This book has been published with the help of a grant from the Federation for the
Humanities and Social Sciences, through the Awards to Scholarly Publications Program,
using funds provided by the Social Sciences and Humanities Research Council of Canada.

University of Toronto Press acknowledges the financial assistance to its publishing
program of the Canada Council for the Arts and the Ontario Arts Council, an agency of
the Government of Ontario.

Contents

Tables

PROVINCIAL POLICY LABORATORIES

1

Introduction: Theorizing about Provinces as Provincial Laboratories for Policy Diffusion and Transfer

BRENDAN BOYD

The origins of Canada's public health care system have taken on the status of national myth. Tommy Douglas, a Baptist minister from rural Saskatchewan and the first democratic socialist premier in Canada, introduces a plan for a universal, publicly funded health care system in the province, which is eventually adopted in 1962. A Royal Commission studying the future of health care in Canada recommends the country pursue a nation-wide system based on the Saskatchewan model. The federal government, under Prime Minister Lester B. Pearson, acts on this advice and enacts legislation in 1966, agreeing to share the costs with the provinces. By 1971 all provinces have taken the federal government up on this offer, creating a national system that provides consistent levels of public health care to all citizens across the country. In a 2004 contest run by the Canadian Broadcasting Corporation (CBC) and voted on by the public, Douglas was named the greatest Canadian in the country for his role as the "father of medicare."

Douglas's personal story is undoubtedly compelling. But there is another aspect to the story that is critical to the study of policymaking in Canada. That is the role of policy diffusion, the cross-jurisdictional spread of policies among governments in Canada's federal system. Within a decade, a policy experiment in what was at the time one of the country's smaller and poorer provinces became a national program that is now a fixture in the Canadian policy landscape and a cultural institution in the country. The other nine provinces used Saskatchewan's example, with direction and incentives from the federal government, to develop health care policies in their own jurisdictions resulting in what is effectively a national system. This is not a unique or anomalous occurrence as similar dynamics of policy diffusion can be found in different areas. For example, as part of the *Pan-Canadian Framework on Clean Growth and Climate Change*, the Government of Canada (2016) introduced a system for pricing carbon to be applied as a backstop in any province that did not develop its own system. The design of the federal backstop borrowed from provincial pricing policies that were already operating in British Columbia and Alberta.

Despite these high-profile examples of policy diffusion in Canada, there is surprisingly little academic study of this phenomenon. This book explores the cross-jurisdictional movement of policies among governments in Canada's federal system. The purpose is to increase knowledge about this understudied aspect of policymaking and interjurisdictional dynamics in the Canadian federation. Four broad questions are posed to structure and guide the inquiry: To what extent are policy diffusion and transfer occurring among jurisdictions in Canada's federal system? What does this look like? How well does the literature explain these dynamics in Canada? How can a better understanding of diffusion and transfer inform and contribute to policymaking in the country? This chapter begins by outlining three distinct but related concepts that are necessary to understand interjurisdictional flows of policy information and ideas: policy diffusion, policy transfer, and policy convergence. The discussion focuses on the mechanisms of policy diffusion and suggests that differentiating between levels of policy and considering the role of local factors and context is necessary to establish the link between these mechanisms and the adoption of policy. These concepts have primarily been used to study diffusion at the US state and international level, leaving open the question of how well they apply to Canadian provinces. Several suggestions about what we might expect to see in the study of diffusion in Canada are proposed. This is followed by a discussion of the implications of studying diffusion and the contributions this volume makes to our understanding of interjurisdictional dynamics in Canadian policymaking.

The main component of this edited volume is the six empirical case-study chapters that cover different policy issues across provinces and territories in Canada. In chapter 2, Dave Snow examines the diffusion of parentage policy, the procedures for determining the legal parents of children born through assisted reproduction or surrogacy, across all provincial governments. Heather Millar, in chapter 3, studies policies and regulations in Alberta and New Brunswick that address hydraulic fracturing, which involves horizontal drilling and injection of fluids into geological formations to release natural gas and petroleum. The diffusion of endangered species legislation across all fourteen Canadian governments, including territories, provinces, and the federal level, is the focus of Andrea Olive's research in chapter 4. Matthew Lesch, in chapter 5, explores the role that Ontario's experience played in British Columbia's decision to adopt a harmonized sales tax. Laurel Besco focuses on how greenhouse gas (GHG) emissions in the aviation sector are being dealt with by federal, provincial, and territorial governments in chapter 6. Finally, Jared Wesley examines whether provincial policymakers are learning from each other when addressing the challenge of cannabis legalization under the federal government's framework. Through these six chapters the book explores different methodological but similar theoretical approaches to policy diffusion and transfer studies.

Canada's Federal System

Before jumping into a discussion about the diffusion and transfer of policy in Canada, it is useful to consider a few facts about Canada and its government. As of 2018, the country has 36.7 million people, less than the state of California (39 million). Its per capita gross domestic product (USD$46,194) makes it a mid- to upper-range Organisation of Economic Co-operation and Development (OECD) country. It is a relatively young country. While 1867 marks its independence from Britain, some provinces and territories are much younger – Newfoundland did not join confederation until 1949 and Nunavut only became a territory (separating from the Northwest Territories) in 1999.

In total, Canada's federal system is made up of fourteen governments: the federal government, ten provinces, and three territories. The country's constitution recognizes the federal and provincial orders of government and divides sovereignty between them. Specifically, sections 91 and 92 of the Constitution Act of 1982 define jurisdiction. It is important to note that provinces have ownership over provincial public lands (which is the majority of land in the provinces), health care and hospitals, education, provincial taxation, private property, and matters of a local nature. Unlike American states, Canadian provinces have the responsibility and jurisdiction over natural resources, a difference which makes them extremely powerful compared to their US counterparts. Over time, the provincial governments have increased their role in policymaking as they have fought for more autonomy, and areas under their jurisdiction, such as education and health care, have expanded and increased in importance (Atkinson et al. 2013).

The territories have governing structures similar to the provinces but are created and given responsibilities through the federal government. The three territories include all of mainland Canada north of the 60th parallel (latitude 60° north) and west of the Hudson Bay. While many people associate these territories with the "Arctic," most of the region lies outside the Arctic Circle. Indeed, it is important to note that Northern Ontario and Northern Quebec are part of the Canadian Far North but not part of the territories. Also, Labrador is part of Newfoundland and not a territory. The three territories have small populations, of which about half are Indigenous Peoples (Inuit, First Nation, and Métis). However, they do have governments similar in structure to the provinces and also have representation in Canada's federal Parliament. Like provinces, they have jurisdiction over education, health care, social services, the administration of justice, and municipal government.

Canadian provinces have many institutional similarities, such as the Westminster style of government, which could facilitate policy diffusion. However, provinces also differ in many ways, including population, geography, economies, and political culture (see Table 1.1). In terms of population and GDP, Ontario,

Table 1.1. Canada's Provinces and Territories by Population, GDP, and Share of Public Sector Employees

Province/territory (listed west to east)	Population (2016 census)	GDP (2017, million CAD)	Public sector share of employees (2013, %)
British Columbia	4,648,055	282,204	23.2
Alberta	4,067,175	331,937	20.2
Saskatchewan	1,098,352	79,513	31.3
Manitoba	1,278,365	71,019	29.4
Ontario	13,448,494	825,805	23.2
Quebec	8,164,361	417,173	24.9
New Brunswick	747,101	36,088	28
Nova Scotia	923,598	42,715	28.5
Prince Edward Island	142,907	6,652	34
Newfoundland and Labrador	519,716	33,074	32
Yukon	35,874	2,895	Not calculated
Northwest Territories	41,786	4,856	Not calculated
Nunavut	35,874	2,846	Not calculated

Note: See Di Matteo (2015) for data on public servants.

Quebec, Alberta, and British Columbia stand as the "big four" among Canadian provinces. Together, these provinces make up just over 85 per cent of Canada's population and the national GDP, with the Atlantic provinces, Manitoba, Saskatchewan, and the territories comprising only 15 per cent. In absolute terms, it stands to reason that the four largest provinces would have the largest public sectors. Although measured as a share of total provincial employees, the public sector is smallest in these provinces.

Canada's federal system has been described as one of, if not the most, decentralized in the world (Bakvis and Skogstad 2012). As mentioned above, provincial governments have constitutional authority over many critical policy areas, such as natural resources, education, healthcare, immigration, and agriculture. The classical conception of federalism is that both levels of government would operate in their areas of responsibility without encroaching on each other. However, this has rarely been the case since the latter half of the twentieth century. Federal relations have gone through periods of cooperation, including the building of the welfare state, and periods of competition, for example, changes to the Constitution, fiscal transfers, and regulation of natural resources. Provinces even maintain a role in implementing international treaties, if it falls within their constitutional responsibilities. This means that while the federal government can sign and ratify treaties, it often needs to negotiate with provinces and develop a national consensus to see them realized.

A set of arrangements and programs has been developed to manage federal relations. First ministers' meetings among the prime minister and premiers occur on an ad hoc basis. For example, in 2016, the first ministers met to discuss a national framework to address climate change. Since the mid-2000s, the premiers, without the prime minister, have met annually through the Council of the Federation. There are intergovernmental forums for many ministries, such as education, energy, or immigration, where elected ministers and senior government officials from the federal, provincial, and territorial governments meet regularly to address shared concerns. Inwood, Johns, and O'Reilly (2011) argue that Canada's intergovernmental capacity, the ability for both levels of government to work together to solve public policy problems, must be strengthened because most policy areas now operate with some element of shared jurisdiction.

Specific programs exist to manage fiscal relations between the provinces and the federal government. The federal government collects income and corporate taxes on behalf of most provinces, and five provinces have harmonized their sales taxes with the federal sales tax. The federal government gives money to the provinces for health and social programs through the Canada Health Transfer and the Canada Social Transfer to help maintain these systems. Equalization is a federal program that is designed to ensure provinces can provide a comparable level of public services across the country without enacting onerous levels of taxation on their populations. The formula establishes how much revenue each province would be able to generate using standard taxation rates and provides funding to bring those provinces that are below the national average up to that average. While the exact formula changes over time and has been contested by some provinces, the principle of equalization is enshrined in the constitution and is a symbol of provinces' commitment to membership in the Canadian federal system. These relationships and arrangements can influence and condition the mechanisms of policy diffusion in Canada's federal system, as we will see in the next section.

Diffusion Concepts, Approaches to Policy Change, and Methods

The lack of diffusion studies in Canada is surprising given that the approach originated in the United States, a neighbouring federal system, in order to understand how American states interact with and affect each other in policy development (Walker 1969; Grey 1973). State governments have been hailed as the "laboratories of democracy" for producing innovative policies that could be replicated and spread across the country, even being adopted as federal standards.[1] Diffusion studies in the United States have burgeoned into a robust research program covering a range of policy areas (for reviews, see Berry and Berry 2018; Karch 2007; Shipan and Volden 2008). But this has not been the case in Canada. Two early studies examined diffusion across multiple pieces of legislation in a variety of policy areas to look for patterns of policy adoption based on regional leadership and similarities in socio-economic and political conditions (Poel 1976; Lutz 1989). A handful of studies of provincial diffusion have been conducted in the areas of housing, climate, social and taxation policy, administrative reform, technological innovations, and tobacco control (Béland et al. 2018; Carroll and Jones 2000; Cohn 2005; Gow 1992; Harrison 2013a; Martin and Economic Council of Canada 1979; Boyd 2017, 2019; Studlar 2007). The most comprehensive study of diffusion in Canada is Wallner's (2014, 10) book on education policy, in which she argues that "intergovernmental learning and cooperation can play a vital and meaningful role shaping substate policy activity."

But these works notwithstanding, a tradition of diffusion research comparable to the United States does not exist in Canada. For context, a search of the *Canadian Journal of Political Science* for the term "policy diffusion" only returned one result: a review of a book on international transfer of welfare and tax policy that includes Canada (Cohn 2005). The same search in *Canadian Public Policy* returned a single entry, a study of provincial climate policy (Harrison 2013b). In *Canadian Public Administration* the search returned four results, but only two were focused at the provincial level, focusing on early childhood education and changes in government structure (White and Prentice 2016; Lawlor and Lewis 2014).[2] Diffusion studies also exist at the municipal level in Canada, in the areas of public health, municipal smoking by-laws, physical activity promotion, the use of consultants, and ride sharing policies (Momani and Khirfan 2013; Nykiforuk et al. 2007; Olstad et al. 2015; Politis et al. 2014; Shields n.d.).

It is possible that the US federal system, with fifty states, lends itself to studies of policy diffusion. The study of policy diffusion typically involves quantitative analysis of a large number of cases and examination of the broader patterns and timing of policy adoption across jurisdictions. It proposes and tests high-level explanations for its findings, including geography, politics, or socio-economic development. For example, Boushey (2010) tracks the spread of 133 policies across all fifty states and suggests the pattern of adoption depends on four factors: the receptivity of states, the nature of the policy, the presence of advocacy groups, and the external policy environment during the time of diffusion. This type of analysis is less suited to the ten provinces and three territories in the Canadian federation. It is more difficult to clearly identify these large patterns of diffusion or offer conclusions about what has caused them. More will be said on methods of inquiry later in this chapter. For now, it is sufficient to note that a lack of quantitative studies does not mean that policy ideas do not cross provincial lines and influence policy development. It means that different approaches and methods of studying the phenomenon are required.

Mechanisms of Diffusion

The study of diffusion mechanisms identifies the processes through which policies spread. This approach provides insight into why and how governments have sought knowledge about an existing policy outside their government and how they have used that knowledge at home. While many frameworks of diffusion mechanisms have been proposed, they typically include *learning*, adopting a policy because it has been deemed effective somewhere else; *competition*, ensuring similar policies as other jurisdictions to avoid the loss of economic activity; *imitation*, copying another jurisdiction's policy exactly; *coercion*, when a policy is forced on jurisdictions by a higher level of government; and *normative pressures*, where jurisdictions feel compelled or obligated to adopt a policy for moral reasons (Berry and Berry 2018; Shipan and Volden 2008).

The most common diffusion mechanism identified among Canadian provinces is competition where jurisdictions adopt similar policies to their neighbours' in order to attract or retain economic activity such as trade, investment, and labour that can move to locations providing the most favourable policy conditions (Atkinson et al. 2013; Galeotti et al. 2000; Harrison 2006). If a policy in another jurisdiction reduces costs to its economy, then investment, goods, and people may shift there from other jurisdictions that do not adopt it. Thus, governments monitor their counterparts and act to ensure their own policies do not render their jurisdiction uncompetitive and at risk of losing economic activity. This has been described by a plethora of metaphors such as a "race to the bottom," "capital flight," and "voting with your feet" (Harrison 2006; Cuddington 1986; Tiebout 1956, respectively). The implications of competition are viewed as positive or negative, depending on who benefits and who does not. Nevertheless, the result is the diffusion of policy across multiple jurisdictions as they respond to each other's policy actions.

In addition to competition, coercion from the central government is typically assumed to be the other prominent mechanism of substate diffusion in federations (Wallner 2014). In short, the federal government may intervene to push provinces to adopt its preferred policy. Of course, coercion does not necessarily mean the use of legal recourse to impose uniform adoption of a single policy across the country. The federal government can provide incentives, for example financial assistance or political support, to promote a policy response. In many cases the federal government establishes standards, benchmarks, or frameworks but gives provinces the flexibility to pursue different options within them. The federal government's spending power is particularly influential in this regard. It provides funding to the provinces for programming and services in many areas, including health, social, infrastructure, immigration, justice, and the environment, to name only a few. In most cases, these transfers are conditional and can be clawed back if certain guidelines or standards are not met (Marland and Wesley 2016). Arguably, the best-known example is the Canada Health Transfer, which helps provinces pay for the cost of health care services on the condition that they meet the requirements of the Canada Health Act: they are publicly administered, portable, universally available and accessible, and cover all medically necessary services. The extent and detail that is proscribed in the conditions attached to various short-term and long-term funding agreements is a continual source of contestation between the federal and provincial governments. Nevertheless, federal spending is a powerful tool that can lead to the diffusion of policies across the country. Another example would be the *Pan-Canadian Framework on Clean Growth and Climate Change* that requires provinces to establish a carbon pricing benchmark but gives them flexibility when choosing how to meet it, through a tax or a trading system (Government of Canada 2016). All revenue collected is returned to the province in which it originated to provide an incentive, or lessen the disincentive, to complying.

As Harrison (2006, 14) notes: "People, goods, and cash are not the only things that cross borders. So do ideas, both as information and as norms and values." The study of diffusion mechanisms such as learning and imitation, which focus on the exchange of information and ideas, is also referred to as policy transfer. Dolowitz and Marsh (2000, 4) define policy transfer as "the process by which knowledge about policies, administrative arrangements, institutions and ideas in one political system (past or present) is used in the development of policies, administrative arrangements, institutions and ideas in another political system." The process of cross-jurisdictional information exchange has also been referred to as *lesson-drawing* (Rose 1993) or *pinching ideas* (Schneider and Ingram 1988). The policy transfer approach focuses on the cross-pollination of policy knowledge among countries at the international level, typically attributed to forces of globalization and developments in information and communication technologies that have shrunk the globe (Evans 2009). Like diffusion mechanisms, the approach can be used to understand the micro-level processes and dynamics by which policies move from one jurisdiction to another by imitation, emulation, and learning (Wolman 1992). One of the most commonly used frameworks for studying transfer, developed by Dolowitz and Marsh (2000), directs scholars to answer five questions: Who is involved in the process? What is transferred? From where are lessons drawn? What degree of transfer occurs? How voluntary or coercive is transfer?

The policy transfer literature also elaborates the ways in which policymakers use information from other jurisdictions (Dolowitz and Marsh 2000; Evans 2009; Rose 1993). The exact number of categories and terminology differ but most frameworks involve *copying*, replicating the policy as it exists; *emulation*, using the ideas behind the policy to create a new one; *combination*, adopting a mixture of several policies to create a new one; and *inspiration*, meaning a policy in another jurisdiction drives a change, but the design of the resulting policy is not influenced by the original. It is possible to distinguish between copying, imitating, or emulating a policy and a process of learning based on the experience that another jurisdiction has had with that policy. Stone (1999, 52) notes that policy learning is analytically distinct from imitation and cites the work of Hall (1993) in arguing that "the emphasis is on cognition and the redefinition of interests on the basis of new knowledge which affects the fundamental beliefs and ideas behind policy approaches." Lesch, in chapter 5 of this volume, uses insights from the literature on decision making to probe this distinction further and suggests that when perfunctory emulation is occurring rather than learning, we will observe that limited time and resources are spent to study policy reforms, that limited deliberation and consultation with experts will occur, and that the sources of information used will be highly selective.

The distinction between learning and imitation leads to an important empirical question about policy transfer among provinces: To what extent is it used as a rational process of policy evaluation, systematically examining the effectiveness of policies and the likelihood they would perform similarly in the adopting jurisdiction? Alternatively, to what extent is transfer used as a shortcut in policy analysis and design, which replaces more in-depth analytical processes such as experiments, pilot projects, formal modelling, and cost-benefit analysis? Dolowitz and Marsh's (2000) definition of policy transfer leaves open the possibility of either, and evidence from outside Canada suggests both are at least possible. Mossberger and Wolman's (2003) review of several case studies suggests that transfer tends to fall short of their criteria for a rational process of evaluating policies and is closer to the "lesson-drawing" envisioned by Rose (1993) or Schneider and Ingram's (1988) "pinching ideas." However, Legrand (2012) finds that in the case of welfare program reform, the Tony Blair government in the United Kingdom was drawn to the effectiveness of US policy under the Clinton administration as well as the sophistication of its evaluation techniques.

Whether policymakers draw lessons through a rational process of learning or mimic ideas from other jurisdictions as a shortcut in policy analysis and design, policy transfer is often thought of as a technical process where bureaucratic officials mine other jurisdictions for examples of programs that could be used to solve problems at home. However, political factors also affect how lessons are drawn (Robertson 1991) and information from other jurisdictions is used by a variety of actors, including politicians, interest groups, and international organizations to further their respective interests (Dolowitz and Marsh 2000). Bennett (1991a) outlines four ways policymakers use information from other jurisdictions in the policy processes: (1) placing an issue on the political agenda, mollifying political pressure, (2) providing an exemplar, (3) indicating the range of options available, or (4) reinforcing decisions that have already been made.

The Dolowitz and Marsh (2000) framework has primarily been used to study international policy transfer. Thus, more work is needed to determine the extent of policy learning and imitation among Canadian governments operating in a federal system and their relationship to competition and coercion. As noted above, the literature suggests a testable hypothesis: that competition and central coercion are expected to be the most prevalent mechanisms of diffusion among Canadian provinces. The other possible outcome, which Wallner (2014) suggests has occurred in education policy, is that imitation and learning will play a larger role than the literature accounts for. Wallner argues that learning through intergovernmental organizations can lead to horizontal cooperation among provinces, which could include common goals, strategies, and accountability mechanisms. This could lead to an additional mechanism, not outlined in standard diffusion frameworks, where jurisdictions face pressures to adopt similar policies because they rely on their collective participation to achieve their own goals. Finally, Wallner suggests that federal involvement and provincial cooperation may be mutually exclusive, as horizontal learning is more likely to occur in areas where jurisdiction is certain and there is less chance of a federal government pre-empting provincial initiatives.

As Table 1.2 shows, most authors in this volume used the common diffusion framework. In some cases, they further refined these categories, such as Millar's distinction between technical and political learning, and Olive's separation of direct and indirect coercion. Several authors used different wording for similar concepts. For example, Millar and Wesley use *emulation*, Besco uses *mimicry*, and Lesch uses *bounded learning* to describe a process of imitation. Drawing on the literature on institutional decision-making, Lesch uses bounded learning to focus specifically on the political ramifications of a policy. He also uses the terms *competitive emulation*, equivalent to competition, and *sociocultural emulation*, equivalent to normative pressures. As Lesch is focused on internal institutional-learning processes, he does not consider the mechanism of coercion. By contrast, Wesley studies policy transfer within a federally designed policy and legal framework; thus, he does not consider voluntary learning or normative pressures.

Policy Convergence

A closely related concept to policy diffusion and transfer is *policy convergence*, which occurs when policies in two or more jurisdictions become more similar over time (Bennett 1991b). As Besco notes, convergence is a possible result of policy diffusion and transfer; as the spread of a policy causes similarities among the responses of two or more jurisdictions. Convergence is also a process and needs to be looked at overtime rather than by comparing a snapshot of policies in two or more jurisdictions (Bennett 1991b). The question is not whether policies are the same at any point but, rather, if a pattern of increasing similarity or diversity is observed. The distinction between diffusion and convergence highlights an empirical challenge. There is an obvious difference between the transfer of information and ideas about a policy and the diffusion or transfer of that policy itself (Radaelli 2005; Stone 2012), and we should not assume that the former always leads to the latter. Put another way, just because knowledge about a policy in one jurisdiction

Table 1.2. Mechanisms of Diffusion in Empirical Chapters of This Volume

	Mechanisms of Diffusion				
	Competition	Coercion	Normative Pressure	Learning	Imitation
Conceptual framework (Berry and Berry 2018; Shipan and Volden 2008)	Ensuring similar policies to avoid loss of economic activity	A policy is forced on a jurisdiction by a higher authority	Jurisdictions feel compelled or obliged to a adopt a policy for moral reasons	Adopting a policy deemed effective somewhere else – updating beliefs based on a policy from somewhere else	Copying another jurisdiction's policy exactly
Snow (chapter 2)	Competition	Coercion	Normative Pressure	Learning	Imitation
Millar (chapter 3)	Competition	Coercion	Normative Pressure	Learning – Technical and political (including benchmarking) – the goal is not always adoption – negative learning	Emulation Synthesis – goal is adoption or policy change
Olive (chapter 4)	Competition	Coercion – direct and indirect	Normative pressure, as a subset of coercion	Learning	Imitation – even symbolic
Lesch (chapter 5)	Competitive emulation	Coercion	Sociocultural emulation	Learning	Bounded emulation or bounded political learning
Besco (chapter 6)	Competition	Coercion		Learning	Mimicry
Wesley (chapter 7)	Competition	Imposed alignment			Emulation

is put forward in the policy process of another jurisdiction, it does not necessarily mean that will lead to policy adoption.

It is even possible that the use of information about policy in another jurisdiction could cause policymakers to avoid a similar course of action at home, which Dolowitz and Marsh (2000) refer to as a negative lesson. Negative lessons learned from another jurisdiction could tell policymakers that the policy was ineffective, that it could become politically controversial, or that it would be a poor fit in their own jurisdiction. While negative lessons do not receive as much attention as situations where transfer leads to policy adoption, they are an important aspect of cross-jurisdictional information sharing, which needs to be included in the study of policy diffusion mechanisms. Illical and Harrison (2007) demonstrate that Canada's federal government learned negative lessons, particularly regarding private property and business interests, and about endangered species policy when creating the national Species at Risk Act. Similarly, in Lesch's chapter on tax reform, he finds that many provinces avoided adopting a harmonized sales tax because of the unpopularity of the federal government's shift to a goods and services tax in the 1980s. The presence of negative lessons provides another way to distinguish between the mechanisms of imitation, where the outcome would always be policy adoption, and learning, where multiple outcomes are possible, including transfer, termination, or additional innovations (Stone 1999).

Finally, it is worth noting that convergence can also be caused by similar responses arising independently in multiple jurisdictions that are addressing a similar problem or experiencing similar conditions. Two governments may have similar responses to an issue, but this does not necessarily mean that policymakers in one jurisdiction have borrowed, learned, or responded to the actions of other jurisdictions. It could be due to similarities in the local features of the jurisdictions, including economic conditions, the ideology and interests of the government, or the nature of the problem. In short, similar policies in two or more jurisdictions do not necessarily mean that diffusion mechanisms are responsible. It is essential that studies of policy diffusion demonstrate that knowledge about an external policy was present and played a critical role in decision making that led to policy adoption (Bennett 1991b).

Policy Diffusion and Policy Change

Studying whether policy diffusion leads to policy adoption is complicated. It goes beyond the identification of diffusion mechanisms and requires an understanding of how policy changes. This requires two things: differentiation of the parts or components of policy on which diffusion and adoption can occur, and consideration of how local factors influence and interact with diffusion mechanisms in the process of adoption.

Differentiating the components of policy is part of the dependent variable problem (Howlett and Cashore 2009), which highlights the need to identify clearly what is changing when assessing policy change. Early studies of policy transfer took a kitchen-sink approach when identifying components of policy, including goals, instruments, content, outcomes, administrative institutions, ideas, and values (Bennett 1991b; Dolowitz and Marsh 2000). In a review of the policy transfer approach, Evans (2009) argues in favour of Hall's (1993) typology of policy change: first-order, changes in the settings or details of a policy instrument; second-order, changes in instruments; and third-order, shifts in the broader goals and ideological underpinnings of a policy. Using carbon pricing as an example, a first-order change would involve increasing or decreasing the price that was applied to emissions, from $15 per tonne to $20 per tonne, for example. A second-order change would involve a shift from a carbon tax, which sets a fixed price on emissions, to a cap-and-trade system, which sets an upper limit on the number of emissions that can be produced and allows the price to be established through market trading. Shifting from a carbon price to a regulation or law that makes emitting carbon illegal would also be a second-order change. In this case, the goal is the same, reducing greenhouse gas (GHG) emissions. If a government abandoned its attempts to reduce GHG emissions and address climate change, in favour of maximizing production and economic growth, this would be a first-order change in policy goals. Howlett and Cashore (2009) have critiqued Hall's (1993) framework, establishing a complex six-part typology that differentiates between high-level abstraction, operationalization, and on-the-ground implementation for policy ends and means. They also raise concerns about the assumed pathways of change, particularly related to endogenous and exogenous sources, and highlight the complexity in theorizing and testing causation.

In this volume, the authors follow Evans's (2009) advice and use Hall's (1993) framework as a guide, although they each focus on different elements. Even though political factors and power relationships must not be ignored, policy diffusion and transfer are, at their heart, about learning. Hall's (1993) orders of change framework is based on social learning, the examination of how policymakers adjust their beliefs according to past experiences and new information. This makes it particularly suited to researchers who want to conceptualize and understand how provincial policies have changed, or not, as a result of diffusion of policy knowledge across jurisdictions. The framework allows scholars to capture and explain subtle shifts in policy, like Besco's insights regarding the exclusion of interjurisdictional and international flights in carbon pricing regimes, which are less the outcome of political contestations than a decision maker's knowledge about the policy. It can also explain broader shifts in ideas or paradigms about policy, for example the change in attitudes towards same-sex marriage and trans rights, described by Snow, which are not fully captured by an analysis of political conflicts or government processes.

Table 1.3. Policy Components Covered in Empirical Chapters of This Volume

	Settings (first-order change)	Instruments (second-order change)	Goals and ideas (third-order change)
Snow (chapter 2)	√	√	√
Millar (chapter 3)		√	
Olive (chapter 4)	√	√	
Lesch (chapter 5)		√	
Besco (chapter 6)	√		
Wesley (chapter 7)	√	√	√

The authors use their evidence inductively to elucidate the pathways of change, rather than testing pre-existing theories, which allows them to be sensitive to the concerns raised by Howlett and Cashore (2009). As Table 1.3 shows, the empirical chapters cover a range of different policy components. Besco focuses exclusively on first-order policy settings, examining whether and how provinces, which had all adopted the instrument of carbon pricing, included greenhouse gas emissions from the aviation sector. Lesch investigates British Columbia's adoption of a harmonized sales tax, and Millar tracks the adoption of hydraulic fracking regulations, which both fall under second-order policy instruments. Olive examines instruments, which provinces had adopted endangered species legislation (ESL), as well as settings and how many of the previously agreed-upon criteria each province's legislation met. For example, did the legislation include independent scientific review and are recovery plans required? Two authors cover all three orders of policy. Snow pays attention to settings, such as age, gender, and number of parents permitted; instruments, whether declarations of parentage are made judicially or administratively; and broader goals and ideas, specifically attitudes and perceptions about assisted reproduction and LGBTQ families. Wesley introduces a framework outlining the different levels upon which diffusion could occur: directional, high-level objectives; strategic, mid-level plans to achieve those objectives; and operational, discrete, short-term activities and outputs within a strategy, which track closely onto the goals and ideas, instruments, and settings framework.[3]

Differentiating between policy components provides two insights for the study of diffusion. First, one should not assume that diffusion on one part of a policy necessarily leads to diffusion on another. Second, if diffusion on multiple aspects of policy does occur, one should not assume the mechanism was the same for each part. In her chapter on endangered species legislation, Olive finds that, after signing a 1996 accord committed to the protection of endangered species, the federal and all provincial and territorial governments adopted legislation, signaling diffusion of policy goals and instruments. However, not all jurisdictions' legislation meets the fifteen criteria outlined in the accord, with many governments using more general wildlife acts rather than specific endangered species legislation. Thus, the settings of individual policies remain different across Canadian jurisdictions. Wesley finds that in developing cannabis policy, directional alignment, the third-order of policy components, was achieved among provinces as the federal government set broad public health goals. However, less alignment occurred at the strategic and operational levels as provinces looked inward to replicate local tobacco and alcohol regimes rather than learning from each other.

When diffusion mechanisms are present, it is still necessary to look at the broader policymaking and implementation process to develop a comprehensive understanding of policy adoption decisions (James and Lodge 2003). The literature on policy transfer and diffusion suggests that local factors play an important role in the transition from the diffusion of knowledge to the adoption of policy (for a summary, see Evans 2009). To address these concerns, terms like *policy assemblages* (McCann and Ward 2012), *policy mimesis* (Massey 2009), and *policy translation* (Stone 2012) have been coined to better reflect the complexity of the transfer process, account for local factors, and capture variation in the resulting policies.

In his book on policy diffusion in US states, Karch (2007) outlines the different stages or phases between the transfer of knowledge and policy adoption: agenda setting, where different alternatives are considered; information generation, where examples are studied to determine how they work; customization, where a policy template is molded to fit local conditions, and enactment; where officials decide whether to adopt the instrument. Karch argues that policymakers have discretion in the agenda-setting and exploration stages to look abroad for instruments and lessons to help them solve a problem. Local variables are active in the later stages of the policymaking process leading to customization of transferred policies and influencing final decisions on adoption. Karch argues that organized interests, which aggregate and influence public opinion, are particularly influential on policy decisions in the customization and final adoption stage. He states: "The most influential causal mechanisms during the customization process will be the individuals and organizations that represent and can mobilize potential voting blocs" (13). These organized interests could cause policymakers to alter an instrument to mollify local pressures and influence their final decision on adoption.

The Canadian political system and environment could lead to different patterns of interaction between government and interest groups from those in the United States, which could affect the diffusion process (Montpetit 2005; Presthus 1974). Canada's tradition of executive federalism, where interprovincial relations are primarily conducted through meetings of first ministers and ministers with similar portfolios, often shuts out interest groups and backbench legislators from policy development (Meekison 2004). Therefore, it is plausible that societal interests will play less of a role in the diffusion process in Canada compared to the US.

The tradition of strong executive and majority governments means that Canadian politicians may have more discretion in the customization and adoption phases of diffusion compared to their American counterparts, who must be more responsive to local legislators and organized interests. This is not to say that Canadian governments have free reign to adopt policies from anywhere without any consequences or pushback. But Montpetit (2005) argues that Canada's parliamentary system, with concentration of power in the executive, creates an exclusive network of actors with high levels of interconnection and cohesion of interests and values. He suggests this type of network increases the levels of trust among participants, making communication, deliberation, and policy learning more likely. In contrast, US policy networks are more open, with low interconnection and cohesion, causing strategic and competitive action to be the primary behaviour.

With different processes of intergovernmental relations, the process between the diffusion of knowledge about a policy and its adoption could be distinct in Canada. More empirical and theoretical work is necessary to understand how Canadian diffusion processes differ from those in the US. As a starting point, we might expect to see learning and normative pressures as influential diffusion mechanisms among Canadian governments, compared to competition or imitation, as societal interests are either less influential or more likely to be engaged in deliberative processes with government on policy adoption rather than groups simply advocating for their interests.

In this volume, several authors tackle the challenge of integrating local factors with diffusion mechanisms. Wesley finds that replication of internal policy regimes for tobacco and alcohol were more influential in policy design than the models and experiences of other provinces. Snow examines how legal decisions in provincial courts have contributed to the diffusion of policy. Lesch integrates local and external forces through the concept of *bounded emulation*, where a jurisdiction borrows a policy from another jurisdiction, but the decision is driven by endogenous local interests rather than external pressures. Millar suggests that coherence or fit with domestic institutions is a key variable in explaining instances of cross-jurisdictional learning.

It should be noted that Karch's (2007) framework of different phases of diffusion assumes a linear and rational approach to policymaking based on models of the policy cycle (Howlett, Ramesh, and Pearl 2009). However, many critiques of this approach suggest that it does not reflect the reality of how policy is made (Stone 2002; Lindblom and Woodhouse 1993; Majone 1989; Radin 2013; Wildavsky 1987). Alternative theories of the policy process, such as punctuated equilibrium (Baumgartner and Jones 2009) and the multiple stream approach (Kingdon 2003), tend to emphasize the irrational and political aspects of policymaking. For example, Kingdon (2003) suggests that policymakers frequently develop an affinity for a particular policy solution and seek to attach it to an emerging issue, rather than identifying a problem and then evaluating their response options. This dynamic has been observed with cap-and-trade systems, where a group of experts lobbied to use the policy instrument to address GHG emissions, after originally being deployed to regulate nitrous oxides and sulphur oxides (Betsill and Hoffman 2011; Vob and Simons 2014). Kingdon stresses that the policymaker must also wait for the political conditions to be right, which along with problem and policy make up the three streams. When the streams come together a policy window will open, and policy adoption can occur. The presence of critics and alternative theories does not mean that rational-linear models are of no use in understanding policymaking in general and diffusion in particular. These models are best used as a general guide to elucidate the different functions or activities involved in policymaking. When applying them, it is essential to remember that in practice, phases of the policy cycle can be compressed or skipped entirely, the phases do not always appear in the order outlined by models, and there can be iterations within the cycle (Howlett, Ramesh, and Pearl 2009; Howard 2005). The authors in this volume all use a bottom-up approach, using their evidence to identify the different functions involved in policymaking and the timing and sequence with which they occur, rather than imposing a rigid framework or model of policy development on their chosen subjects of inquiry.

Methodology

As mentioned earlier in this chapter, the relatively small number of governments in the Canadian federation does not lend itself to large-N quantitative studies. Such an approach would involve either examining multiple issue areas or examining a single policy as it evolved over decades across subjurisdictions. For example, looking at every amendment to hunting regulations in every province since 1905 might necessitate a large N approach. However, for most policy transfer scholars in Canada, a qualitative approach is more suitable for an N <15 case study. Rather, the authors in this volume apply qualitative methods to examine a single case study (although consideration of influences from other jurisdictions was required) or a comparative study of several jurisdictions, ranging from two to just over ten. This approach can generate evidence about diffusion mechanisms while still allowing for some generalizability across multiple jurisdictions. With a relatively small number of potential cases in Canada to study on any given policy, this approach seems well-suited to the examination of diffusion dynamics within the country.

While the research design was always qualitative, the authors in this volume relied on different methods and source materials. Common methods included content analysis of written legislation, the Hansards, and written policy documents. However, none of the authors used qualitative software to analyse documents, which has been used in some qualitative transfer studies (de Loe, Murray, Michaels, and Plummer 2016; White and Prentice 2016). Interviews with politicians and/or civil servants were less common as only Millar, Lesch and Wesley personally spoke to policymakers. Finally, it is important to note that while the US and European literature suggests that newspapers and public opinion are important sources of knowledge (see for example, Karch 2007; Pacheco 2012; Piatti Crocker and Tasch 2015), no author in this volume relied upon such material to illustrate the origin of diffusion. Using these data sources in the future could enrich the study of diffusion in Canada.

Qualitative designs of a small number of cases have advantages for the study of diffusion that go beyond the Canadian context. Large-N statistical studies typically fail to consider the different components of policy on which diffusion occurs, which, as already discussed, is essential for understanding if and how diffusion leads to policy change. In large-N studies, the dependent variable is binary, providing a yes or no answer to policy adoption. Howlett and Rayner (2008) argue that this tends to focus diffusion studies on policy settings and instruments (first- and second-order policy components). They suggest that in-depth study of single cases is conducive to analyses of diffusion on broader policy goals and these goals' underlying ideological basis (third-order change) because the values and motivations of individual decision makers can be explored. Qualitative studies of a small number of cases also provide an advantage in studying diffusion on policy settings, as they allow for in-depth investigation of the details of program implementation, rather than simply comparing variation in the provisions outlined in legislation or policy documents. For example, a study examining dozens, or hundreds, of cases of policy adoption would not be aware of any changes that program developers or front-line service delivery agents in any single jurisdiction made to a transferred policy when putting it in place. Thus, qualitative studies that provide fine-grained analysis of the micro-level processes, decisions, and significant events within cases offer a valuable technique for sophisticated study of diffusion mechanisms, one that is not available in large-N quantitative studies.

Contributions to Policymaking in a Federal System

Scholars have been interested in the relationship between Canada's federal system and public policy since the 1970s and attention has risen and fallen along with major issues in the country, such as healthcare, fiscal and budgetary restraint, and the environment (Inwood et al. 2011). Much of this work has examined the impact of the country's federal system, particularly how power and authority is distributed between the federal and provincial governments, on policy outcomes (Inwood et al. 2011). This discussion typically revolves around the trade-off between the coordination and coherence provided by a centralized approach, where decision-making authority is concentrated in the federal government, and the flexibility and responsiveness of decentralization, where power is distributed at the provincial level. An important argument in favour of greater decentralization depends on Canadian provinces' performing the same function frequently attributed to US states, that is, operating as policy laboratories that produce innovative policy solutions that, if successful, can be adopted by their peers.

The study of collective-action problems suggests that individual actors, in this case provinces, are unlikely to work together even when they have common interests, because they have no assurance that others would hold up their end of the bargain (Olson 1971; Hardin 1968). The conventional wisdom has been that a central authority, in this case the federal government, must impose a uniform solution on the parties. However, the work of Nobel Prize-winning economist Elinor Ostrom has challenged the assumption that only a centralized authority can address collective-action problems. Ostrom (1990) argues that local actors will work together when the number of participants is small and there is an opportunity for them to communicate. The glue that holds these actors together is the trust that develops among them, allowing them to establish and enforce mechanisms that hold actors accountable for their actions. This means that provincial cooperation could move beyond one-off instances of learning or borrowing policies and move to a coherent policy system, established through a bottom-up process, potentially comprising common goals, instruments, and settings.

In her study of education policy, Wallner (2014) argues that the dynamics described by Ostrom (1990) are present among provinces in the Canadian federation. Wallner (2014) states:

> The provinces can work together to craft coherent policy systems. Provincial decisions are not made in isolation but rather consideration of the decisions and actions taken by other jurisdictions. Captured by the concepts of interdependence and connectivity, actors such as provincial leaders, education officials, schooling professionals, and other members of the policy community are linked together through formal and informal channels that influence the transmission of policy ideas among them. The economic and legal interdependence created under a federal union and organizational and cultural bonds that can evolve within a federation furnish conduits for disseminating policy ideas and offer varying incentives and opportunities for policy activity. These bonds, by their nature and intensity, generate a structural environment in which ideas move among the jurisdictions. (1)

Yet we do not know enough about whether provinces have played this role, the extent to which they have worked together, and how the experience of their counterparts is informing their policy choices. This volume seeks to take the initial steps and chart a future course that can answer these questions and better understand the role that provinces play as policymakers in Canada.

Provincial diffusion and transfer studies are also important in understanding policy formation in a multi-level governance context. The concept of *multi-level governance* describes the expansion of the network of actors involved in policy decisions, which has grown in number and complexity since the end of the twentieth century, and the diffusion of authority away from national governments (Hooghe and Marks 2001). Multi-level governance is attributable to the forces of globalization and economic liberalization, which have eroded the authority of the state, as well as governance trends, which have sought to devolve power from centralized governments to local actors (Weibust and Meadowcroft 2014). In Canada, it is tempting to treat provinces the same as the federal government, thus also ceding authority to non-state actors. But others have asserted that, in a multi-level governance context, provinces play an increased role in policymaking compared to their federal counterpart (Atkinson et al. 2013). This can be seen in new institutions of collaborative federalism, such as the Council of the Federation, which are designed to address issues that are common to the provinces, without the involvement of the federal government. However, the study of multi-level governance in Canada is limited compared to what exists in the European Union (EU). What does exist focuses on regional governance in North America (Weibust and Meadowcroft 2014; Rabe 2007; Craik, VanNijnatten, and Studer 2013). In studies of the EU, the concept of lower levels of governments as laboratories producing iterative policy learning is placed front and centre in frameworks of experimental governance (Sabel and Zeitlin 2010).

The preceding discussion leads to several questions that are critical to understanding policymaking in Canada's modern federal system. To what extent do provinces learn and borrow innovative policies from each other and is it leading to policy convergence? Have these connections among provinces led to bottom-up policy frameworks and are they replacing the traditional top-down framework of national policymaking in Canada? These questions must be examined across policy fields, including those with different distributions of constitutional authority between the federal and provincial levels, over time, and likely in comparison with other federal systems. By providing empirical case studies of six different policies, this volume seeks to be the initial offering in a new direction of research on Canadian federalism that will contribute to a new understanding of intergovernmental and national policymaking.

Regardless of debates about federal and provincial roles in national policymaking, at a practical level, provinces have experienced an increased policy function as many of the primary areas of government growth in the second half of the twentieth century occurred in areas that are their constitutional responsibility. As Marland and Wesley (2016, 105) state: "Since the advent of the modern welfare state in the aftermath of the Second World War, the provinces have inherited responsibility for the fastest-growing areas of government spending, most notably healthcare and education." Unfortunately, provincial capacity to develop, implement, and evaluate policy has not kept up with the growth in their responsibilities (Atkinson et al. 2013). In this situation, the federal government's spending power takes on increased importance, which, as discussed, could lead to more similarities in provincial policies. We might also expect to see similarities in policies as provinces share experiences in order to find effective policy solutions, without running expensive pilot projects and filling bureaucracy with large policy analyses and evaluation capacities. Scanning other jurisdictions for models and examples that can be borrowed or emulated could be viewed as a cost-effective technique of policy analysis for provincial policymakers as they learn from the successes and failure of their peers rather than having to experience them on their own. This method of analysis is summed up by the phrase "let's not reinvent the wheel," often expressed by policymakers when they begin to explore options for addressing a new issue. Provinces will face these challenges to a different extent because, as mentioned earlier, there is diversity in terms of the size of their bureaucracy and policy capacity. This raises several interesting questions. Do these larger provinces, with the potential for greater policy capacity, act as models for their counterparts, or is it possible for them to coerce smaller provinces to adopt policy? Do regional, political, or cultural similarities have an impact on where provinces look for examples or with whom they must compete? Questions such as these can be answered through further study and application of the processes and dynamics of policy diffusion and transfer.

The previous discussion underscores a normative argument driving the study of policy diffusion: an improved understanding of policy diffusion will contribute to policymaking by helping provinces pool their efforts, rather than going it alone, when addressing critical policy challenges. Of course, there is no guarantee that a policy deemed effective in one jurisdiction will be effective when transferred to another. Dolowitz and Marsh (2000) recognize as much in outlining three conditions for failed transfer: *uninformed transfer*, where the borrowing jurisdiction has insufficient information to properly establish their own version of the policy; *incomplete transfer*, where key elements of the policy are not adopted; and *inappropriate transfer*, where important differences between the original jurisdiction and the borrowing jurisdiction have been ignored during the transfer process. Mossberger and Wolman (2003) set out two criteria for the sound evaluation of a policy in another jurisdiction: an awareness of policies, including scope, adequacy, and accuracy of the information; and an assessment of transfer, considering similarity of problems and goals, the policy's performance, and differences in contexts. While it is not yet known, it is unlikely that much of the policy transfer among governments in Canada would reach this bar. As Lesch reminds us, Canada has largely avoided establishing robust intergovernmental institutions that would provide formal opportunities for provinces to learn from each other, much less mechanisms that would ensure learning leads to informed policy development and successful transfer. It is hoped that the findings of this volume and future research in this area will contribute to the practice of intergovernmental policymaking in Canada, including policy analysis techniques and institutional design.

Summary of Empirical Case Studies

The case studies cover a range of policy areas, many of them relatively new. This provides an opportunity to study policy innovation and assess the role that diffusion plays in the early stage of policy development. However, in some cases a final picture of diffusion across the entire country is less clear as these processes of policy development are still in progress. This drawback is offset by the inclusion of chapters on endangered species legislation (ESL) and sales taxes, where policy development has gone through at least a full cycle, and there is more certainty about the final outcomes of diffusion. In the case of ESL, diffusion patterns and potential causes can be examined over almost fifteen years, providing greater insight into the temporal aspects of diffusion.

In the next chapter, Snow notes that every province except New Brunswick has now adopted some form of parentage policy in statute or regulation. He finds that learning and normative pressures were salient in the diffusion of policy and highlights the court system as a potential driver of these mechanisms, particularly in creating normative pressures that can create comprehensive policy changes that go beyond what court decisions mandate.

In chapter 3, Millar finds that Canadian provinces do look to their provincial counterparts, in addition to US states, as examples of policy development for hydraulic fracturing regulations. She contends that, in the energy sector, economically well-off provinces, such as Alberta, tend to be viewed as policy leaders. Millar also finds that political learning is essential in this area as the technical complexity of energy policy is often exacerbated through public opposition. Institutional design is a key aspect of this learning and ensuring regulators are aware of and can respond to stakeholder consultations and public deliberations can support policy development.

In chapter 4, Olive finds that there has been diffusion of endangered species legislation caused by competition and normative pressures and attributes this to the presence of the federal government. However, she notes that there is still variation in the content of the legislation adopted across jurisdictions, highlighting that diffusion can occur on some parts of policy but not others.

Looking at sales tax reform in chapter 5, Lesch outlines the empirical conditions that need to be satisfied to demonstrate rational learning as opposed to perfunctory imitation. He finds that bounded emulation was the cause of policy diffusion as British Columbia's policymakers contended with environmental limitations and cognitive constraints in a more boundedly rational process of decision making. Lesch's chapter provides a unique approach, undertaking a fine-grained analysis of the decision-making process in a single province throughout policy development and the influence of another province that had adopted the policy earlier. His chapter demonstrates the value of in-case analysis to examine the micro-level processes of decision making and the role of external exemplars.

This approach provides rich description of how diffusion mechanisms are salient as well as providing compelling causal assertations about their role in policy adoption.

In Canadian greenhouse gas emissions policy, the aviation sector provides a challenge as flights occur within a province or territory, across provinces or territories, and from a province or territory to another country. In chapter 6, Besco finds learning played an important role in the regulation of GHGs from intrajurisdictional flights. Competition was likely a larger concern for interjurisdictional flights and coercion from the federal government to provinces and territories played a role in international flights, as the federal government had to meet its international commitments.

Legalizing cannabis presents one of the most high-profile policy challenges that Canadian governments have faced in the last few decades. In chapter 7, Wesley finds that alignment at the direction level, on broad policy objectives, has occurred due to the direction and guidance of the federal government. At the lower levels of policy development, strategic (how objectives are achieved) and operation (how those strategies are implemented), de-alignment has been more common. Wesley indicates that this is because policymakers have largely looked inward to replicate existing regimes for tobacco and alcohol rather than imitating or learning lessons from their counterparts. Local factors, such as the ideologies of governing parties, political culture, and economic circumstances within each province contributed to this decision. This is an important reminder that regional and provincial differences in Canada are often working against diffusion and convergence, even in a policy area where alignment at the highest level has already been established and the conditions for diffusion appear to be favourable.

Conclusion

This chapter has demonstrated that there is a paucity of empirical, theoretical, and practical knowledge about policy diffusion among jurisdictions within Canada's federal system. This volume provides six empirical cases studies that cover economic, social and health, energy, and environment policy areas. It offers insight into whether policy diffusion is occurring in Canada and what it looks like. Given that the preponderance of theoretical work on diffusion has focused on US states or the international context, there is a need to assess whether these frameworks can be applied to diffusion in Canada, whether they need to be adapted or whether new frameworks need to be developed. While these questions cannot be fully answered in a single volume, we identify several instances where diffusion in Canada may be different and propose what we might expect to see in the cases studies. Our call to authors did not specify an analytical framework or required literature; however, all six authors independently referenced or applied similar frameworks outlining the mechanisms of diffusion, highlighting their salience across different policy fields and reinforcing the value of the approach. Finally, debate about the impact of Canada's federal system on policy development has at times referred to the potential benefit of cross-jurisdictional experimentation and diffusion and bottom-up approaches to national policy development. But whether and how this has occurred has not been widely researched. As such, this volume will contribute to our understanding of the provincial role in Canadian policymaking and provide insights for policymakers who wish to compete, learn lessons, imitate, or even coerce their counterparts in the country's federal system.

NOTES

1 This phrase was first used by US Supreme Court Justice Louis Brandeis in 1932 in *New State Ice Co. v. Liebmann*.
2 The other two entries focused on municipal governments and a comparison of Canada and the European Union.
3 Wesley's terminology is likely more familiar to policy practitioners and could be useful to them in understanding and thinking strategically about engaging in learning and emulation.

WORKS CITED

Atkinson, Michael M., Daniel Beland, Gregory Marchildon, Kathleen McNutt, Peter W.B. Phillips, and Ken Rasmussen. 2013. *Governance and Public Policy in Canada: A View from the Provinces*. Toronto: University of Toronto Press.

Bakvis, Herman, and Grace. Skogstad, G. 2012. *Canadian Federalism: Performance, Effectiveness and Legitimacy*. Don Mills, ON: Oxford University Press.

Baumgartner, Frank R., and Bryan D. Jones. 2009. *Agendas and Instability in American Politics*. Chicago: University of Chicago Press.

Béland, Daniel, Anahely Medrano, and Philip Rocco. 2018. "Federalism and the Politics of Bottom-Up Social Policy Diffusion in the United States, Mexico, and Canada." *Political Science Quarterly* 133 (3): 527–60. http://doi.wiley.com/10.1002/polq.12802.

Bennett, Colin J. 1991a. "How States Utilize Foreign Evidence." *Journal of Public Policy* 11 (1): 31–54. https://www.cambridge.org/core/journals/journal-of-public-policy/article/how-states-utilize-foreign-evidence/7F68726B35CA6AA226510B0C03C7C1A2.

– 1991b. "What Is Policy Convergence and What Causes It?" *British Journal of Political Science* 21: 215–33. https://www.jstor.org/stable/193876.

Berry, Frances Stokes, and William D. Berry. 2018. "Innovations and Diffusion Models in Policy Research." In *Theories of the Policy Process*, edited by Christopher Weible and Paul Sabatier, 253–97. Boulder, CO: Westview Press.

Betsill, Michele, and Matthew Hoffman. 2011. "The Contours of 'Cap and Trade': The Evolution of Emissions Trading Systems for Greenhouse Gases." *Review of Policy Research* 28 (1): 83–106.

Boushey, Graeme T. 2010. *Policy Diffusion Dynamics in America.* Cambridge: Cambridge University Press. http://ebooks.cambridge.org/ref/id/CBO9780511778834.

Boyd, Brendan. 2017. "Working Together on Climate Change: Policy Transfer and Convergence in Four Canadian Provinces." *Publius: Journal of Federalism* 47 (4): 546–71.

– 2019. "A Province under Pressure: Alberta Climate Change Policy and the Influence of the United States." *Canadian Journal of Political Science* 52 (1): 183–99.

Carroll, Barbara Wake, and Ruth J. E. Jones. 2000. "The Road to Innovation, Convergence or Inertia: Devolution in Housing Policy in Canada." *Canadian Public Policy/Analyse de Politiques* 26 (3): 277. https://www.jstor.org/stable/3552401.

Cohn, Daniel. 2005. "Regressive Taxation and the Welfare State: Path Dependence and Policy Diffusion." *Canadian Journal of Political Science/Revue canadienne de science politique* 38 (4): 1079–80. http://www.journals.cambridge.org/abstract_S0008423905309978.

Craik, Neil, Isabel Studer, and Debra VanNijnatten, eds. 2013. *Climate Change Policy in North America: Designing Integration in a Regional System.* Toronto: University of Toronto Press.

Cuddington, John. 1986. *Capital Flight: Estimates, Issues and Explanations.* The World Bank. http://documents.worldbank.org/curated/en/736611492123483697/pdf/CPD8551000Capi0es00and0explanations.

de Loe, Robert, Daniel Murray, Sarah Michaels, and Ryan Plummer. 2016. "Policy Transfer Among Regional-Level Organizations: Insights from Source Water Protection in Ontario." *Environmental Management* 58 (1): 31–47.

Di Matteo, Livio. 2015. "An Analysis of Public and Private Sector Employment Trends in Canada, 1990–2013." Fraser Institute. https://www.fraserinstitute.org/sites/default/files/analysis-of-public-and-private-sector-employment-trends-in-canada.

Dolowitz, David P., and David Marsh. 2000. "Learning from Abroad: The Role of Policy Transfer in Contemporary Policy-Making." *Governance* 13 (1): 5–23. http://doi.wiley.com/10.1111/0952-1895.00121.

Evans, Mark. 2009. "Policy Transfer in Critical Perspective." *Policy Studies* 30: 243–68.

Galeotti, Gianluigi, Pierre Salmon, and Ronald Wintrobe. 2000. *Competition and Structure: The Political Economy of Collective Decisions: Essays in Honor of Albert Breton.* Cambridge: Cambridge University Press.

Government of Canada. 2016. *Pan-Canadian Framework on Clean Growth and Climate Change.* Environment and Climate Change Canada. http://publications.gc.ca/collections/collection_2017/eccc/En4-294-2016-eng.pdf.

Gow, James Iain. 1992. "Diffusion of Administrative Innovations in Canadian Public Administrations." *Administration & Society* 23 (4): 430–54. http://journals.sagepub.com/doi/10.1177/009539979202300402.

Grey, Virginia. 1973. "Innovation in the States: A Diffusion Study." *American Political Science Review* 67 (4): 1174–85.

Hall, Peter. 1993. "Policy Paradigms, Social Learning, and the State: The Case of Economic Policymaking in Britain." *Comparative Politics* 25 (3): 275–96.

Hardin, Garrett. 1968. "The Tragedy of the Commons." *Science* 168:1243–8.

Harrison, Kathryn. 2006. *Racing to the Bottom? Provincial Interdependence in the Canadian Federation.* Vancouver: UBC Press.

– 2013a. "Federalism and Climate Policy Innovation: A Critical Reassessment." *Canadian Public Policy* 39(Supplement 2): S95–108. https://utpjournals.press/doi/10.3138 /CPP.39.

– 2013b. "Federalism and Climate Policy Innovation: A Critical Reassessment." *Canadian Public Policy* 39(Supplement 2): S95–108.

Hooghe, Liesbet, and Gary Marks. 2001. *Multi-Level Governance and European Integration.* Oxford: Rowman & Littlefield.

Howard, Cosmo. 2005. "The Policy Cycle: A Model of Post-Machiavellian Policy Making." *Australian Journal of Public Administration* 64 (3): 3–13.

Howlett, Michael, and Benjamin Cashore. 2009. "The Dependent Variable Problem in the Study of Policy Change: Understanding Policy Change as a Methodological Problem." *Journal of Comparative Policy Analysis: Research and Practice* 11 (1): 33–46. https://doi.org/10.1080/13876980802648144.

Howlett, Michael, M Ramesh, and Anthony Pearl. 2009. *Studying Public Policy: Policy Cycles and Policy Subsystems.* 3rd ed. Don Mills, ON: Oxford University Press.

Howlett, Michael, and Jeremy Rayner. 2008. "Third Generation Policy Diffusion Studies and the Analysis of Policy Mixes: Two Steps Forward and One Step Back?" *Journal of Comparative Policy Analysis: Research and Practice* 10 (4): 385–402. https://doi.org /10.1080/13876980802468816.

Illical, Mary, and Kathryn Harrison. 2007. "Protecting Endangered Species in the US and Canada: The Role of Negative Lesson Drawing." *Canadian Journal of Political Science* 40 (2): 367–94.

Inwood, Gregory J., Carolyn M. Johns, and Patricia O'Reilly. 2011. *Intergovernmental Policy Capacity in Canada: Inside the Worlds of Finance, Environment, Trade, and Health.* Montreal: McGill-Queen's University Press.

James, Oliver, and Martin Lodge. 2003. "The Limitation of 'Policy Transfer and 'Lesson Drawing' for Public Policy Research." *Political Studies Review* 1: 179–93.

Karch, Andrew. 2007. *Democratic Laboratories: Policy Diffusion among the American States.* Ann Arbor: University of Michigan Press.

Kingdon, John. 2003. *Agendas, Alternatives, and Public Policies.* 2nd ed. New York: Longman.

Lawlor, Andrea, and J.P. Lewis. 2014. "Evolving Structure of Governments: Portfolio Adoption across the Canadian Provinces from 1867–2012." *Canadian Public Administration* 57 (4): 589–608. http://doi.wiley.com/10.1111/capa.12088.

Legrand, Timothy. 2012. "Overseas and Over Here: Policy Transfer and Evidence-Based Policy-making." *Policy Studies* 33 (4): 329–48. https://doi.org/10.1080/01442872.2012.695945.

Lindblom, Charles, and Edward Woodhouse. 1993. *The Policy-Making Process.* Toronto: Prentice Hall.

Lutz, James. 1989. "Emulation and Policy Adoptions in the Canadian Provinces." *Canadian Journal of Political Science* 22(1): 147–54. doi: https://doi.org/10.1017/S0008423900000883.

Majone, Giandomenico. 1989. *Evidence and Argument in the Policy Process.* Chelsea, MI: Bookcrafters Inc.

Marland, Alex, and Jared Wesley. 2016. *Inside Canadian Politics.* Don Mills, ON: Oxford University Press.

Martin, Fernand, and Economic Council of Canada. 1979. *The Interregional Diffusion of Innovations in Canada.* Hull, QC: Economic Council of Canada. http://www.worldcat.org/title/interregional-diffusion-of-innovations-in-canada/oclc/6197961.

Massey, Andrew. 2009. "Policy Mimesis in the Context of Global Governance." *Policy Studies* 30 (3): 383–95. https://doi.org/10.1080/01442870902888940.

McCann, Eugene, and Kevin Ward. 2012. "Policy Assemblages, Mobilities and Mutations: Towards a Multidisciplinary Conversation." *Political Studies Review* 10 (3): 325–32.

Meekison, J. Peter. 2004. "The Annual Premiers' Conference: Forging a Common Front." In *Reconsidering the Institutions of Canadian Federalism*, edited by Peter J. Meekison, Hamish Telford, and Harvey Lazar, 141–82. Montreal: McGill-Queen's University Press.

Momani, Bessma, and Luna Khirfan. 2013. "Explaining the Use of Planning Consultants in Ontario Cities." *Canadian Public Administration* 56 (3): 391–413. http://doi.wiley.com/10.1111/capa.12027.

Montpetit, Éric. 2005. "Westminster Parliamentarism, Policy Networks, and the Behaviour of Political Actors." In *New Institutionalism*, edited by André Lecours, 225–44. Toronto: University of Toronto Press.

Mossberger, Karen, and Wolman, Harold. 2003. "Policy Transfer as a Form of Prospective Policy Evaluation: Challenges and Recommendations." *Public Administration Review* 63 (4): 428–40.

Nykiforuk, Candace I.J., John Eyles, and H. Sharon Campbell. 2007. "Smoke-Free Spaces over Time: A Policy Diffusion Study of Bylaw Development in Alberta and Ontario, Canada." *Health & Social Care in the Community* 16 (1): 64–74. http://www.ncbi.nlm.nih.gov/pubmed/18181816.

Olson, Mancur. 1971. *The Logic of Collective Action.* Cambridge, MA: Harvard University Press.

Olstad, Dana Lee, Elizabeth J. Campbell, Kim D. Raine, and Candace I.J. Nykiforuk. 2015. "A Multiple Case History and Systematic Review of Adoption, Diffusion,

Implementation and Impact of Provincial Daily Physical Activity Policies in Canadian Schools." *BMC Public Health* 15: Article 385. http://www.ncbi.nlm.nih.gov/pubmed /25885026.

Ostrom, Elinor. 1990. *Governing the Commons: The Evolution of Institutions for Collective Action.* Cambridge: Cambridge University Press.

Pacheco, Julianna. 2012. "The Social Contagion Model: Exploring the Role of Public Opinion on the Diffusion of Antismoking Legislation across the American States." *Journal of Politics* 74(1): 187–202.

Piatti-Crocker, Adriana, and Laman Tasch. 2015. "Veil Bans in Western Europe: Interpreting Policy Diffusion." *Journal of International Women's Studies* 16 (2): 15–29.

Poel, Dale. 1976. "The Diffusion of Legislation among the Canadian Provinces: A Statistical Analysis." *Canadian Journal of Political Science* 9 (4): 605–26.

Politis, Christopher E., Michelle H. Halligan, Deb Keen, and Jon F. Kerner. 2014. "Supporting the Diffusion of Healthy Public Policy in Canada: The Prevention Policies Directory." *Online Journal of Public Health Informatics* 6 (2): e177. http://www.ncbi .nlm.nih.gov/pubmed/25379125.

Presthus, Robert. 1974. "Interest Group Lobbying: Canada and the United States." *The Annals of the American Academy of Political and Social Science* 413: 44–57. https://www .jstor.org/stable/1040566.

Rabe, Barry. 2007. "Beyond Kyoto: Climate Change Policy in Multilevel Governance Systems." *Governance: An International Journal of Policy, Administration, and Institutions* 20 (3): 423–44.

Radaelli, Claudio. 2005. "Diffusion Without Convergence: How Political Context Shapes the Adoption of Regulatory Impact Assessment." *Journal of European Public Policy* 12 (5): 924–43.

Radin, Barry. 2013. *Beyond Machiavellianism: Policy Analysis Reaches Midlife Crisis.* 2nd ed. Washington, DC: Georgetown University Press.

Robertson, David Brian. 1991. "Political Conflict and Lesson-Drawing." *Journal of Public Policy* 11 (1): 55–78.

Rose, Richard. 1993. *Lesson-Drawing in Public Policy: A Guide to Learning across Time and Space.* Chatham, NJ: Chatham House.

Sabel, Charles, and Jonathan Zeitlin, eds. 2010. *Experimentalist Governance in the European Union.* London: Oxford University Press.

Schneider, Anne, and Helen Ingram. 1988. "Systematically Pinching Ideas: A Comparative Approach to Policy Design." *Journal of Public Policy* 8 (1): 61–80.

Shields, Lisa. 2016. "Driving Decision-Making: An Analysis of Policy Diffusion and Its Role in the Development and Implementation of Ridesharing Regulations in Four Canadian Municipalities." MPA research report, University of Western Ontario. https://localgovernment.uwo.ca/resources/docs/research_papers/2016/Shields,%20 Lisa%20-%202016%20-%20PUBLIC.pdf.

Shipan, Charles, and Craig Volden. 2008. "The Mechanisms of Policy Diffusion." *American Journal of Political Science* 52 (4): 840–57. https://www.jstor.org/stable/pdf/25193853.

Stone, Debra. 2002. *Policy Paradox: The Art of Political Decision Making*. New York: Norton.

Stone, Diane. 1999. "Learning Lessons and Transferring Policy across Time, Space and Disciplines." *Politics* 19 (1): 51–9.

– 2012. "Transfer and Translation of Policy." *Policy Studies* 33(6): 483–99.

Studlar, Donley. 2007. "Ideas, Institutions and Diffusion: What Explains Tobacco Control Policy in Australia, Canada and New Zealand?" *Commonwealth and Comparative Politics* 45 (2): 164–84.

Tiebout, Charles. 1956. "A Pure Theory of Local Expenditures." *Journal of Political Economy* 64 (5): 416–24.

Vob, Jan-Peter, and Arno Simons. 2014. "Instrument Constituencies and the Supply Side of Policy Innovation: The Social Life of Emissions Trading." *Environmental Politics* 23 (5): 735–54. https://doi.org/10.1080/09644016.2014.923625.

Walker, Jack. 1969. "The Diffusion of Innovations among the American States." *American Political Science Review* 63 (3): 880–99.

Wallner, Jennifer. 2014. *Learning to School: Federalism and Public Schooling in Canada*. Toronto: University of Toronto Press.

Weibust, Inger, and James Meadowcroft. 2014. *Multilevel Environmental Governance: Managing Water and Climate Change in Europe and North America*. London: Edward Elgar Publishing.

White, Linda, and Susan Prentice. 2016. "Early Childhood Education and Care Reform in Canadian Provinces: Understanding the Role of Experts and Evidence in Policy Change." *Canadian Public Administration* 59 (1): 26–44. http://doi.wiley .com/10.1111/capa.12156.

Wildavsky, A. 1987. *Speaking Truth to Power: The Art and Craft of Policy Analysis*. 2nd ed. New Brunswick, NJ: Transaction Publishers.

Wolman, Harold. 1992. "Understanding Cross National Policy Transfers: The Case of Britain and the US." *Governance: An International Journal of Policy and Administration* 5 (1): 27–45.

2

Parentage Policy Diffusion in the Canadian Provinces

DAVE SNOW

Introduction

Canada has much to offer comparative political scientists when understanding the factors that affect subnational policymaking. Canada is one of the most decentralized federations in the developed world in terms of fiscal capacity, and provinces have primary policymaking authority in important fields such as health and education (Banting and McEwan 2018). Provinces have considerable space to develop public policy, independent of direction from the federal government. By the same token, they have the ability to share information, to learn, and, ultimately, to decide whether to emulate policies previously enacted by other governments.

The developing literature on policy diffusion and transfer can help explain how and why provinces adopt policy on the basis of other provinces' experiences. Policy diffusion – whereby governments adopt policies that emulate "previous policies by other governments" – is a broad umbrella term that applies to multiple processes and outcomes (Berry and Berry 2018, 308; see also Boyd, chapter 1 of this volume). In this chapter, I examine the diffusion of parentage policy, a field of provincial jurisdiction that concerns the procedures for determining the legal parents of children born through assisted reproduction or surrogacy. As an increasing number of children are born through assisted reproduction every year, these rules are an important way for governments to impede or promote diverse forms of family formation. The last decade has seen remarkable change in this field, as every province, with the exception of New Brunswick, has adopted some form of parentage policy in its statutes or regulations.

This chapter uses a qualitative approach by providing a comparative analysis of former legislation, current legislation, written judicial decisions, and policy documents pertaining to parentage from each of the ten Canadian provinces. As Boyd notes in chapter 1, a qualitative approach best enables the assessment of diffusion mechanisms in Canada. Drawing from Berry and Berry (2018), I argue that two mechanisms of diffusion have been especially important for explaining changes to parentage policy: learning and normative pressure. There is evidence, particularly from Alberta, British Columbia, and Ontario that provinces are learning from the successes and failures of other provinces' policies as they develop their own rules for parentage. There is also evidence that shifting norms – particularly norms regarding the acceptance of LGBTQ relationships, surrogacy, and, more recently, trans-inclusiveness and multi-parent families – have affected more recent provincial policies. By contrast, there is little evidence that provinces are changing their parentage policies for reasons of economic competitiveness, federal government coercion, or out of a desire to imitate other governments.

The analysis in this chapter also points to the importance of courts as institutions that can promote policy diffusion, both in terms of policy learning and normative pressure. Provincial courts have been key drivers of change to parentage policy in Alberta, British Columbia, and Ontario, and judges have also rendered decisions in Saskatchewan and New Brunswick. In each of these provinces, judicial decisions have moved parentage policy in a less restrictive direction. Moreover, in the realm of parentage, provinces have not merely complied with the technical requirements of a judicial decision and tweaked their policies. Instead, judicial decisions have tended to lead to comprehensive change. Even when a decision only mandates a change to a precise policy "setting," provincial legislatures have often responded in a way that overhauls the policy settings, instruments, and even overarching goals of parentage policy (see Hall 1993). The dual factors of judicial decisions and changing norms surrounding assisted reproduction and family building have been mutually reinforcing, as the normative pressure of a judicial decision creates the impetus for large-scale policy reform, especially in cases involving the Canadian Charter of Rights and Freedoms.

This chapter proceeds in four sections. The first briefly explores the policy diffusion literature. The second section provides an overview of parentage policy in Canada and describes three phases of policy development: permitting lesbian co-mothers to be recognized as legal parents if their partner underwent assisted reproduction; permitting parentage transfer in the case of surrogacy; and, most recently, recognizing the status of LGBTQ families beyond same-sex couples. In the third section, I note how these parentage changes have occurred contemporaneously with other developments: lesbian mothers were granted presumptions of parentage in the wake of some provinces' (and ultimately the federal government's) legalization of same-sex marriage; surrogacy laws were introduced during a period where assisted reproduction became more common; and recent reforms aimed at supporting LGBTQ families have occurred during a period of growing awareness of transgender issues. The final section concludes with a call for future studies of policy diffusion to explore the role of the judiciary more closely.

Mechanisms of Policy Diffusion and Parentage Policy

The literature on policy diffusion contains terminological uncertainty: different studies speak of policy transfer, learning, competition, lesson-drawing, convergence, coercion, and imitation, and not always with consistency (Dobbin, Simmons, and Garrett 2007; Graham, Shipan, and Volden 2012; Shipan and Volden 2008). Dobbin, Simmons, and Garrett (2007, 450) provide a useful conception of what diffusions theorists share, whether those theorists study the intranational or international dimensions of diffusion: it is "the view that the policy choices of one [jurisdiction] are shaped by the choices of others, whereas conventional accounts of policy choices point only to domestic conditions." The acknowledgement of extra-domestic sources of policy change is the essential ingredient in policy diffusion.

In chapter 1, Boyd describes Berry and Berry's (2018) five mechanisms of policy diffusion (see Table 1.2). The first is *policy learning*, which occurs when "policymakers in one jurisdiction derive information about the effectiveness (or success) from previously adopting governments" (Berry and Berry 2018, 256). With learning, the lessons need not be positive; the goal, ultimately, is to determine best practices. The other four mechanisms are *policy imitation*, when policymakers emulate other governments independent of any evaluation of a policy's effectiveness; *competition,* when a jurisdiction adopts a policy to achieve an economic advantage over one's neighbours; *coercion,* when a more powerful jurisdiction takes action that encourages a weaker jurisdiction to adopt a policy; and *normative pressure,* the voluntary adoption of a policy "widely adopted by other governments ... because of shared norms" (Berry and Berry 2018, 311).

Berry and Berry's (2018, 314) categorization is not mutually exclusive, insofar as "multiple mechanisms may underlie a policy's diffusion." It is, nevertheless, a useful guide for understanding how and why policies diffuse in a given policy field and within given jurisdictions, which helps scholars understand the institutional mechanisms that give rise to diffusion. This is especially important for parentage policy, which I define as "the rules concerning the procedures and eligibility requirements used to determine legal parenthood for children born through assisted conception or surrogacy." Parentage policy, which in Canada is entirely under provincial jurisdiction, is distinct from adoption, as parentage policy seeks to recognize parenthood at birth and avoid the various hoops through which prospective adoptive parents must jump. In a previous study (Snow 2018, 87), I developed a ten-point scale for measuring parentage policy in terms of restrictiveness versus permissiveness, with permissive policy defined by "fewer legal barriers for intended parent(s)." Table 2.1 and Table 2.2 below, which are reproduced from Snow (2018), describe the ten measures of parentage permissiveness and the Canadian provinces' location along the parentage policy spectrum.

Table 2.1. Ten Measures of Parentage Permissiveness

Ten Measures of Parentage Permissiveness
1. Assisted Conception: Female Partner
2. Assisted Conception: More Than Two Parents
3. Surrogacy: Heterosexual Parents
4. Surrogacy: Two Female Parents
5. Surrogacy: Two Male Parents
6. Surrogacy: Single Female Parent
7. Surrogacy: Single Male Parent
8. Surrogacy: No Genetic Relation Requirement
9. Gestational Surrogacy as Contract
10. Traditional Surrogacy as Contract

Table 2.2. Parentage Policy Permissiveness in Canada

Restrictive <--> Permissive							
1	2	3	4	5	6	7	8
MB	SK* (1)				AB	NL	BC
QC	NB* (0)				NS		ON
PE							

* In part because of judicial decisions (legislative total in parentheses).
Source: Snow (2018, 88 and 107).

While this scale describes the current policy framework for parentage within Canadian provinces, it does not explore three aspects of parentage policy variation that are important for understanding mechanisms of policy diffusion. First, the scale lacks a temporal dimension: it takes a snapshot in time but does not explore the way in which early adopters shaped policy change in the other provinces. Second, it does not account for when jurisdictions create administrative rather than judicial parentage declarations. In British Columbia's 2011 law and Ontario's 2016 law, for example, there has been an increased emphasis on establishing parentage administratively rather than judicially. Third, the scale does not consider the more recent instantiation of trans-inclusive language beyond gender binaries and beyond two-parent households on a child's birth registration. As the subsequent analysis will show, these three factors – a focus on time, administrative declarations, and trans-inclusive language – can help situate Canadian provinces' parentage policy changes in light of the different mechanisms of policy diffusion noted above. Before doing so, it is necessary to first explore other Canadian changes to family policy that occurred prior to and alongside parentage policy reform in the early 2000s.

Laying the Groundwork: LGBTQ Rights, the Courts, and the *Assisted Human Reproduction Act*

During the 1990s and early 2000s, the LGBTQ rights movement made a number of concrete gains in terms of spousal recognition through the Supreme Court of Canada. In *Egan v. Canada* (1995), although the Supreme Court narrowly upheld a provision that excluded same-sex couples from accessing federal benefits in the Old Age Security Act, it unanimously agreed that sexual orientation constituted an "analogous ground" of discrimination in the Canadian Charter of Rights and Freedoms. In *M v. H.* (1999), the Supreme Court held by an 8–1 margin that Ontario's exclusion of the word "spouse" from its Family Law Act violated equality rights and was not a reasonable limit on those rights. This led federal and provincial governments across the country to amend numerous statutes, including the federal government's Modernization of Benefits and Obligations Act, to comply with the ruling.

These legal victories were soon followed by successful provincial challenges to marriage laws. Between 2003 and 2004, provincial appeal courts in Quebec, British Columbia, and Ontario held that the traditional heterosexual definition of marriage was an unreasonable violation of same-sex couples' equality rights (*Barbeau v. British Columbia* 2003; *Catholic Civil Rights League v. Hendricks* 2004; *Halpern v. Canada (Attorney General)* 2003). Subsequent trial court decisions in Saskatchewan, Manitoba, Nova Scotia, New Brunswick, Newfoundland and Labrador, and the Yukon came to the same conclusion. In 2004, the Supreme Court of Canada did not answer the question of whether the traditional heterosexual definition of marriage violated same-sex couples' Charter rights, though it did unanimously hold that same-sex marriage "flows from" the Charter (*Reference re Same-Sex Marriage* 2004, para. 43). The federal government subsequently legalized same-sex marriage in the 2005 Civil Marriage Act. Canadian courts were thus a crucial factor in policy diffusion for LGBTQ families: because of the unified structure of Canada's judicial decision, the Supreme Court of Canada's Charter decisions shaped and harmonized provincial laws, even in areas of provincial jurisdiction.

During the same period, the use of assisted reproduction techniques and fertility treatment centres increased. In 1993, the Royal Commission on New Reproductive Technologies recommended a centralized framework for assisted reproduction policy to be administered almost exclusively by the federal government. However, it recognized that laws concerning the legal parenthood of children born through assisted reproduction – what would come to be known as parentage policy – was an area of provincial jurisdiction. Keeping with the Commission's desire for national uniformity, it recommended that provinces adopt identical parentage legislation clarifying who is a parent across the country, with the proviso that the "legal status" of children "cannot differ from province to province" (Royal Commission on New Reproductive Technologies 1993, xxvi).

The dual themes of uniformity and urgency coloured the Commission's recommendations, yet neither urgency nor uniformity have characterized parentage policy in Canada since that time. The federal government eventually created comprehensive legislation in the form of the 2004 Assisted Human Reproduction Act, which did not legislate for parentage, and thus there was no federal coercion for parentage. This delayed federal framework for assisted reproduction, which left much of the field to be governed by medical self-regulation, created little incentive for provinces to reform their parentage laws to reflect the changing ways in which many Canadians were building their families. As such, the first phase of parentage policy reform and diffusion in Canada stemmed not from shifting norms surrounding assisted reproduction per se, but instead around shifting norms, values, and policy changes for same-sex couples in the courts.

Phase One: Recognition of Lesbian Co-Mothers

Although reference is often made to "LGBTQ litigation" to describe policy changes in the Canadian courts in the 1990s and early 2000s, those policy changes were largely directed at same-sex couples in long-term relationships. Those couples won victories that created more inclusive definitions of "family," "parent," or "spouse" in the cases noted above. Though it is impossible to determine causation, there is little doubt that judicial decisions had an impact on changing norms surrounding LGBTQ relationships in Canada, particularly gay and lesbian relationships around the turn of the millennium (Smith 2005). The subsequent shift in public opinion has been remarkable. In 1997, two years after the Supreme Court of Canada held that sexual orientation was a prohibited ground of discrimination under the Charter, only 41 per cent of Canadians supported same-sex marriage. By 2007, two years after same-sex marriage was legalized, that number was 53 per cent; by 2017, it was 75 per cent (Giguère 2017).

Just as public opinion surrounding homosexuality and same-sex marriage was shifting, provinces began to remove restrictive barriers to children born into some (though not all) LGBTQ families. In 2002, Quebec became the first province to legislate a legal presumption of paternity to same-sex spouses, regardless of whether they were married or in a civil union (Nelson 2013, 339). Quebec parents using third-party reproductive material were presumed to be parents once the child was born, and were given the same rights and obligations as parents of children born through heterosexual intercourse (*Civil Code of Québec*, LRQ, c. C-1991). However, Quebec retained strict rules for surrogacy arrangements, which are rendered null and void by Article 541 of its Civil Code. Because a gay male couple would require a woman to gestate and carry a child to term, and

because Quebec's provision banning surrogacy arrangements prevented the transfer of parentage from a female surrogate to a male intended parent, Quebec's law
thus recognized parentage for lesbian couples who conceive using assisted reproduction, but not for gay male couples.

Quebec's legal framework initiated a phase of parentage policy reform that
made manifest a biological issue inherent in building families using assisted reproduction: that to afford the same legal parental rights to gay men and women,
surrogacy must be legally sanctioned, and parentage transfer from the surrogate
to an intended father must be facilitated. However, contemporaneous progressive legal changes to LGBTQ relationships were not accompanied by progressive
legal changes to surrogacy. The 2004 federal Assisted Human Reproduction Act
(AHRA) created criminal prohibitions for payment for eggs, sperm, embryos, and
surrogacy, including prohibitions on paying a surrogate, advertising "consideration" to a surrogate, and acting as an intermediary for surrogacy. The legislation permits compensation for expenditures incurred while being a surrogate or
donating eggs, but bans compensation beyond those expenditures. This had the
consequence of restricting the supply of surrogates and egg donors by preventing
women from being paid for the time and effort associated with surrogacy.

As the federal government was restricting payment for surrogacy, provincial
governments (with the minor exception of Alberta, discussed below) were, unsur-
prisingly, in no hurry to legislate for surrogacy within their own jurisdictions. Yet
they did follow Quebec's lead on parentage for lesbian mothers, whether pushed
by a judicial decision or pulled by other forces. Ontario was one jurisdiction
pushed by a judicial decision. In *Rutherford v. Ontario* (2006), two lesbian co-
mothers challenged that the Ontario's Vital Statistics Act violated their Charter
right to be free from discrimination because the law only allowed a child to have
one mother and one father on the statement of live birth. The trial judge agreed
that the Act violated the Charter, holding that the mothers required a change to
the "institution of parentage ... in light of their needs and experiences of what is
normal in our society" (*Rutherford v. Ontario* 2006, para. 192). Ontario amended
its legislation in 2009 to allow the woman giving birth and an "other parent" to
be presumed as parents in the case of assisted reproduction. However, like Quebec, Ontario made no amendments pertaining to surrogacy, even though a 2008
Ontario Superior Court of Justice case had granted a parentage declaration to a
heterosexual couple who had been intended parents through a surrogacy arrangement (*M.D. et al. v. L.L. et al.* 2008).

During the same time period, other provinces amended their parentage policy
to permit lesbian mothers to be parents. Although Manitoba had updated its legislation prior to 2003[1] to include a provision that a birth registration for a "child
born to a woman as a result of artificial insemination" shall be completed with the
consent of a "woman and her husband or common-law partner," it was not until
2008 that the province changed "husband" to the gender-neutral "spouse." In

2009, Prince Edward Island amended its Child Status Act (section 9(2)) to include "assisted conception" as a means "other than sexual intercourse" that includes "the fertilization of the mother's ovum outside of her uterus and subsequent implantation of the fertilized ovum in her." In 2009, Saskatchewan amended its Vital Statistics Act to recognize the female partner – an "other parent [… in a] spousal relationship at the time of the child's birth who intends to participate as a parent" – of the woman giving birth. Notably, neither Ontario, Prince Edward Island, Saskatchewan nor Manitoba amended its legislation to permit parentage transfer with respect to surrogacy.

Phase Two: Surrogacy Declarations in Nova Scotia, Newfoundland and Labrador, and Alberta

There were, however, three provinces that amended their legislation during this time period (2002–9) to include provisions for surrogacy and assisted conception: Alberta, Nova Scotia, and Newfoundland and Labrador. Alberta was actually the first province to include a section on surrogacy in its Family Law Act in 2003, though its provision only enabled parentage to be transferred from the surrogate to a woman whose egg was used in assisted reproduction. Unlike the five provinces listed above, Alberta's law did not apply to same-sex couples.

Nova Scotia and Newfoundland and Labrador, however, went even further by creating explicit provisions to enable parentage transfer in the case of surrogacy, as well as legally recognizing lesbian co-mothers in the case of assisted reproduction. In 2007, Nova Scotia created regulations pursuant to its Vital Statistics Act (Birth Registration Regulations) that recognized the gender-neutral spouse of a woman giving birth as the "other parent," albeit with an additional hurdle (in the form of a signed declaration) if the couple were unmarried. The regulations also enabled a court to make a declaration of parentage in the case of a surrogacy arrangement, provided one of the intended parents "has a genetic link to the child." According to Nova Scotia's regulations, for surrogacy there must be two intended parents – no more, no less. In 2009, Newfoundland and Labrador overhauled its Vital Statistics Act to permit the birth mother's "father or other parent" to be listed as the child's parent along with the woman giving birth. At the same time, it amended its legislation to allow its registrar general to "register the intended parents as the parents of the child" in the case of a surrogacy arrangement, provided a declaration of motherhood or fatherhood is made.

While far from comprehensive, two of Canada's smallest provinces built on the Quebec example allowing parentage addition for lesbian co-mothers and – unlike Ontario, Manitoba, Saskatchewan, and Prince Edward Island – added provisions for surrogacy as well. Notably, in both Nova Scotia and Newfoundland and Labrador, the surrogacy provision was added at the same time as the provision allowing the birth mother's female partner to be added as a parent. There are marginal differences between the two provinces – Nova Scotia's is limited to two intended parents, while Newfoundland and Labrador's legislation does not specify how many parents a child can have – but in neither case is the sexual orientation of the intended parents in a surrogacy arrangement explicitly mentioned.

Alberta's 2003 surrogacy law, by contrast, was limited to transferring parentage from the surrogate to an intended mother. Moreover, it did not recognize that the birth mother could have a female co-parent. This male-only partner provision was successfully challenged in the Alberta Court of Queen's Bench in *Fraess v. Alberta* (2005). Just as an Ontario judge would rule in *Rutherford* in 2006, the Alberta judge in *Fraess* held that the law was not a justifiable limit on the equality rights of same-sex couples. Alberta consequently overhauled its Family Law Act in 2010 to allow for same-sex partners. This overhaul brought Alberta's rules for lesbian mothers into line with the five provinces listed above, but it also made Alberta the first province to pass comprehensive surrogacy legislation. Alberta's surrogacy framework assumes the surrogate and the child's genetic father are the parents of the child, and it permits parentage to be transferred from the surrogate to another person whose reproductive material was used to create the child. The partner (male or female) of this person can also apply for a declaration of parentage, which must be made by a judge.

With the benefit of hindsight, Alberta's legislation was both path-breaking and limited. It was path-breaking because it set out an extensive surrogacy regime and put clear rules in place regarding who gets to be a parent and how parentage is transferred to same-sex couples. Alberta was also the first Canadian jurisdiction to state, in law, that surrogacy arrangements are not valid if the surrogate herself does not consent after birth. However, the law was limited insofar as at least one intended parent must be genetically related to the child, and insofar as a judge cannot transfer parentage if the declaration "would result in the child having more than 2 parents" (section 8(12)(b)). As in Newfoundland and Labrador and Nova Scotia, Alberta's legislation ultimately left parentage declarations for surrogacy in the hands of judges. Each of these features – genetic relation, two or fewer parents, and judicial declarations – were explicitly avoided in the two most recent pieces of parentage legislation: British Columbia's Family Law Act and Ontario's All Families Are Equal Act.

Phase Three: Learning, Adaptation, and Comprehensiveness in British Columbia and Ontario

Two cases in British Columbia's courts granted parentage declarations in the case of surrogacy, even though the law made no provision for such declarations (*Rypkema v. H.M.T.Q. et al.* 2003; *B.A.N. v. J.H.* 2008). Subsequently, British Columbia followed Alberta by overhauling its Family Law Act in 2011. British Columbia's legislation differs from Alberta's in the three respects identified above:

it does not require a genetic relation between the intended parents and the child in the case of surrogacy; it permits a child to have three parents, provided the birth mother is one of those parents; and it establishes most parentage for surrogacy administratively rather than judicially. At the time, these three changes made British Columbia the province with the fewest legal barriers for intended parents using assisted reproduction and surrogacy.

British Columbia's policy innovation has clearly influenced subsequent proposals for parentage policy reform. In 2015, Manitoba introduced the Family Law Reform Act, which sought to reform its parentage legislation along the lines of British Columbia's model, with one exception: that genetic relation would be required for parentage transfer to occur following surrogacy. However, Manitoba's bill died on the order paper with the 2016 election and was not introduced by the new government after the election. A consultation paper from the Law Reform Commission of Saskatchewan (2018) approvingly cited British Columbia (and Alberta and Ontario) on a number of occasions in making the case for reform. But British Columbia's most tangible influence was when Ontario adopted its All Families Are Equal Act in 2016, after the Ontario Superior Court held that the Children's Law Reform Act violated the Charter equality rights of children on the basis of their parents' sexual orientation, gender identity, and use of assisted reproduction (*Grand et al. v. Ontario* 2016).

Although passed by a Liberal majority government, Ontario's legislation drew heavily from Cy and Ruby's Act, a private member's bill introduced by NDP Member of Provincial Parliament Cheri DiNovo, which itself had drawn explicitly from British Columbia's Family Law Act. Jennifer Mathers McHenry, a lawyer, activist, and parent of Cy and Ruby (the children after whom the law was named) said the following about crafting the bill:

> We took a look at a number of jurisdictions. British Columbia in particular has had much more expansive parental recognition for a number of years and that was one of the jurisdictions that we took a look at. The bill that we drafted was not modelled after it necessarily, but inspired by it. We took steps to have the legislation be a little bit smoother and a little bit broader. (TVOntario 2016 at 13:35)

Like British Columbia and Alberta, Ontario's final legislation creates a comprehensive framework for parentage in the case of assisted conception and surrogacy. Like British Columbia (and unlike Alberta), Ontario's law seeks to establish parentage after surrogacy administratively rather than judicially (hence "a little bit smoother"); it removes the requirement for a genetic relation between the intended parents and the child; and it permits a child to have more than two parents.

As Mathers McHenry noted above, the law is "a little bit broader." Whereas British Columbia allows only up to three parents, including the birth mother,

Ontario allows a child to have up to four parents, including the birth mother. It also allows a child to have more than four parents in exceptional circumstances, although in such instances a judicial declaration is required. Generally, judicial orders are not required provided a number of conditions are met, such as each party receiving independent legal advice and the child being conceived through assisted reproduction rather than intercourse. Ontario also introduced an innovation for parentage transfer: a surrogate cannot relinquish her parental rights for the first seven days after a child is born, during which parental responsibility is shared with the intended parents.

Finally, the law is infused with trans- and gender-inclusive language. Ontario has replaced the terms "mother" and "father" in the Children's Law Reform Act and Vital Statistics Act with "parent," and also removed most references to relations "by blood" or "natural parents." Even the person giving birth is referred to as a gender-neutral "birth parent" (in Alberta's and British Columbia's legislation, the term is "birth mother"). The replacement of mother and father with "parent" – which was the most contentious aspect of the law during legislative committee hearings (Snow 2017, 341–4) – was one of many ways in which Ontario's law seeks to be more trans-inclusive, moving beyond parental recognition for same-sex couples to parental recognition for three-plus-parent and non-gender-conforming families.

Discussion: Policy Change through Learning and Normative Pressure

The above analysis demonstrates that there has been gradual policy diffusion of parentage policy in the Canadian provinces, and that such diffusion has been in a more permissive direction. What have been the mechanisms of such diffusion? Returning to the framework used in Chapter 1 (see also Berry and Berry 2018), it is first important to note the mechanisms by which policy has *not* diffused. There was little outright *imitation* of Canadian provinces' parentage policy diffusion, where a government "cop[ies] the actions of another in order to look like that other." Instead, the adaptations seem to have been driven by knowledge of policy effectiveness, rather than the desire to "appear to be the same" as the previously adopting government (Shipan and Volden 2008, 842). There is also no evidence that any of these policies were adopted for the purposes of *competition* to achieve economic advantages over other provinces. Nor has there been *coercion*: the federal government has no jurisdiction over parentage, and it has not created any incentives for provinces to adopt any particular type of parentage policy. Indeed, the seeming lack of any federal interest or involvement in parentage policy is one of the reasons the field has developed so unevenly over the past two decades. The one small exception to this is the federal Assisted Human Reproduction Act, which, by banning payment for surrogacy, obviously prevents provinces from regulating such payment.

Instead, *learning* has been the key mechanism of policy diffusion, particularly in the most recent phase of parentage policy change, from the passage of legislation in Alberta (2010), British Columbia (2011), and Ontario (2016). Alberta initially created the most comprehensive rules for surrogacy in the country but placed limitations on the number of parents; it required a genetic relationship for surrogacy to occur; and it retained the judiciary as the sole actor granting parentage declarations. British Columbia learned from this experience in adapting its own policy: it created a similarly comprehensive surrogacy regime, but removed the genetic requirement, allowed three-parent families in certain circumstances, and moved most parentage decisions from the judiciary to the bureaucracy. Ontario adapted its legislation based on British Columbia's experience: to make its legislation "a little bit smoother and a little bit broader," it used trans-inclusive language, permitted a child to have four or more parents, and removed judicial declarations from surrogacy, except in the case of a dispute. Moreover, it is clear that the judges themselves are learning from similar decisions in other provinces. An Ontario court in *Rutherford* (2006) cited an Alberta court in *Fraess* (2005) in finding a Charter violation, while an Ontario court in *M.D. et al. v. L.L. et al.* (2008) approvingly cited a British Columbia court from *Rypkema v. H.M.T.Q. et al.* (2003) when granting a declaration of parentage. While provincial court decisions are not binding in other provinces, these cases show that Ontario courts clearly found extra-provincial decisions to be persuasive when dealing with novel areas, and that judicial decisions in Alberta and British Columbia had an indirect impact on Ontario's legislative reforms.

It is also clear that *normative pressure* – the most nebulous of all the mechanisms of diffusion – has also been a key factor explaining parentage policy change in the Canadian provinces. As defined by Berry and Berry (2018, 257), normative pressure occurs when a government adopts a policy "because it observes that the policy is being widely adopted by other governments" and "chooses to conform" because of shared norms. While Berry and Berry assert that "multiple mechanisms" of diffusion can occur, it is methodologically difficult to disentangle learning from normative pressure. For example, to what extent was Ontario's 2016 All Families Are Equal Act the result of learning about policy instruments from the British Columbia government, and to what extent was it the result of changing attitudes and beliefs over family-making and assisted reproduction? Polling data confirms shifting public attitudes towards same-sex marriage and transgender rights, and the last several years have seen increasing media visibility surrounding trans issues (Angus Reid Institute 2016; Giguère 2017; Taylor 2015). Although learning clearly played a role, so too did greater awareness of LGBTQ families.

Along with learning, it is clear that normative pressure to adopt LGBTQ-friendly policy therefore deserves attention as an explanatory factor for parentage policy reform. Indeed, the three "phases" of parentage reform above largely map onto three interrelated value changes in Canada: values toward monogamous homosexuality (narrowly defined) and same-sex marriage; values toward assisted reproduction and surrogacy;[2] and values toward LGBTQ individuals, particularly those whose gender identity does match the gender they were assigned at birth. Obviously, these beliefs and attitudes are related: most LGBTQ organizations advocate on behalf of same-sex couples and the trans community, while the availability of assisted reproductive technologies and surrogacy enables family-building opportunities for LGBTQ families. Yet there were specific times at which these discrete issues grew into public consciousness and manifested into courtroom litigation. Just as progressive value change towards same-sex marriage preceded value change towards trans individuals, so too did Charter challenges for same-sex marriage precede Charter challenges on the basis of gender identity.

In terms of parentage policy diffusion, the three phases of policy reform track onto the extent to which citizen norms and beliefs surrounding these issues grew into public consciousness. Beginning with Quebec, seven provinces from 2002–9 adapted their parentage policies to allow the lesbian partner of the woman giving birth to be recognized as a parent. Although Alberta was the first jurisdiction to create surrogacy policy (in 2003), it was not until Nova Scotia's 2007 legislation that parentage policy reform shifted to explicitly recognizing surrogacy for non-heterosexual couples. Newfoundland and Labrador, Alberta, British Columbia, and Ontario subsequently introduced policy for surrogacy, each of which gradually increased in comprehensiveness and, in the last two cases, shifted parentage declarations from the judiciary to the bureaucracy. This maps onto a period, from the mid-2000s to the present day, where surrogacy has been normalized, particularly in popular culture.

In chapter 1, Boyd surmised that larger provinces, with their increased policy capacity, might be most likely to "act as models for their counterparts." The current chapter demonstrates that population size has indeed been the strongest predictor of parentage policy leadership rather than political culture or regional proximity (see Besco, chapter 6 of this volume). Quebec kickstarted parentage policy change by recognizing lesbian co-mothers in 2002, and while Nova Scotia and Newfoundland did innovate slightly during the second phase of parentage reform, it is Alberta, British Columbia, and now Ontario that have engaged in wholesale reform, serving as models for other provinces. The four most populous provinces have taken the lead on parentage policy change at various stages, whether by creating entirely new policies or adapting other provinces' policies based on their experience.

Conclusion

From the preceding analysis, four broad conclusions can be drawn. First, parentage policy diffusion has occurred in the Canadian provinces in three phases: the allowance of lesbian co-mothers to be declared parents in cases of assisted conception; the allowance of parentage to be transferred in the case of surrogacy; and, most recently, a more comprehensive approach that moves beyond two-parent families, genetic relation requirements, and gender binaries. Second, there are two mechanisms by which parentage policy has diffused in the Canadian provinces: learning and normative pressure. These mechanisms are in contrast to those in other Canadian studies of diffusion identified by Boyd in chapter 1, in which he suggested that competition and coercion might be the most prevalent mechanisms of provincial diffusion. The contrast is, however, consistent with the prominence of learning in Alberta's and New Brunswick's hydraulic fracturing policies (Millar, chapter 3 of this volume) and provincial greenhouse gas emissions for intrajurisdictional flights (Besco, chapter 6 of this volume), though Besco also finds evidence of competition and coercion.

Third, the judiciary has often been the institutional venue in which the process of diffusion begins. In all three provinces that have comprehensively reformed their parentage policy in the last decade (Alberta, British Columbia, and Ontario), policy reform was precipitated by judicial decisions, and in two cases they were Charter decisions. Like many Charter cases initiated by LGBTQ individuals, the prominent parentage cases were examples of "venue shopping" (Guiraudon 2000), where individuals and activists unable to change policy through provincial legislatures shifted their attention to the courts and achieved success (Smith 2005). Fourth, and most surprisingly, the scope of the provincial reforms, particularly in the three provinces that comprehensively overhauled their legislation, has gone well beyond the requirements of the judicial decision themselves. This suggests that diffusion is not merely about compliance with judicial decisions. While a judicial decision may act to "trigger" policy reform, once the decision to reform has been made, provinces are first looking to their neighbours, then drawing from changing beliefs and norms to adapt policy in a less restrictive direction. As Karch (2007, 13) predicts, diffusion in Canadian parentage policy was most common in the early stages of policymaking (agenda setting and information generation), whereas innovations based on local factors and feedback from organized interests were more prominent at the latter stages (customization and enactment).

To understand what is happening, it is useful to refer back to Peter's Hall's (1993, 278) conception of policymaking as a process involving first-, second-, and third-order change (see Table 1.3 in chapter 1). For parentage policy, first-order change involves adjusting precise settings, such as the age, gender, and number of parents permitted; second-order change involves changing the policy instruments, such as whether parentage declarations are made judicially or administratively; and third-order change involves the goals and values that inform the law, such as expanding the definition of what constitutes a parent or family. In Alberta, British Columbia, and Ontario, a judicial decision preceded parentage policy change (*Rypkema v. H.M.T.Q. et al.* 2003; *Fraess v. Alberta* 2005; *Grand et al. v. Ontario* 2006). In each case, the judicial decision only required a change to the "precise settings" of existing parentage policy by specifying that the province ought to allow certain individuals to be parents. Yet each province ultimately decided to overhaul its entire parentage policy, making explicit changes to the settings, instruments, and even goals of that policy area that went beyond what the judicial decision recommended (see Snow 2017, 340–1). In this sense, judicial decisions themselves may be acting as something analogous to "inspiration," where a final policy outcome "does not actually draw upon the original" solution (Dolowitz and Marsh 2000, 13). While the judiciary has not been the sole cause of parentage policy change, it has certainly been the most important institutional venue for kickstarting change to the policy status quo.

This chapter demonstrates that scholars examining the policy process need to pay close attention to the way judicial decisions interact with policy change. In a recent edited collection on courts and policy impact, Minh Do (2018, 21) argues that "[w]hen examining the policy influence of courts, scholars often do not explicitly use theories of public policy that explain policy change." Boyd's comprehensive review of the Canadian and international literature on policy diffusion (see chapter 1 of this volume) makes clear that the judiciary has too often been ignored in diffusion studies as well. Theories of the policy process tend to ignore courts, while law and politics scholars minimize formalized theories of the policy process. Do (2018, 35) makes a strong case that "policy theories can help accurately identify the nature and scope of the judiciary's policy influence, thereby improving our understanding of the courts' policymaking role."

Using the case of parentage policy, this chapter has shown the utility of isolating different mechanisms of policy diffusion to explain areas that have been highly affected by judicial decisions. It is not the first to emphasize the role of the judiciary: as Hollander and Patapan (2016, 15) note, courts have played a major role in the way in which morality policy has diffused throughout the United States, particularly given decisions at the Supreme Court level. Yet this chapter shows that subnational as well as national courts can play a role in diffusion and can do so with respect to more "latent" morality policies that are capable of being defined in moral terms (Hollander and Patapan 2016, 18). By focusing on the discrete mechanisms by which policy diffuses, future studies can better understand how the judiciary shapes such diffusion. While normative pressure stemming from changing public opinion is an important factor, so too is the normative authority stemming from a judicial decision.

NOTES

1 Information on precise date of amendment unavailable, as the Canadian Legal Information Institute (CanLII) only contains information on this legislation back to 1 January 2003.

2 While public opinion data confirms that Canadians are increasingly supportive of same-sex marriage and trans rights more broadly (Angus Reid Institute 2016; Giguère 2017), there is no publicly available data on Canadian attitudes towards assisted reproduction or surrogacy.

WORKS CITED

Angus Reid Institute. 2016. "Transgender in Canada: Canadians Say Accept, Accommodate, Move On." 7 September. http://angusreid.org/transgender-issues/.

Banting, Keith G., and Nicola McEwan. 2018. "Inequality, Redistribution and Decentralization in Canada and the United Kingdom." In *Constitutional Politics and the Territorial Question in Canada and the United Kingdom*, edited by Michael Keating and Guy Laforest, 105–34. London: Palgrave MacMillan.

Berry, Frances Stokes, and William D. Berry. 2018. "Innovation and Diffusion Models in Policy Research." In *Theories of the Policy Process*, 4th ed., edited by Christopher M. Weible and Paul A. Sabatier, 253–97. Boulder, CO: Westview Press.

Do, Minh. 2018. "Lessons from Public Policy Theories: Ask about Policy Change First, Courts Second." In *Policy Change, Courts, and the Constitution*, edited by Emmett Macfarlane, 21–39. Toronto: University of Toronto Press.

Dobbin, Frank, Beth Simmons, and Geoffrey Garrett. 2007. "The Global Diffusion of Public Policies: Social Construction, Coercion, Competition or Learning?" *Annual Review of Sociology* 33: 449–72.

Dolowitz, David P., and David Marsh. 2000. "Learning from Abroad: The Role of Policy Transfer in Contemporary Policy-Making." *Governance: An International Journal of Policy and Administration* 13 (1): 5–24.

Giguère, Alain. 2017. "Are You in Favour of Same-Sex Marriage? 74% of Canadians and 80% of Quebecers Support It (and Death in Venice by Benjamin Britten)." CROP. 17 November. https://www.crop.ca/en/blog/2017/207/.

Graham, Erin R., Charles R. Shipan, and Craig Volden. 2012. "Review Article: The Diffusion of Policy Diffusion Research in Political Science." *British Journal of Political Science* 43 (3): 673–701.

Guiraudon, Virginie. 2000. "European Integration and Migration Policy: Vertical Policy-making as Venue Shopping." *Journal of Common Market Studies* 38 (2): 251–71.

Hall, Peter A. 1993. "Policy Paradigms, Social Learning and the State: The Case of Economic Policy-Making in Britain." *Comparative Politics* 25 (3): 275–97.

Hollander, Robyn, and Haig Patapan. 2016. "Morality Policy and Federalism: Innovation, Diffusion, and Limits." *Publius: The Journal of Federalism* 47 (1): 1–26.

Karch, Andrew. 2007. *Democratic Laboratories: Policy Diffusion among the American States*. Ann Arbor: University of Michigan Press.

Law Reform Commission of Saskatchewan. 2018. *Assisted Reproduction and Parentage: Consultation Paper*. Saskatoon: Law Reform Commission of Saskatchewan. https://lawreformcommission.sk.ca/Assisted-Reproduction-Parentage-Consultation-Paper.pdf.

18

Nelson, Erin. 2013. *Law, Policy, and Reproductive Autonomy*. Portland, OR: Hart Publishing.

Royal Commission on New Reproductive Technologies. 1993. *Proceed with Care: Final Report of the Royal Commission on New Reproductive Technologies*. Ottawa: Minister of Government Services Canada.

Shipan, Charles R., and Craig Volden. 2008. "The Mechanisms of Policy Diffusion." *American Journal of Political Science* 52 (4): 840–57.

Smith, Miriam. 2005. "Social Movements and Judicial Empowerment: Courts, Public Policy, and Lesbian and Gay Organizing in Canada." *Politics and Society* 33 (2): 327–53.

Snow, Dave. 2017. "Litigating Parentage: Equality Rights, LGBTQ Mobilization and Ontario's *All Families Are Equal Act*." *Canadian Journal of Law and Society* 32 (3): 329–48.

– 2018. *Assisted Reproduction Policy in Canada: Framing, Federalism, and Failure*. Toronto: University of Toronto Press.

Taylor, Trey. 2015. "Why 2015 Was the Year of Trans Visibility." *Vogue*, 29 December. https://www.vogue.com/article/2015-year-of-trans-visibility.

TVOntario. 2016. "LGBTQ Parenting Rights in Ontario." *The Agenda with Steve Paikin*, 29 June. https://www.youtube.com/watch?v=KHrr7qYD2g4.

CASES CITED

B.A.N. v. J.H., [2008] BCSC 808, 294 DLR (4th) 564.

Barbeau v. British Columbia, [2003] BCCA 251 (CanLII).

Catholic Civil Rights League v. Hendricks, [2004] 238 D.L.R (4th) 577, 2004 CanLII 20538 (QC CA).

Egan v. Canada, [1995] 2 S.C.R. 513.

Fraess v. Alberta (Minister of Justice and Attorney General) [2005] A.B.Q.B. 889.

Grand et al. v. Ontario (Attorney General) [2016]. (Ontario Superior Court of Justice Interim order and minutes of settlement; FS-16-20779).

Halpern v. Canada (Attorney General), [2003] 172 O.A.C 276.

M. v. H., [1999] 2 S.C.R. 3.

M.D. et al. v. L. L. et al. [2008] 90 O.R. (3d) 127.

Reference re Same-Sex Marriage, [2004] 3 S.C.R. 698, 2004 SCC 79.

Rutherford v. Ontario (Deputy Registrar General) [2006] 81 O.R. (3d) 81.

Rypkema v. H.M.T.Q. et al. [2003] B.C.S.C. 1784.

3

Interjurisdictional Transfer of Hydraulic Fracturing Regulations among Canadian Provinces

HEATHER MILLAR

Introduction

Canadian energy and environmental policy scholars have long noted the potential for economic competitiveness to drive policy convergence in provincial regulation (Harrison 2006). In a highly decentralized federal system in which provinces retain constitutional authority over natural resources (Gattinger 2015), the presumption is that provincial governments are incentivized to "race to the bottom" with regard to environmental regulation in order to attract ongoing industry development (Boyd 2017; Harrison 2006; Rabe 2014). Recent analysis of environmental regulation among oil and gas producing provinces in Canada finds broad convergence, exemplified by the creation of independent regulators, limited attention to cumulative effects, and lack of opportunities for public engagement (Carter, Fraser, and Zalik 2017). Environmental scholars in both Canada and the United States have also noted that, while some jurisdictions seem intent to "race to the bottom," in other situations the opposite is also true, as governments "race to the top" in order to gain competitive advantage over international and domestic competitors through more stringent environmental regulation such as clean energy standards (Vogel 2000; Harrison 2006). In the case of climate policy, researchers have documented the potential for subnational jurisdictions to function as "laboratories of democracy," by generating innovative policy designs which can diffuse across state and provincial boundaries (Rabe and Borick 2013; Bernstein and Hoffmann 2018).

As Boyd argues in the introduction of this volume, an alternative approach to explaining variation in provincial regulation is to turn to literature on policy diffusion and transfer. Scholars examining the role of information sharing and learning in the Canadian context have documented the influence of lesson drawing from the United States in a variety of environmental domains, from air pollution, pesticides and toxic substances (Hoberg 1991) to species-at-risk (Illical and Harrison 2007) to climate policy (Boyd 2017). Primary mechanisms of policy transfer from the United States to Canada have included both voluntary processes of technical learning and emulation, as well as more coercive mechanisms driven by the desire to conform to international norms (Dolowitz and Marsh 2000; Harrison 2006). Yet despite the attention to Canadian uptake of ideas from its southern neighbour, less is known with regard to the potential for information sharing and learning among provinces within Canada (Boyd 2017; Boyd, introduction of this volume).

This chapter addresses this limitation by identifying the role of interprovincial policy transfer in provincial regulation of hydraulic fracturing in Canada. Hydraulic fracturing, or "fracking" as it is more commonly known, is an unconventional method of oil and gas production that has fundamentally transformed the oil and gas industry in North America (Neville et al. 2017). Through the use of new technologies enabling the combination of horizontal drilling and multistage hydraulic fracturing,[1] both US state governments and Canadian provinces have been able to exploit previously inaccessible reserves of oil and natural gas (United States Energy Information Administration [US EIA] 2013). Despite these economic benefits, the extraction process has garnered a range of environmental critiques from both academic and activist communities, as groups have raised the potential for groundwater contamination, habitat fragmentation, air pollution, chemical spills, and seismic activity, among others (Council of Canadian Academies [CCA] 2014; Neville et al. 2017). In both Canada and the United States, subnational governments have responded to these challenges by implementing a variety of regulatory frameworks, ranging from layering of new regulations onto existing conventional frameworks, to developing more comprehensive suites of regulations designed specifically for hydraulic fracturing, to adopting precautionary approaches such as moratoria and bans (Carter and Eaton 2016; Millar 2019).

The case of hydraulic fracturing presents a compelling empirical puzzle for the examination of Canadian interjurisdictional information sharing for a number of reasons. First, as an area of natural resource development, we would expect that provincial governments would be responsive to the potential risks of interprovincial competition, resulting in lowered stringency of environmental standards. Yet empirical evidence finds that in the cases of Alberta and New Brunswick both provinces have experimented with introducing more comprehensive regulatory frameworks than the economic conditions seem to warrant (Carter and Eaton 2016; Government of New Brunswick 2013a). Second, government officials in both provinces are engaged in networks of officials, both with US and Canadian regulators, creating an opportunity for both north-south and horizontal information sharing between provinces (Gattinger and Aguirre 2016). Given these conditions, to what degree, if any, do Canadian regulators draw on the experiences of other provinces to guide their decisions?

This chapter proceeds in the following manner: the next section provides a brief review of the literature on policy transfer and learning, focusing on the mechanisms of technical learning and political learning. The third section examines two cases of hydraulic fracturing regulatory change in Alberta and New Brunswick, focusing on initial responses of governments to the emerging issue in 2008–13. The analysis finds that although both governments engaged in processes of information sharing with US government regulators, government officials in New Brunswick also engaged in cross-provincial processes of technical learning, drawing extensively on Alberta's regulatory framework for conventional oil and gas. The research also finds that officials in Alberta engaged in a process of political learning from the US, resulting in a comprehensive regulatory framework.

Policy Transfer and Learning

As Boyd notes in the introduction of this volume, citing Dolowitz and Marsh (2000, 7), policy transfer refers to the "process by which knowledge about policies, administrative arrangements, institutions and ideas in one political system (past or present) is used in the development of policies, administrative arrangements, institutions and ideas in another political system." Emerging out of the policy diffusion literature that focused on the spread of policy innovations across space (Dolowitz and Marsh 1996), studies on policy transfer tend to examine the specific decision-making dynamics internal to different jurisdictions with close attention to both the content that is transferred and the role of learning processes (Stone 2017, 58). As Boyd distinguishes in the introduction, the content of policy transfer can range from broad policy goals, ideas, and ideologies, to specific program recommendations, such as instruments and settings (Dolowitz and Marsh 2002; Hall 1993). Scholarly consensus on different mechanisms of policy transfer is less cohesive. In addition to mechanisms of competition, coercion, learning, and emulation that are well established in the policy diffusion literature (Dobbin, Simmons, and Garrett 2007; Boyd, introduction of this volume), policy transfer scholars have also identified the role of normative pressure in which governments take voluntary action to meet perceived external standards (Dolowitz and Marsh 2002; Boyd 2017). Policy transfer scholars have developed a range of terms to capture the learning process through which policymakers draw on the experiences of other jurisdictions, including "lesson-drawing" (Rose 1991), technical learning (Boyd 2017), and "negative lesson drawing" (Illical and Harrison 2007), among others. Despite the breadth of scholarship, researchers have struggled to identify necessary conditions for policy learning to occur (Dunlop and Radaelli 2013).

   To begin addressing these limitations, this chapter narrows its focus to discern the influence (if any) of two mechanisms of interprovincial policy transfer on subsequent regulatory outcomes: technical learning and political learning. I define technical learning as a process in which actors update their *beliefs about the efficacy* of a particular policy instrument or setting based on new information from different jurisdictions, epistemic communities, or past experiences (Dunlop and

Radaelli 2013; Hall 1993; Boyd 2017). In contrast, I define processes of political learning as a mechanism of policy change in which policy elites update their perceptions of *the political feasibility* of a given solution, also based on information gained either across time or space (May 1992; Rose 1991; Illical and Harrison 2007). While technical lesson drawing often leads policymakers to attend to epistemic communities and scientific knowledge (Dunlop and Radaelli 2013), political learning can be activist-driven in which a broader sector of advocates focus government's attention on the electoral pitfalls of a particular course of action (Hoberg 1991; Harrison 2006; Stone 2017).

Drawing on the classic work by Rose (1991) on the conditions of policy transfer, as well as scholarship in the policy learning tradition (Hall 1993; May 1992; Dunlop and Radaelli 2013), I propose two necessary conditions for interprovincial policy transfer to occur. First, policymakers must understand themselves to be facing a degree of policy uncertainty whether because of (a) challenges of complexity stemming from an inability to discern cause-effect, or (b) challenges of ambiguity stemming from a lack of consensus among officials, citizens, and interest groups as to the core dimensions of the policy problem and the most appropriate solution (Wellstead, Cairney, and Oliver 2018). The premise is that conditions of uncertainty make it difficult for policymakers to know their interests, incentivizing and activating a search for more information (Rose 1991).

Second, provincial institutional structures must facilitate a "fit" between the lesson and the local context (Illical and Harrison 2007, 391). Although the dynamics of federalism suggest that broad institutional contexts in each province are similar, especially in English-speaking provinces, the governance of different policy areas can vary, with decision-making power split across multiple ministries or departments, for example. Rose (1991) also suggests that a key condition for policy transfer is the existence of intergovernmental institutions, namely professional fora, conferences, and exchanges through which information sharing can occur.[2]

This chapter uses process tracing to gather pattern, account, and sequence evidence (Beach 2016) in the support of the presence/absence of technical and political learning in the formulation and adoption of hydraulic fracturing regulation in New Brunswick and Alberta. The study examines second order change (see Table 1.3 in chapter 1) in regulatory instruments; as noted above, both provinces implemented more comprehensive regulatory frameworks for hydraulic fracturing rather than relying on their existing conventional oil and gas regulatory regimes. Research on learning and policy change suggests that technical learning is more likely to be conducive to regulatory rather than paradigmatic change (Hall 1993; Rietig 2018); as such, hydraulic fracturing provides a case in which we can anticipate that technical learning would play a role in regulatory development. Evidence is drawn from analysis of provincial policy reports, strategies, and regulations; federal reports; corporate documents; policy briefs from environmental non-governmental organizations; newsmedia articles and secondary academic literature; as well as fifteen semi-structured interviews conducted with government officials, environmental advocates, and industry representatives in New Brunswick and Alberta in 2014–15. In-depth process tracing (Beach 2016) is particularly well suited for the study of interprovincial policy transfer in that it provides an opportunity to examine the flow of content (e.g., ideas about specific regulatory instruments) between jurisdictions as well as the specific political dynamics internal to each province influencing regulatory tailoring and adoption (Boyd, introduction of this volume).

Provincial Regulation of Hydraulic Fracturing

Hydraulic fracturing is an unconventional method of oil and gas extraction that uses the technological innovation of combining horizontal drilling with high volume, multistage hydraulic fracturing to access reserves in low permeable rock, the most profitable of which has been natural gas from shale and oil from tight sands (CCA 2014; Neville et al. 2017). Emerging out of technical innovations developed in the Texan Barnett shale in the late 1990s and early 2000s, the extraction of shale gas has transformed North American energy production and flows, fundamentally restructuring global gas markets and positioning the US as a net exporter rather than importer of natural gas (US EIA 2017). Canadian unconventional production has boomed in the north east of British Columbia in the Horn River and Montney Basins, the Duvernay Formation in Alberta, and the Bakken shale in Saskatchewan (Carter, Fraser, and Zalik 2017). Resources have also been identified in Quebec, New Brunswick, Nova Scotia, and Newfoundland, with more limited potential in Ontario and Manitoba (US EIA 2013).

At the same time that hydraulic fracturing has proliferated across North America, so too have concerns regarding environmental harms. Academic experts have drawn attention to a substantial degree of scientific uncertainty regarding potential groundwater contamination, seismic activity, habitat fragmentation, and increased greenhouse gas (GHG) emissions resulting from the practice (Schultz et al. 2018; Olive 2018). Environmental groups, local citizens, and Indigenous governments across Canada have also expressed strong opposition to hydraulic fracturing, generating substantial ambiguity as to the perceived trade-offs between environmental harms and economic benefits (Neville & Weinthal 2016; Carter & Eaton 2016).

Regulatory responses among Canadian provinces have been varied, although scholars have identified a broad east/west division, with Western provinces generally pursuing development and Eastern provinces slowing or delaying the process (Olive 2016). As one of the first provinces to engage in substantial production, British Columbia initially relied on its pre-existing regulatory framework developed for conventional oil and gas, layering on single-issue regulations to address specific harms such as chemical disclosure (BC Oil and Gas Commission 2011).

Similarly, Saskatchewan has introduced very little new regulation, relying on its traditional regulatory framework (Carter and Eaton 2016; Olive and Valentine 2018). In contrast, as of writing, moratoria have been adopted in Quebec, New Brunswick, and Newfoundland, and Nova Scotia has implemented a legislated ban[3] (Montpetit, Lachapelle, and Harvey 2016; Carter and Eaton 2016; Olive 2016). Between these poles lie the positions of the Alberta Energy Regulator and the Progressive Conservative government of David Alward in New Brunswick, both of which have pursued more comprehensive regulatory frameworks designed to address specific environmental, social, and health concerns regarding hydraulic fracturing (Carter and Eaton 2016; Government of New Brunswick 2013a). This chapter examines these cases to identify the degree to which processes of technical and political learning served to influence regulatory design.

New Brunswick's Rules for Industry

In January 2011, newly elected New Brunswick premier David Alward established a high-level Natural Gas Steering Committee to coordinate the development of new rules for unconventional gas production. The government also established a staff-level Natural Gas Group to review regulatory frameworks in other jurisdictions and, in early 2012, the government released a formal discussion paper based on the regulatory review (New Brunswick Natural Gas Group 2012b). The discussion paper presented a comprehensive regulatory regime designed specifically for shale gas management, setting out standards for well construction, waste management, and flaring and venting, among others. Following the release of the discussion paper, the government hired Dr. Louis LaPierre, an emeritus professor of biology from the University of Moncton to head a two-month public consultation tour in the summer of 2012 (Huras 2012a, 2012b). In the fall of 2012 the government released LaPierre's consultation report; LaPierre's prime recommendation was to establish a New Brunswick Energy Institute that would provide peer-reviewed research to inform policy development (LaPierre 2012). The government proceeded to establish the Energy Institute in 2013 and appointed LaPierre to lead it (Mazerolle 2013a).

In February 2013, the New Brunswick government released *Responsible Environmental Management of Oil and Natural Gas Activities in New Brunswick: Rules for Industry*, a regulatory framework that included ninety-seven new rules (Huras 2013a). The framework included regulations on a wide variety of instruments, ranging from seismic testing to well casing, wastewater management, transportation, and storage, GHG emissions, and well monitoring and remediation (Government of New Brunswick 2013a; Huras 2013b). The government followed up on the framework in May 2013, releasing its *Oil and Natural Gas Blueprint* that identified six strategic objectives for implementing the framework, together with corresponding recommended actions (Government of New Brunswick 2013b).

Technical Learning in New Brunswick

The New Brunswick case illustrates the importance of the necessary condition of policy uncertainty to prompt a deliberate search beyond a jurisdiction. Prior to the election, the Progressive Conservatives had landed on the mandate of "responsible development" with regard to shale gas, promising to "support the responsible expansion of the natural gas sector while ensuring the safety and security of homeowners and our groundwater supply" (Progressive Conservative Party of New Brunswick [PCNB] 2010). The platform position was seen as a signal to energy producers that New Brunswick was open to industry despite the ban on exploration and mining of uranium in the province, as well as an alternative to the perceived "background deals" that plagued the previous Liberal government regarding the failed sale of New Brunswick power to Quebec (Macdonald and Lesch 2015; PCNB 2010). The core policy challenge facing the Alward government was how to engage in responsible development – that is, how to determine the appropriate regulatory instruments and settings that would ensure New Brunswick had a strong regime. According to Premier Alward:

> Post-election, we did a tremendous amount of work as a government … what became clear to us was that the regulatory work hadn't been completed in New Brunswick adequately for a developed industry, so we took the next couple of years really to look at what the industry is, what type of regulatory systems are in place in the US and Western Canada, brought a very, what I believe was an outstanding team together to look at the regulatory regimes, what worked well, what hasn't worked well, both from a public safety perspective, but also from a regime for revenue and that whole piece as well.[4]

One of the core challenges facing the New Brunswick government was that, although the province had a history of oil and gas development, the existing legislative and regulatory framework was limited, without the variety of regulatory tools common in the larger oil and gas producing provinces.[5] Rather than develop draft legislation, the group decided it would be swifter and more feasible to develop a comprehensive set of rules for industry. These rules could be appended to the Environmental Impact Assessment (EIA) regulation, which was enforceable under the Clean Environment Act (Department of Environment and Local Government 2012) as well as conditions for other approvals under the Oil and Natural Gas Act, the Clean Air Act, and the Clean Water Act (New Brunswick Natural Gas Group 2012b). Thus, from the perspective of decision makers, the key problem to be solved was one of policy complexity, namely how to capture economic benefits of shale gas development while also protecting public safety.

Bureaucrats appointed to the Natural Gas Group were seconded from Natural Resources and Environment and Local Government, creating an ad hoc institutional bridge between the two historically disparate departments. Members of the Natural Gas Group embarked on a number of research delegations to meet with regulators, industry, and environmental organizations in a number of US and Canadian jurisdictions, including Pennsylvania, Arkansas, British Columbia, and Alberta (Foster 2011a, 2011b; Morris 2011). Staff were able to build on existing north-south networks developed through New Brunswick's participation in Interstate Oil and Gas Compact Commission (IOGCC) conferences[6] as well as interprovincial forums such as the Energy and Mines Ministers' Conference (2013). Consultations included in-person meetings as well as discussions of draft documents developed by the Natural Gas Group.[7] The discussion paper released in 2012 draws on a wide range of regulatory frameworks from other jurisdictions, scientific research, and policy reports issued by both industry associations and environmental groups[8] (New Brunswick Natural Gas Group 2012a). In particular, the discussion paper draws heavily on Alberta regulatory frameworks in a number of places, with specific references to well construction, casing, venting, blowout prevention, well abandonment, and noise control directives issued by the Environmental Resources Conservation Board (ERCB), the Alberta regulator at the time (New Brunswick Natural Gas Group 2012b). The subsequent *Rules for Industry* includes twelve references to eight different ERCB directives, as well as reference to site restoration criteria developed by Alberta Environment (Government of New Brunswick 2013a).

Thus, the New Brunswick case presents a seemingly textbook example that illustrates the role of technical learning in facilitating interjurisdictional policy transfer between provinces. Bureaucrats were faced with substantial policy complexity, namely how to modernize the existing oil and gas regulatory framework. In the absence of strong scientific consensus on how to mitigate risks, officials turned to the experiences of regulators in other jurisdictions to shape policy design.[9] Although the government officials involved in policy design consulted with a range of regulators from both Canada and the United States, the approved regulatory framework draws most heavily on standards developed by Alberta, copying the perceived "leader" in oil and gas regulation in Canada. Although the government stopped short of copying Alberta's regulatory structure by establishing an independent energy regulator, the government did establish a new Department of Energy and Mines in 2012, making Minister Craig Leonard responsible for the hydraulic fracturing file (Government of New Brunswick 2012).

At the same time, the New Brunswick case illustrates the limitations of policy transfer and the importance of local factors in determining the shape of policy design (Boyd 2017). Interview data and case analysis indicate that LaPierre's recommendation to develop and implement the New Brunswick Energy Institute was a distinct, homegrown attempt to respond to growing resistance to shale gas development in the province (Mazerolle 2013b). As Leonard noted, "It got to the point where the average person was simply saying 'I don't know who to believe anymore' … So the concept was, let's go to the one area that still has credibility in our society, which is the academics, they are supposed to be unbiased, well trained, and experts in their fields and we'll set up this institute."[10] Although the initial promise of the Energy Institute was hindered by a subsequent scandal regarding LaPierre's credentials,[11] the case demonstrates the ways in which institutional change can be motivated by local rather than cross-jurisdictional concerns.

Alberta's Play-Based Regulation

Alberta has a highly developed regulatory regime for conventional oil and gas development, but it has only begun to develop regulatory responses specific to multistage horizontal hydraulic fracturing in recent years. In January 2011, following an internal review of its regulatory framework for coalbed methane, shale gas, and tight gas, the ERCB, which was the independent regulator at the time, released an initial report detailing the characteristics of regulatory regimes in eight other jurisdictions in Canada and the United States (ERCB 2011).

Towards the end of 2011, Energy Minister Ted Morton announced a "regulatory overhaul" in response to public concern regarding multistage hydraulic fracturing focused on developing best practices for the ERCB. The government was concurrently considering the development of a "single-desk" regulator (Penty 2011), and a year later the Redford government introduced the Responsible Energy Development Act (REDA) for discussion and debate in the house. REDA combined the regulatory functions of the ERCB with relevant elements housed with Alberta Environment, with the aim to create a "one-stop-shop" regulator for the oil and gas industry (Henton 2012; Ernst and Young Global [EY] 2015). REDA was passed in November 2012 by the legislature under the Redford government and was proclaimed in June 2013, establishing the Alberta Energy Regulator (AER) and replacing the ERCB (Gerein 2012; AER 2013b).

In December 2012, the ERCB released its "Discussion Paper: Regulating Unconventional Oil and Gas in Alberta," outlining a new regulatory approach to address hydraulic fracturing that included "play-focused regulation" (ERCB 2012a), an approach which was subsequently termed "play-based regulation" (PBR). PBR is a more comprehensive regime that aims to coordinate industry proponents on an area-based approach rather than a well-by-well approach. Key aspects of the regulatory design include closer attention to cumulative effects, increased expectations for stakeholder engagement, and streamlining of the application process (EY 2015). The board invited written feedback on the new approach from citizens and stakeholders (ERCB 2012b). The AER subsequently piloted its new play-based regulation (PBR) in the Duvernay shale play near Fox Creek, Alberta (AER 2014, 2016; EY 2015). In addition to play-based regulation, the regulator also issued two new directives focused specifically on chemical disclosure and well-to-well communication. Directive 059, Well Completion and

Data Filing Requirements, was issued in December 2012 and requires producers to disclose chemical composition of fracture fluids and water use on fracfocus.ca (ERCB 2012c). In May 2013, the ERCB issued new regulatory requirements for managing subsurface well integrity under Directive 083, Hydraulic Fracturing – Subsurface Integrity (AER 2013a).

Technical and Political Learning in Alberta

The Alberta case illustrates the ways in which jurisdictions with significant regulatory capacity engage in processes of technical learning from both epistemic communities and networks of regulators. Although government officials within the ERCB were keeping abreast of technical developments in the United States throughout the 2000s, by 2008 they were aware that horizontal drilling and hydraulic fracturing was quickly becoming the norm among operators in Alberta.[12] In response, the ERCB undertook a three-pronged approach in 2010; two internal task groups would examine regulatory risks and emerging scientific developments while another team would review regulatory developments in other jurisdictions (ERCB 2011). Initial risk identification highlighted the policy complexity of the issue, both from a scientific perspective with regard to addressing subsurface integrity (including well-to-well communication) and groundwater monitoring, as well as a regulatory management approach with regard to water withdrawals, well spacing, and production intensity (ERCB 2011).

To formulate new standards, government officials relied on informal and formal connections with regulators across Canada and the United States. In Canada, top level officials in Alberta, Saskatchewan, and British Columbia participated at the time in the Western Regulators Forum (Government of Canada 2018). Alberta has also been an international member of the IOGCC since 1996 (IOGCC, n.d.a, n.d.b). The jurisdictional review team consulted with regulators from British Columbia and Saskatchewan, as well as Michigan, Louisiana, Pennsylvania, Oklahoma, Texas, and New York (ERCB 2011). Evidence suggests that government officials within the ERCB drew in part on British Columbia's experiences managing well-to-well communication as well as industry input in the development of Directive 83[13] (ERCB 2011; AER 2013a). Similarly, examination of British Columbia's management of water withdrawals also suggested regional approaches to water management (ERCB 2011), an element of regulatory design which was ultimately incorporated into the cumulative effects objective of the PBR (ERCB 2012a; EY 2015; AER 2016).

In addition to technical learning from the United States and British Columbia, the Alberta case also illustrates the ways in which political learning can inform the development of more comprehensive regulatory regimes. Between 2008 and 2010, regulators were increasingly aware of the growing public concern and media attention to the potential for hydraulic fracturing to contaminate groundwater.[14]

In 2010, US documentary filmmaker Josh Fox released *Gasland*, a feature-length film focusing on the contamination of wells in local communities in Pennsylvania and the growth of fracking in the US oil and gas industry (Fox 2010). Research finds that the film generated considerable attention in both US and Canadian contexts by providing an opportunity for activists to highlight environmental and health risks (Vasi et al. 2015; Eaton and Kinchy 2016). At this time, regulators were beginning to document an increase in public inquiries to its regional offices regarding the higher degree of intensity around shale gas wells, evident in increased trucking for example.[15] Together with stories of policy failure from US states, local concerns served to drive up issue salience with the Alberta regulator. As one government official noted:

> To be fair to Albertans too, there were a number of start-up problems in the United States. Several US states had no history of oil and gas, they had no foundation nor experience. No foundation of regulatory oversight, no effective service industries, etcetera. In that regard there were some documented problems that we would like to think would never happen here because of our rules, there's always compliance and assurance, but the rules are in place to avoid some of the situations that triggered the media coverage. But we had to explain that to Albertans. So part of this is the technical shift, some of it's the regulatory process shift, and some of it is a continued and accelerated engagement and involvement of the public.[16]

The ERCB (2011, 5) jurisdictional review also highlighted public concern as an issue, wryly noting, "Increasing public, media, and government attention is being focused on the potential for hydraulic fracturing of shale gas reservoirs to contaminate useable water aquifers with fracturing fluid chemicals and natural gas, despite no proven cases of hydraulic fracturing of deep zones having caused such a problem." The report subsequently refers to the New York moratorium and the use of chemical disclosure rules as key regulatory responses to addressing landowner concerns (29). Interview data confirms that regulators were also aware of the moratorium in Quebec.[17] Thus, the threat of burgeoning negative public opinion throughout the Eastern provinces and the United States provided regulators with insight into *what not to do*: maintaining the status quo had left US and Canadian regulators susceptible to contentious politics. Within this context, the ERCB's decision to join British Columbia in using fracfocus.ca and the introduction of PBR provides an example of political learning or, in this case, negative lesson drawing. To avoid public outcry regarding water contamination snowballing in other jurisdictions, regulators ratcheted up the stringency of regulation, akin to the process that Hoberg (1991) refers to as activist-driven learning.

At the same time, as in New Brunswick, the Alberta case illustrates the importance of local institutional context in guiding regulatory design. Concurrent with the development of the PBR and Directives 59 and 83, the government was also engaged in substantial institutional reform and redesign as a result of REDA. The establishment of the new Alberta Energy Regulator provided an institutional opening for the government to signal an increased attention to both cumulative effects and stakeholder engagement, a shift that was exemplified in the creation of a new Stakeholder and Government Engagement Division within the organizational structure (AER 2018). In effect, the institutional reorganization provided a window of opportunity for government officials to signal to the public that the regulator was responsive and attentive to public concerns.[18] As Stone (2017, 61) observes, "Negative lessons can have symbolic value and power in de-railing the proposals of opponents." Although critics have attacked REDA for streamlining the approvals process (Ecojustice 2013; Carter, Fraser, and Zalik 2017), the regulator has been able to operationalize some of the concepts developed in the initial discussion paper more fully into the PBR framework that was piloted in Fox Creek in 2014 (ERCB 2012a; AER 2016).

Discussion

The cases explored above illustrate the different ways that processes of technical and political learning influenced the design of provincial regulation of hydraulic fracturing in Canada. Several key features of the cases stand out in comparative perspective. First, the two cases suggest that, faced with policy complexity, policy "leaders" in Canada are more likely to look to the US for inspiration than to their provincial peers, evident in Alberta's participation in the IOGCC and close attention to regulatory practices in US oil producing states. A similar dynamic is also evident in "laggard" provinces such as New Brunswick, which also turned to US states to guide its regulatory development. At the same time, the cases illustrate that provinces are attuned to regulatory developments in other jurisdictions, even on the other side of the country, evident in New Brunswick's incorporation of Alberta's directives into its regulatory framework and Alberta's examination of British Columbia's water management practices. More research is needed within the Canadian context as to the drivers of regulatory "leadership." As in the international context, although geography and proximity play a role in policy transfer, so do values and ideologies (Stone 2017). Similar to Besco's (chapter 6 of this volume) findings that Manitoba has aligned itself as a "western" province with regard to aviation emissions, despite its geographic proximity to Ontario, the New Brunswick case demonstrates that provinces can learn from their more distant counterparts if they are perceived to be ideologically close. In the energy sector, the desire to be seen as a "have" province – namely to be a fossil fuel powerhouse such as Alberta, British Columbia, Saskatchewan, or Newfoundland – may drive attention to these provinces as policy leaders and could have a significant effect on policy design.

Second, these case studies support the need for continued attention to the role of institutional factors in guiding the type and degree of policy transfer. Even despite the strong similarities in provincial institutional contexts, such as higher levels of regulatory discretion in Canada because of the parliamentary system for example (Illical and Harrison 2007), variation in provincial institutional structures matters. While Snow (chapter 2 of this volume) finds that judicial decisions can spur processes of learning, this study finds that institutional factors can also shape how learning processes unfold, influencing policy formulation and design. As the New Brunswick case illustrates, the ad hoc creation of the Natural Gas Group in effect insulated bureaucrats from political pressures, fostering a process of technical learning. Conversely in Alberta, the contingent restructuring of the AER prompted regulators to respond to public concerns, packaging its regulatory framework in a more forward-facing design.[19] These findings suggest that there is value in considering the influence of administrative features such as the division of responsibility across departments, ad hoc working groups, public consultations, and independent agencies on processes of policy transfer.

Third, the cases suggest the need for renewed attention to the dynamics of political learning. The New Brunswick case illustrates the ways in which it is difficult for regulators to attend to both policy complexity and political ambiguity at the same time. Although New Brunswick bureaucrats engaged in multifaceted processes of technical learning to inform the regulatory framework, government officials were unprepared for the strength of public opposition to shale gas. Although the government attempted to respond to these concerns by establishing the Energy Institute, the timing of reforms was considered to be too little too late in the public eye, ultimately spurring electoral loss. Conversely, regulators in Alberta were able to anticipate and respond in a timely and comprehensive way to public concerns by developing play-based regulation, dampening opportunities for public debate. These findings support Boyd's assertion (introduction of this volume) that societal interests are more likely to influence policy design during processes of policy adoption rather than formulation. In the context of Karch's (2007) framework, although technical learning may be more likely in the agenda setting and exploration stages, political learning may be much more common during processes of customization (Boyd, introduction of this volume). More research is needed as to the conditions facilitating different modes of technical and political learning and the influence of these processes on provincial policy design (Dunlop and Radaelli 2013).

Conclusion

This chapter illustrates that under conditions of policy complexity, provincial energy regulators can and do turn to their US and Canadian peers to inform regulatory design. The study of the hydraulic fracturing in New Brunswick and Alberta illustrates that, even in the field of energy production, in which we would expect economic competition to have a substantial effect on regulatory outcomes, information sharing and lesson drawing can play a significant role in determining regulatory design. Through formal membership in US state organizations, regional fora, and informal networks, regulators seek input on regulatory instruments and settings, drawing on evidence in other jurisdictions. Moreover, the findings of these cases suggest that under certain conditions, even independent provincial regulators can be responsive to public concerns and political risks. Whether subsequent reforms achieve more durable and democratic outcomes is a matter for further empirical study.

NOTES

1 Other terms for the process include "hydro-fracking," "fraccing," and "high volume hydraulic fracturing." For the purposes of this chapter, I use the term "hydraulic fracturing" to encompass the entire process of extraction, including well pad construction, well drilling and completion, the transportation of water and chemicals to the well pad, the actual "frack" of injecting pressurized water into the well, and the disposal of produced waters.

2 Scholars working in the advocacy coalition framework note that professional fora play a similar role in facilitating policy-oriented learning (Jenkins-Smith et al. 2014; Weible 2008).

3 Quebec implemented its initial moratorium in 2012, Newfoundland in 2013, and New Brunswick in 2014 (Cousineau, Marotte, and Seguin 2012; Government of Newfoundland and Labrador 2013; McHardie 2016).

4 David Alward, phone interview with author, 1 December 2014.

5 Craig Leonard, phone interview with author, 18 November 2014.

6 Bruce Northrup, phone interview with author, 6 November 2014.

7 Anonymous, interview with author, 19 November 2014.

8 The discussion paper was released with a companion document of references that is thirty-six pages long, including references to legislation and regulation in Alberta, British Columbia, Colorado, Delaware, Maryland, Michigan, Montana, New Jersey, New Mexico, New York, Nova Scotia, Pennsylvania, Philadelphia, Quebec, Saskatchewan, Texas, West Virginia, and Wyoming.

9 Anonymous, interview (19 November).

10 Leonard, interview.

11 In September 2013, it emerged that LaPierre had long been misrepresenting his master's and doctoral degrees as achieved in environmental science, rather than environmental education, and as a result LaPierre stepped down from the Energy Institute (Berry 2013).

12 Government officials, interview with author, 9 July 2015, Calgary, Alberta.

13 Government officials, interview.
14 Government officials, interview.
15 Government officials, interview.
16 Government officials, interview.
17 Government officials, interview.
18 Anonymous, phone interview with author, 25 August 2015.
19 Anonymous, interview (25 August).

WORKS CITED

Alberta Energy Regulator (AER). 2013a. "Directive 083: Hydraulic Fracturing – Subsurface Integrity." Calgary: Energy Resources Conservation Board. https://www.aer.ca/regulating -development/rules-and-directives/directives/directive-083.

– 2013b. "Alberta Energy Regulator Directors Get Down to Business with First Meeting." News release. https://web.archive.org/web/20170803115543/https://www.aer.ca /documents/news-releases/AERNR2013-02.pdf.

– 2014. "Frequently Asked Questions: Play-Based Regulation (PBR) Pilot Project." Calgary: AER. https://www.aer.ca/documents/about-us/PBR_FAQ_20141204.pdf.

– 2016. "Evaluation of the Alberta Energy Regulator's Play-Based Regulation Pilot." Calgary: AER. https://www.aer.ca/documents/about-us/PBR_EvaluationReport _June2016.pdf.

– 2018. "Organizational Structure." Calgary: AER. http://www.aer.ca/providing -information/about-the-aer/who-we-are/aer-organizational-structure#stake.

BC Oil and Gas Commission. 2011. "Industry Bulletin 2011–33: Submission Information for Disclosure of Hydraulic Fracturing Fluids." BC Oil and Gas Commission. https://www.bcogc.ca/node/6067/download.

Beach, Derek. 2016. "It's All about Mechanisms – What Process-Tracing Case Studies Should Be Tracing." *New Political Economy* 21 (5): 463–72. https://doi.org/10.1080 /13563467.2015.1134466.

Bernstein, Steven, and Matthew Hoffman. 2018. "The Politics of Decarbonization and the Catalytic Impact of Subnational Climate Experiments." *Policy Sciences* 51: 189–211.

Berry, Shawn. 2013. "LaPierre Fallout Ripples to Shale Gas File." *The Times – Transcript*, 20 September, sec. A. http://search.proquest.com.myaccess.library.utoronto.ca /canadiannews/docview/1433961471/F4D1133986BD47DBPQ/11?accountid=14771.

Boyd, Brendan. 2017. "Working Together on Climate Change: Policy Transfer and Convergence in Four Canadian Provinces." *Publius: The Journal of Federalism* 47 (4): 546–71. https://doi.org/10.1093/publius/pjx033.

Carter, Angela V., and Emily M. Eaton. 2016. "Subnational Responses to Fracking in Canada: Explaining Saskatchewan's 'Wild West' Regulatory Approach." *Review of Policy Research* 33 (4): 393–419. https://doi.org/10.1111/ropr.12179.

Carter, Angela V., Gail S. Fraser, and Anna Zalik. 2017. "Environmental Policy Convergence in Canada's Fossil Fuel Provinces? Regulatory Streamlining, Impediments, and Drift." *Canadian Public Policy* 43 (1): 61–76.

Council of Canadian Academies (CCA). 2014. "Environmental Impacts of Shale Gas Extraction in Canada: The Expert Panel on Harnessing Science and Technology to Understand the Environmental Impacts of Shale Gas Extraction." Ottawa: CCA. http://www.scienceadvice.ca/uploads/eng /assessments%20and%20publications%20and%20news%20releases /shale%20gas/shalegas_fullreporten.pdf.

Cousineau, Sophie, Bertrand Marotte, and Rheal Seguin. 2012. "Quebec Gas in Peril as PQ Signals Ban." *Globe and Mail*, 21 September, sec. B.

Department of Environment and Local Government. 2012. "A Guide to Environmental Impact Assessment in New Brunswick." Fredericton, NB: Government of New Brunswick. http://www2.gnb.ca/content/dam/gnb/Departments/env/pdf/EIA-EIE /GuideEnvironmentalImpactAssessment.pdf.

Dobbin, Frank, Beth Simmons, and Geoffrey Garrett. 2007. "The Global Diffusion of Public Policies: Social Construction, Coercion, Competition, or Learning?" *Annual Review of Sociology* 33 (1): 449–72. https://doi.org/10.1146/annurev.soc .33.090106.142507.

Dunlop, Claire A., and Claudio M. Radaelli. 2013. "Systematising Policy Learning: From Monolith to Dimensions." *Political Studies* 61 (3): 599–619. https://doi.org/10.1111 /j.1467-9248.2012.00982.x.

Eaton, Emily, and Abby Kinchy. 2016. "Quiet Voices in the Fracking Debate: Ambivalence, Nonmobilization, and Individual Action in Two Extractive Communities (Saskatchewan and Pennsylvania)." *Energy Research & Social Science*, 20 (October): 22–30. https://doi .org/10.1016/j.erss.2016.05.005.

Ecojustice. 2013. "Legal Backgrounder: Bill 2 Responsible Energy Development Act." https://www.ecojustice.ca/wp-content/uploads/2015/03/REDA-backgrounder -May-2013.pdf.

Energy and Mines Minister's Conference. 2013. *Responsible Shale Development Enhancing the Knowledge Base on Shale Oil and Gas in Canada*. Yellowknife, NWT: Government of Canada. http://www.nrcan.gc.ca/sites/www.nrcan.gc.ca/files/www/pdf/publications /emmc/Shale_Resources_e.pdf.

Energy Resources Conservation Board (ERCB). 2011. "Unconventional Gas Regulatory Framework – Jurisdictional Review." Calgary: ERCB. http://www.aer.ca/documents /reports/r2011-A.pdf.

– 2012a. "A Discussion Paper: Regulating Uncoventional Oil and Gas in Alberta." Calgary: ERCB. https://static.aer.ca/prd/documents/projects/URF/URF_DiscussionPaper _20121217.pdf.

– 2012b. "News Release 2012-12-17 (NR2012-13) ERCB Seeking Feedback on Regulatory Approach for Unconventional Development." Calgary: ERCB. https:// www.aer.ca/documents/news-releases/NR2012-13.pdf.

– 2012c. "Bulletin 2012–25: Amendments to Directive 059: Well Drilling and Completion Data Filing Requirements in Support of Disclosure of Hydraulic Fracturing Fluid Information." Calgary: ERCB. http://www.aer.ca/documents /bulletins/Bulletin-2012-25.pdf.

Ernst & Young Global [EY]. 2015. "Alberta's Oil and Gas Sector Regulatory Paradigm Shift: Challenges and Opportunities." https://www.eyjapan.jp/industries/oil/knowledge /pdf/2015-04-24-01.pdf.

Dolowitz, David, and David Marsh. 1996. "Who Learns What from Whom: A Review of the Policy Transfer Literature." *Political Studies* 44 (2): 343–57.

– 2000. "Learning from Abroad: The Role of Policy Transfer in Contemporary Policymaking." *Governance* 13, no. 1: 5–23.

Foster, James. 2011a. "U.S. Gas Rules Explored; N.B. Delegation Checks out Natural Gas Regulations Stateside." *The Times – Transcript*, 25 January, sec. International. http://search.proquest.com.myaccess.library.utoronto.ca/canadiannews/ docview/847084602/CBA9BE4CE19A4849PQ/16?accountid=14771#.

– 2011b. "We'll Do It Right: DNR Minister; Northrup Says Shale Gas to Proceed Safely or Not at All." *The Times – Transcript*, 14 March, sec. Main. http://search.proquest. com.myaccess.library.utoronto.ca/canadiannews/docview/856748655/8C58322F19D 6469DPQ/4?accountid=14771#.

Fox, Josh, dir. 2010. *Gasland*. New York: HBO Documentary Films.

Gattinger, Monica. 2015. "A National Energy Strategy for Canada: Golden Age or Golden Cage of Energy Federalism?" In *Canada: The State of the Federation 2012: Regions, Resources, and Resiliency*, edited by Loleen Berdahl, Andre Juneau, and Carolyn Hughes Tuohy, 39–70. Montreal: McGill-Queen's University Press.

Gattinger, Monica, and Rafael Aguirre. 2016. "The Shale Revolution and Canada-United States Energy Relations: Game Charger or Deja Vu All Over Again?" In *International Political Economy*, edited by Greg Anderson and Christopher J. Kukucha, 409–35. Toronto: Oxford University Press.

Gerein, Keith. 2012. "MLAs Endure All-Nighter to Pass Energy Bill." *Calgary Herald*, 22 November, sec. News.

Government of Canada. 2018. "Western Regulators Forum Terms of Reference." 25–28 June. https://www.cer-rec.gc.ca/en/safety-environment/western-regulators-forum /trmsrfrnc-eng.pdf.

Government of New Brunswick. 2012. "New Members of Executive Council Sworn In." News release, 9 October. http://www2.gnb.ca/content/gnb/en/news/news_release .2012.10.0930.html.

– 2013a. *Responsible Environmental Management of Oil and Natural Gas Activities in New Brunswick: Rules for Industry*. Fredericton: Government of New Brunswick. http:// www2.gnb.ca/content/dam/gnb/Corporate/pdf/ShaleGas/en/RulesforIndustry.pdf.

– 2013b. "The New Brunswick Oil and Natural Gas Blueprint." Fredericton: Government of New Brunswick. https://www2.gnb.ca/content/dam/gnb/Departments/en/pdf /Publications/ONGEnglishFinal.pdf.

Government of Newfoundland and Labrador. 2013. "Minister Provides Position on Hydraulic Fracturing." Department of Natural Resources. http://www.releases.gov .nl.ca/releases/2013/nr/1104n06.htm.

Hall, Peter A. 1993. "Policy Paradigms, Social Learning, and the State: The Case of Economic Policymaking in Britain." *Comparative Politics* 25 (3): 275–96.

Harrison, Kathryn, ed. 2006. *Racing to the Bottom? Provincial Interdependence in the Canadian Federation.* Vancouver: UBC Press.

Henton, Darcy. 2012. "Energy Bill Seen as 'Train Wreck'; Province Defends Plan to Simplify Approvals." *Calgary Herald*, 5 November, sec. News.

Hoberg, George. 1991. "Sleeping with an Elephant: The American Influence on Canadian Environmental Regulation." *Journal of Public Policy* 11 (1): 107–31. https://doi.org/10.1017/S0143814X00004955.

Huras, Adam. 2012a. "N.B. Proposes Shale Gas Rules; Bruce Fitch Says Regulations Will Be 'the Strongest in North America.'" *The Times – Transcript*, 18 May, sec. Main.

– 2012b. "Havelock Audience Opposes Shale Gas; Consultation Tour on Shale Gas Development Continues." *The Times – Transcript*, 19 June.

– 2013a. "N.B. to Release Shale Gas Rules Today; Regulations Aimed at Setting Parameters for Development of Industry." *The Times – Transcript*, 15 February, sec. Main.

– 2013b. "New N.B. Shale Gas Regulations Are Questioned; Opposition Parties Worried about Compromise, Enforcement." *The Times – Transcript*, 16 February, sec. Job.

Illical, Mary, and Kathryn Harrison. 2007. "Protecting Endangered Species in the US and Canada: The Role of Negative Lesson Drawing." *Canadian Journal of Political Science / Revue Canadienne de Science Politique* 40 (2): 367–94.

Interstate Oil and Gas Compact Commission (IOGCC). n.d.a. "Member States." IOGC. http://iogcc.publishpath.com/member-states.

– n.d.b. "IOGCC International: Achieving Through Cooperation." Oklahoma City, OK: Interstate Oil and Gas Compact Commission. http://iogcc.ok.gov/Websites/iogcc /Images/International%20English.pdf.

Jenkins-Smith, Hank C., Daniel Nohrstedt, Christopher M. Weible, and Paul A. Sabatier. 2014. "The Advocacy Coalition Framework: Foundations, Evolutions, and Ongoing Research." In *Theories of the Policy Process*, edited by Paul A. Sabatier and Christopher M. Weible, 3rd ed., 183–223. Boulder, CO: Westview Press.

Karch, Andrew. 2007. *Democratic Laboratories: Policy Diffusion among the American States.* Ann Arbor: University of Michigan Press.

LaPierre, Louis. 2012. "The Path Forward." Fredericton: Government of New Brunswick. http://www2.gnb.ca/content/dam/gnb/Corporate/pdf/ShaleGas/en/ThePathForward .pdf.

Macdonald, Douglas, and Matthew Lesch. 2015. "Management of Distributive Conflicts Impeding Expansion of Interprovincial Hydroelectricity Transmission." *Journal of Canadian Studies/Revue d'études Canadiennes* 49 (3): 191–221.

May, Peter J. 1992. "Policy Learning and Failure." *Journal of Public Policy* 12 (4): 331–54.

Mazerolle, Brent. 2013a. "N.B. Has Huge Shale Gas Potential: LaPierre; Head of New Energy Institute Discusses Province's Future Energy Developments with Moncton Audience." *The Times – Transcript*, 7 February, sec. Main.

– 2013b. "Energy Institute Starts Work." *The Times – Transcript*, 17 August, sec. A.

McHardie, Daniel. 2016. "New Brunswick Extends Fracking Moratorium, Energy Minister Says." *CBC News*, 27 May. http://www.cbc.ca/news/canada/new-brunswick /arseneault-fracking-commission-report-1.3602849.

Millar, Heather. 2019. "Managing Uncertainty: Risk Narratives and Learning in Provincial Hydraulic Fracturing Regulation in Canada 2006–2016." PhD diss., University of Toronto.

Montpetit, Éric, Erick Lachapelle, and Alexandre Harvey. 2016. "Advocacy Coalitions, the Media, and Hydraulic Fracturing in the Canadian Provinces of British Columbia and Quebec." In *Policy Debates on Hydraulic Fracturing: Comparing Coalition Politics in North America and Europe*, edited by Christopher M. Weible, Tanya Heikkila, Karin Ingold, and Manuel Fischer, 53–79. New York: Springer.

Morris, Chris. 2011. "Minister Investigating Shale Gas Exploration; Margaret Ann Blaney Headed to Pennsylvania next Week." *The Times – Transcript*, 12 May, sec. Main. http://search.proquest.com.myaccess.library.utoronto.ca/canadiannews/docview /866011324/8C58322F19D6469DPQ/17?accountid=14771#.

Neville, Kate J., Jennifer Baka, Shanti Gamper-Rabindran, Karen Bakker, Stefan Andreasson, Avner Vengosh, Alvin Lin, Jewellord Nem Singh, and Erika Weinthal. 2017. "Debating Unconventional Energy: Social, Political, and Economic Implications." *Annual Review of Environment and Resources* 42 (1): 241–66. https://doi.org/10.1146 /annurev-environ-102016-061102.

Neville, Kate J., and Erika Weinthal. 2016. "Mitigating Mistrust? Participation and Expertise in Hydraulic Fracturing Governance." *Review of Policy Research* 33 (6): 578–602. https://doi.org/10.1111/ropr.12201.

New Brunswick Natural Gas Group. 2012a. "Responsible Environmental Management of Oil and Gas Activities in New Brunswick: List of References." Fredericton: Government of New Brunswick. https://www2.gnb.ca/content/dam/gnb/Corporate /pdf/ShaleGas/en/ListOfReferences.pdf.

– 2012b. "Responsible Environmental Management of Oil and Gas Activities in New Brunswick Recommendations for Public Discussion." Fredericton: Government of New Brunswick. http://www2.gnb.ca/content/dam/gnb/Corporate/pdf/ShaleGas/en /RecommendationsDiscussion.pdf.

Olive, Andrea. 2016. "What Is the Fracking Story in Canada?" *The Canadian Geographer / Le Géographe Canadien*, 60 (1): 32–45. https://doi.org/10.1111/cag.12257.

– 2018. "Oil Development in the Grasslands: Saskatchewan's Bakken Formation and Species at Risk Protection." *Cogent Environmental Science* 4 (1): 1443666. https://doi .org/10.1080/23311843.2018.1443666.

Olive, Andrea, and Katie Valentine. 2018. "Is Anyone out There? Exploring Saskatchewan's Civil Society Involvement in Hydraulic Fracturing." *Energy Research & Social Science* 39 (May): 192–7. https://doi.org/10.1016/j.erss.2017.11.014.

Penty, Rebecca. 2011. "Fracking Fears Spur Review of Oilpatch Regulations; Provinces Commited to Registry to Disclose Use of Chemicals." *Calgary Herald*, 30 December, sec. Calgary Business.

Progressive Conservative Party of New Brunswick (PCNB). 2010. "Putting New Brunswick First ... FOR A CHANGE." Fredericton: PCNB. https://www.poltext.org/sites /poltext.org/files/plateformes/nb2010pc_plt_en_13072011_132739.pdf.

Rabe, Barry G. 2014. "Shale Play Politics: The Intergovernmental Odyssey of American Shale Governance." *Environmental Science & Technology*, February. https://doi.org /10.1021/es4051132.

Rabe, Barry G., and Christopher Borick. 2013. "Conventional Politics for Unconventional Drilling? Lessons from Pennsylvania's Early Move into Fracking Policy Development." *Review of Policy Research* 30 (3): 321–40. https://doi.org/10.1111/ropr.12018.

Rietig, Katharina. 2018. "The Links Among Contested Knowledge, Beliefs, and Learning in European Climate Governance: From Consensus to Conflict in Reforming Biofuels Policy." *Policy Studies Journal* 46 (1): 137–59. https://doi.org/10.1111/psj.12169.

Rose, Richard. 1991. "What Is Lesson-Drawing?" *Journal of Public Policy* 11 (1): 3–30. https://doi.org/10.1017/S0143814X00004918.

Schultz, R., G. Atkinson, D. W. Eaton, Y. J. Gu, and H. Kao. 2018. "Hydraulic Fracturing Volume Is Associated with Induced Earthquake Productivity in the Duvernay Play." *Science* 359 (6373): 304–8. https://doi.org/10.1126/science.aao0159.

Stone, Diane. 2017. "Understanding the Transfer of Policy Failure: Bricolage, Experimentalism and Translation." *Policy & Politics* 45 (1): 55–70. https://doi .org/10.1332/030557316X14748914098041.

United States Energy Information Administration (US EIA). 2013. "Technically Recoverable Shale Oil and Shale Gas Resources: An Assessment of 137 Shale Formations in 41 Countries Outside the United States." Washington, DC: U.S. Department of Energy. http://www.eia.gov/analysis/studies/worldshalegas/.

– 2017. "Annual Energy Outlook 2017." Washington, DC: U.S. Department of Energy. https://www.eia.gov/outlooks/aeo/.

Vasi, Ion Bogdan, Edward T. Walker, John S. Johnson, and Hui Fen Tan. 2015. "'No Fracking Way!' Documentary Film, Discursive Opportunity, and Local Opposition against Hydraulic Fracturing in the United States, 2010 to 2013." *American Sociological Review* 80 (5): 934–59. https://doi.org/10.1177/0003122415598534.

Vogel, David. 2000. "Environmental Regulation and Economic Integration." *Journal of International Economic Law* 3 (2): 265–79. https://doi.org/10.1093/jiel/3.2.265.

Wellstead, Adam, Paul Cairney, and Kathryn Oliver. 2018. "Reducing Ambiguity to Close the Science-Policy Gap." *Policy Design and Practice* 1 (2): 115–25. https://doi .org/10.1080/25741292.2018.1458397.

Weible, Christopher M. 2008. "Expert-Based Information and Policy Subsystems: A Review and Synthesis." *Policy Studies Journal* 36 (4): 615–35. https://doi.org/10.1111 /j.1541-0072.2008.00287.x.

4

Endangered Species Legislation in Canada: Convergence that Matters

ANDREA OLIVE

In 1995, public workshops were held across Canada to determine what criteria should be included in a national approach to wildlife conservation. In 1996, the provinces,[1] the territories, and the federal government signed the National Accord for the Protection of Species at Risk (henceforth, the Accord) and agreed to create similar species at risk policies. Twenty years later, have we seen policy convergence? If so, is it a result of policy transfer and learning? If not, where have species at risk policies failed to take root and why? In answering these questions, this chapter has three broad purposes: (1) to examine innovation and diffusion of endangered species[2] legislation (ESL) across Canada; (2) to examine the quality and character-istics of ESLs; and, (3) to determine if late adopters learned from prior policy. The overall argument is that there has been ESL innovation in all jurisdictions with convergence on very specific criteria. Diffusion and convergence can be explained by competition between the provinces and coercion from the federal government.

The chapter proceeds in six parts. In the first section, I briefly introduce the literature on policy innovation and convergence by examining theories of policy transfer. In section two, I provide a short overview of wildlife legislation and ESL in Canada, with close attention to the 1996 Accord and its agreed-upon criteria. This section concludes with a few hypotheses based on the literature within the political context. The third part is an explanation of the methods and data collec-tion, while section four presents the results. The hypotheses are reviewed in sec-tion five, in light of the results, and the concluding section reflects on the overall findings.

Policy Innovation and Convergence

Walker (1969, 881) defines a policy innovation as a "program or policy which is new to the state adopting it." This simplified definition suggests that any jurisdic-tion adopting any type of ESL is engaged in policy innovation. Taking this idea of innovation a step further, Knill (2005, 768) defines convergence as "any increase in the similarity between one or more institutional characteristics across a given set of political jurisdictions." As illustrated in a number of chapters in this book, there is a lot of theorization about why a state might adopt a new policy and why we might see convergence over time. These processes are different and should be treated separately.

A commonly accepted definition of policy transfer is a process by which "knowledge about policies, administrative arrangements, institutions, and ideas in one political setting (past or present) is used in development of policies, administrative arrangements, institutions, and ideas in another political setting" (Dolowitz and Marsh 2000, 5). Policy diffusion, a related concept stemming more from scholarship on international relations, is commonly defined as "a process through which policy choices in one country affect those made in a second country" (Marsh and Sherman 2009, 270: see also Simmons and Elkins 2004). For our purposes here, transfer and diffusion will be treated as complementary core concepts.[3]

Drawing on the introductory chapter by Boyd in this volume, my research engages with the common diffusion framework shown in Table 1.2 (Berry and Berry 2018; Shipan and Volden 2008). Like other authors, I see typical explanations for transfer/diffusion as competition, coercion, emulation/imitation, or learning (Simmons, Dobbin, and Garrett 2008) and operationalize these concepts in similar ways. However, when it comes to coercion, I make a distinction between direct and indirect force and include "normative pressure" as a type of indirect force/coercion. This is based on my understanding of literature that examines policy diffusion and convergence in Canada and the United States.

Coercion suggests that policies diffuse through "physical force, the manipulation of economic costs and benefits, and even the monopolization of information" (Dobbin, Simmons, and Garrett 2007, 454). Essentially, one government forces another government to adopt a policy (Dolowitz and Marsh 1996). However, the "force" can be "indirect coercive transfer," where the role of externalities influences a government to adopt a new policy. Hoberg (1991), for example, suggests that American policies could put Canada at an economic disadvantage and thereby indirectly coerce Canada towards policy innovation. Dolowitz and Marsh (1996, 348) also agree that "there is little doubt that externalities, which result from interdependence, push government to work together to solve common problems." So, for example, when the United States adopted new emissions standards for light cars and trucks, Canada was pressured to do so as well, given that auto manufacturing is integrated across the border.

Relatedly, Dolowitz and Marsh (1996, 349) point out that "international consensus may act as a push factor." Here the coercion is again indirect, as the international community can pressure countries into conforming with international norms. And similarly, at the domestic level, Baumgartner and Jones (2009) argue that the federal government can be a catalyst for encouraging subnational jurisdictions to adopt new policy. In the same way that the international community pressures countries, the federal government can pressure provinces. Or, the coercion can be more direct, where the federal government will incentivize policy adoption, create regulatory burdens for non-adoption, or even outright demand policy adoption. Thus, similar to competition, coercion can be the "unsolicited external force that limit actor's choices" (Klingler-Vidra and Schleifer 2014, 270).

Outside of this narrower conception of coercion, this chapter uses the common diffusion framework (Table 1.2 in chapter 1 of this volume), similar to that used by other authors, to explain policy diffusion. Indeed, there is ample literature to suggest that policy innovation in any given jurisdiction is the result of one of those four mechanisms. The questions then become: Should we expect policy convergence? Given enough time, will all states adopt similar policies? The convergence literature provides a caution to pay careful attention to which ideas do and do not spread. Glick and Hays (1991, 836) point out that, "instead of a single policy spreading uniformly throughout the states, policymaking may exhibit initial innovation, varied diffusion, and reinvention over time." A policy may change in form over time or may be copied into a different political context or system where changes are necessary. Klingler-Vidra and Schleifer (2014, 264) suggest that "as they diffuse, norms, ideas, and practices often change in form and content" such that policies "are transformed, leading to less than full convergence" (267). Thus, all countries might have a child welfare policy, but policies will look considerably different across states in terms of substance (White & Prentice 2016).

The passage of time adds a dimension to policy innovation that allows for lesson- drawing. Late adopters can modify policy innovations based on the experience of early adopters (Hays 1996, 631). But when innovation occurs through learning, it may lead to expansion in policy scope (Hays 1996, 633). Innovation or "reinvention" shows that "later adopters feel free to adapt these innovative policies to suit their individual needs and circumstances and, more importantly, that there are lessons to be learned from patient observation (Hays 1996, 647). Indeed, Klingler-Vidra and Schleifer (2014) suggest that coercion, competition, and emulation mechanisms are conducive to more convergence, whereas learning facilitates less convergence. As states learn, they adapt and adjust their policies.

Endangered Species Legislation in Canada

During the second wave of environmentalism (1960s and 1970s), the federal government passed the Canadian Wildlife Act and created the Committee on the Status of Endangered Wildlife in Canada (COSEWIC). This committee assesses all native wildlife in Canada and makes scientific recommendations about species status (i.e., endangered, threatened, etc.). The impetus for COSEWIC came from environmental activists and scientists who saw "the creation of a single national list of endangered species as essential to a coherent, science-based program of species protection" (Bocking 2001, 119). Indeed, the creation of COSEWIC was necessary if the Canadian government was going to make any claim to protecting wildlife.

This became especially clear when Canada ratified the United Nation's Convention on Biological Diversity in 1993. With no domestic ESL to speak of, this was a rather bold move. In 1995 the government released its first draft of ESL, which was very limited (to federal lands) and very discretionary (leaving habitat protection to ministerial discretion). While disappointing to environmental groups, the draft proposal highlighted the limited authority of the federal government on this issue (Elgie 2009; Amos, Harrison, and Hoberg 2001). Provinces have authority over Crown lands and private property, which are critical for endangered species that need their habitat protected for long-term survival. The federal government does have jurisdiction over migratory birds, aquatic species, and federal lands. And it also retains ownership over Crown lands in the territories, which is not an insignificant amount of land.

If anything, the ESL draft of 1995 signalled a need to work closely with the provinces. This is why the Accord was necessary. The federal government held public consultations across the country, and, in 1996, the environment minister from each province met to discuss and agree upon a national approach to endangered species' protection. Each signatory to the Accord agreed to participate in the Canadian Endangered Species Conservation Council and recognize the COSEWIC as a source of independent advice on the status of species at risk nationally. All jurisdictions also agreed to "establish complementary legislation and programs that provide for effective protection of species at risk throughout Canada" (Government of Canada 1996). The goals for the complementary legislation were fairly specific in that it included fifteen criteria. Essentially, all species at risk laws in Canada should

1. address all native wild species;
2. provide an independent process for assessing the status of species at risk;
3. legally designate species as threatened or endangered;
4. provide immediate legal protection for threatened or endangered species;
5. provide protection for the habitat of threatened or endangered species;
6. provide for the development of recovery plans within one year for endangered species and two years for threatened species;
7. ensure multi-jurisdictional cooperation for the protection of species that cross borders through the development and implementation of recovery plans;
8. consider the needs of species at risk as part of environmental assessment processes;
9. implement recovery plans in a timely fashion;
10. monitor, assess, and report regularly on the status of all wild species;
11. emphasize preventive measures to keep species from becoming at risk;

12. improve awareness of the needs of species at risk;
13. encourage citizens to participate in conservation and protection actions;
14. recognize, foster, and support effective and long-term stewardship by resource users and managers, landowners, and other citizens; and
15. provide for effective enforcement.

These criteria set a high bar for ESL. At the time, in 1996, no existing provincial or federal piece of legislation came close to meeting even half of these criteria, let alone all fifteen. In fact, criteria 6 through 14 were virtually unheard of in Canadian policy. If we consider each criterion, we see there are real differences in the importance each places on species at risk and their feasibility, for politicians trying to realize each in a regulatory framework. The first two criteria speak to the evolving role of wildlife science in the 1970s and 1980s because science could by then provide "essential information regarding the status of endangered species" (Bocking 2001, 125). However, the jump from criteria 2 to 3 – from independent scientists assessing the status to politicians legally designating a species as endangered or threatened – is huge. In hindsight, it turned out to be the most controversial aspect of species at risk laws across Canada (Elgie 2009; Mooers et al. 2007).

Criteria 4, 5, and 6 are, perhaps, equally as controversial as criterion 3, but for economic reasons. Legally protecting a species as well as its habitat could, and often does, put a significant burden on industries like agriculture and forestry, among others. And policymakers protecting species and/or habitat can encounter opposition from Indigenous Peoples. Moreover, the fact that these plans must be implemented in a timely fashion, as per criterion 8, suggests that provinces cannot create symbolic species lists with aspirational recovery plans. Instead, the Accord criteria are ambitious and create the potential for serious opposition from landowners and industry inside each province. This makes follow-through on the 1996 Accord politically difficult. As Amos, Harrison, and Hoberg (2001, 150) suggest, stringent species at risk legislation can engender some political support from voters, but it has the "potential to generate strong and enduring opposition from those who would pay the price."

The goal of multi-jurisdictional cooperation on recovery plans, criterion 7, is a challenge for federalism where provinces are sovereign decision makers when it comes to public and private lands. However, the early 1990s was marked by cooperation between government jurisdictions through harmonization and Canadian-wide standards. Thus, the presence of criterion 7 is not surprising, since the Accord was "developed in the spirit of an ongoing federal-provincial harmonization exercise" and thereby designed to "ensure a seamless web of protective legislation across all Canadian jurisdictions" (Amos, Harrison, and Hoberg 2001, 141). Moreover, since wildlife science had evolved and more was known about ecosystems and habitat, it made sense to take a multi-jurisdictional cooperative approach.

Considering species at risk in environmental assessment plans, criterion 8 puts regulatory, scientific, and economic burdens on the provinces. It is both time-consuming and expensive to evaluate land prior to development projects and use the presence or absence of species as part of the decision-making process. Criteria 10 and 15 speak to monitoring and enforcement, which should be part of all public policy. Criteria 11 through 14 are about the process of implementing ESL whereby citizens must be made aware and included in the stewardship of species at risk. In the case histories of ESL in Canada provided by Amos, Harrison, and Hoberg (2001) and Bocking (2001), there is no indication that these criteria were controversial. More broadly, Bocking (2001, 125) suggests that "new wildlife and endangered species policies were generally seen by government and public alike as part of a larger response to environmental concerns."

Immediately following the Accord, the federal government introduced Bill C-65, which would have been the country's first national ESL. Environmental groups and scientists immediately argued that the bill was too weak to be effective, whereas industry groups and landowners worried about habitat regulations and the lack of compensation and incentives for affected parties (Elgie 2009; see also Amos, Harrison, and Hoburg 2001). Over 130 amendments were made to the bill but an early election in April 1997 left the bill on the table. Without federal legislation, provinces began to fill the void with their own legislation. Between 1996 and 2000, when the next federal bill was introduced, eight provincial policies were amended or enacted. In early April of 2000, the federal government introduced the Species at Risk Act (SARA) into Parliament. An early election meant SARA was once again left in limbo. When the Liberal Party won another mandate, SARA was reintroduced and became law in December 2002. Provincial governments had always maintained that wildlife was their jurisdiction (Bocking 2001). Prior to the Accord, only six provinces had ESL, and, of these, only two (Quebec and Manitoba) had paid particular attention to the needs of endangered species, whereas the other four were more concerned with hunting and fishing regulations.

Expectations

Based on the policy literature and the legislative context of ESL in Canada, we could expect to see three things:

1. Policy innovation to occur in all provinces and territories that signed the Accord.
2. Policy convergence with the Accord criteria over time.
   a. The least convergence with criteria that impart economic or regulatory costs since these criteria would have the most opposition from landowners and industry stakeholders. Specifically, these would be criteria 2, 3, 4, 5, 8, and 9.

3. Policy learning to occur.
   a. Very late adopters may diverge from Accord criteria on the basis of learning.

Canada's ESL is a case study of policy diffusion and convergence, but it is unlike standard models of diffusion where one jurisdiction innovates and others later adopt a similar (or the same) policy. In those cases, there are no prior discussions or agreements about what policy should, ideally, look like. In Canada, relevant governments gathered and agreed upon the substance and diffusion of the ESL policy. Nevertheless, this chapter suggests that Canadian ESL is an excellent case of policy diffusion and convergence exactly because it demonstrates how policy diffusion occurs unevenly, and how convergence is not guaranteed even when agreed upon. (This is a bit similar to the situation discussed by Wesley in chapter 7 of this volume, where all jurisdictions agreed to create cannabis policy because of federal direction – but then did so in different ways.) As this chapter will demonstrate, in 2019 there was still variation across jurisdictions and, more importantly, the most recent legislation is looking more like policy reinvention than convergence.

Methodology

This chapter relies on Hall's (1993) typology of policy change as described in chapter 1 of this volume. (Also see Table 1.3 in chapter 1.) I examine "settings" (or "first-order changes") and "instruments" (or "second-order changes") as dependent variables in the diffusion of ESL in Canada. Specifically, I examine not only which provinces adopted ESL (instruments) but also how many of the fifteen Accord criteria (settings) were included in the legislation once passed. I am not looking at the ideological underpinnings of the policy (which would be "third-order changes") in each province as those goals were already agreed upon in the Accord discussions. To examine broader goals would be a different project, focused on Canada's larger biodiversity strategy as opposed to just endangered species legislation.

This study is a qualitative examination of fourteen jurisdictions – all provinces and territories plus the federal government. The arguments presented about instruments (the passage of policy) and settings (the fifteen criteria) required in-depth analysis of each provinces/territories' ESL history. To examine the extent of policy convergence, I examined each piece of ESL that was passed into law in each province. To find these laws, I searched the Legislative Assembly bill-finder website and consulted government websites and secondary literature. Once a bill was located, it was carefully read to see if the fifteen criteria from the Accord were met. I coded each as a dichotomous yes/no evaluation of the laws, such that regulation applies to all native species (yes or no), regulation categorizes species into endangered and threatened (yes or no), and so on through all criteria. (I assessed the language of the written law, not the implementation of those laws.)

To examine the extent of policy learning, I examined the legislative debates and the committee hearings, where available, for each endangered species or wildlife act in each jurisdiction. These documents were retrieved from the online databases of provincial legislative assemblies. Each debate was read with careful attention to mentions of federal legislation (Bill C-65 or SARA), the Accord, or other provincial legislation/programs. Again, these were recorded as dichotomous yes/no evaluations that were then supported by quotations taken from the legislative debates.

Unfortunately, as mentioned again below, background policy papers and white papers are not available for systematic and comparative review. The analysis here relies upon bills and legislative debates. Ideally, it would be best to interview decision-makers as to what sources they consulted when devising ESL in their province. However, given that over twenty pieces of ESL are analysed, there would be literally hundreds of policymakers dating back to 1996. Thus, the legislative debates serve as the next-best way to uncover the extent to which policymakers were drawing on previous examples of ESL. But this is a limitation on the extent and types of claims that can be made about learning and emulation. Since legislatures are not where policy is considered and developed in the Westminster system, direct insight into emulation is not possible. However, examination of the language of bills and of general discussion in the Legislative Assembly can still provide evidence of influence.

Data and Results

In total, I found twenty-nine pieces of ESL as listed in Table 4.1. The first law was passed in 1971 in Ontario, and the most recent law was passed in Manitoba in 2013. While I am interested in what happened after the 1996 Accord, it is important to provide a fuller picture, because some provinces had an institutional legacy of existing policy while others did not. This history likely influenced the discussion and debate at the 1996 Accord as some provinces already had specific criteria in their existing policies and may have been reluctant to make changes (Amos, Harrison, and Hoberg 2001).

The list of ESL includes amendments to existing laws (as noted; but only when the amendments changed the substance of the law and not just the list of species) as well as the creation of new laws. One thing that stands out immediately – some provinces enact "wildlife" acts while other provinces enact "endangered species" or "species at risk" acts. This distinction is not simply rhetorical. In provinces where the policy is a "wildlife act" the intent of the law is to regulate human-wildlife interactions, especially in terms of hunting and fishing. However, wildlife acts are included in this list when they include specific provisions for endangered species.

When examining policy transfer and learning, it is not the presence of legislation but "the stringency of these regulations" that is of crucial importance (Ringquist 1994, 30). Table 4.2 presents the results of comparing ESL against the

Table 4.1. Provincial Endangered Species Legislation, 1971–2019

Year	Province	Act
1971	Ontario	Endangered Species Act
1973	New Brunswick	Endangered Species Act
1980	British Columbia	Wildlife Act
1980	New Brunswick	Fish and Wildlife Act
1984	Alberta	Wildlife Act
1988	Prince Edward Island	Wildlife Conservation Act
1988	Northwest Territories	Wildlife Act
1989	Quebec	Act Respecting Threatened or Vulnerable Species
1989	Nova Scotia	Wildlife Act
1990	Manitoba	Endangered Species Act
1990	Newfoundland	Wild Life Act
1990	Ontario	Endangered Species Act
1993	Manitoba	Endangered Species Act – Amendments
1996	New Brunswick	Endangered Species Act
1996	Alberta	Wildlife Act – Amendments
1996	British Columbia	Wildlife Act – Amendments
1997	Quebec	Act Respecting Threatened or Vulnerable Species – Amendments
1998	Nova Scotia	Endangered Species Act
1998	Saskatchewan	Wildlife Act
1998	Prince Edward Island	Wildlife Conservation Act
2000	Alberta	Wildlife Act – Amendments
2001	Newfoundland	Endangered Species Act
2002	Yukon	Wildlife Act (Regulations added in 2012, but not to ESL)
2003	Nunavut	Wildlife Act (Regulations added in 2015, but not to ESL)
2004	British Columbia	Wildlife Act – Amendments
2007	Ontario	Endangered Species Act
2009	Northwest Territories	Species at Risk Act
2012	New Brunswick	Species at Risk Act
2013	Manitoba	Endangered Species and Ecosystems Act

Accord criteria. The rows represent the provincial policy (ordered by year of adoption) and the columns represent the fifteen Accord criteria presented in the order stated previously. The "total" column refers to how many of the Accord criteria the single policy met out of a possible fifteen criteria, and the "total" row at the bottom captures how many of the criteria were met over the years, out of a possible twenty-five attempts.[4] So, for example, criterion 1 (addressing all native species) is met in 15 of the 25 counts of ESL. Note that Table 4.2 includes SARA in italics for illustrative purposes. It is not included in the tally for each criterion at the bottom.

Table 4.2. Provincial Endangered Species Policies by Accord Criteria (1–15), 1971–2014

	1	2	3	4	5	6	7	8	9	10	11	12	13	14	15	Total criteria met
ON 1971	N	N	N	Y	N	N	N	N	N	N	N	N	N	N	N	1
NB 1973	N	N	N	Y	N	N	N	N	N	N	N	N	N	N	N	1
BC 1980	N	N	Y	Y	N	N	N	N	N	N	N	N	N	N	Y	2
AB 1984	N	N	N	N	N	N	N	N	N	N	N	N	N	N	Y	1
QU 1989	N	N	Y	Y	Y	N	N	N	N	N	N	N	N	N	Y	4
MAN 1990	Y	Y	Y	Y	Y	N	N	N	N	N	N	N	N	N	Y	6
MAN 1993	Y	Y	Y	Y	Y	N	N	N	N	Y	N	N	N	N	Y	7
BC 1996	N	N	Y	Y	Y	N	N	N	N	N	N	N	N	N	Y	4
NB 1996	Y	N	N	Y	Y	N	N	N	N	N	N	N	N	N	N	3
AB 1996	N	Y	N	Y	Y	N	Y	N	N	N	N	N	N	Y	Y	6
QU 1997	Y	N	Y	Y	Y	N	N	N	N	N	N	N	N	N	Y	5
SK 1998	Y	N	Y	Y	N	N	Y	N	N	N	N	N	Y	N	Y	6
NS 1998	Y	Y	Y	Y	Y	Y	Y	Y	Y	Y	Y	Y	Y	Y	Y	15
PEI 1998	Y	N	Y	Y	Y	N	N	N	N	Y	N	N	Y	Y	Y	8
AB 2000	Y	Y	Y	Y	Y	Y	N	N	N	N	Y	N	N	N	Y	8
NFLD 2001	Y	Y	Y	Y	Y	Y	Y	N	Y	Y	N	Y	N	N	Y	11
YU 2002	N	N	N	N	Y	N	N	N	N	N	N	N	N	N	N	1
SARA 2002	Y	Y	Y	Y	Y	Y	Y	Y	Y	Y	Y	Y	Y	Y	Y	15
NU 2003	Y	Y	Y	Y	Y	N	Y	N	Y	Y	N	Y	Y	Y	Y	12
BC 2004	Y	N	Y	N	Y	N	N	N	N	N	N	N	N	N	Y	4
ON 2007	Y	Y	Y	Y	Y	Y	Y	N	Y	Y	Y	Y	Y	Y	Y	14
NWT 2010	Y	Y	Y	Y	Y	Y	Y	Y	Y	Y	N	N	Y	Y	Y	13
NB 2013	Y	Y	Y	Y	N	N	N	Y	Y	Y	Y	N	N	Y	Y	10
MAN 2013	Y	Y	Y	Y	Y	N	N	N	N	N	N	Y	Y	Y	Y	9
Totals	**15**	**11**	**17**	**20**	**17**	**5**	**7**	**3**	**6**	**5**	**4**	**5**	**7**	**8**	**17**	

What Table 4.2 most clearly illustrates is that the early policies met very few of the Accord criteria while the later policies met most, if not all, of the criteria. I also note a few trends. First, it was not really until the passage of SARA in 2002 that policies started to converge. After SARA passed, the following six ESLs all included twelve or more criteria. Prior to SARA, only the 1998 Nova Scotia law and the 2001 Newfoundland and Labrador law met more than half of the Accord criteria. Second, those policies that converged with Accord criteria had a regional component: all were east or north of Manitoba. That is to say, the Western provinces did not create policies after SARA. In fact, to this day the Western provinces as well as Yukon and Nunavut have no stand-alone ESL. They are joined by Prince Edward Island, which is the only Eastern province to lack legislation.

Third, if we look at the quality of convergence, we can also see that there is the most convergence on criteria 1, 3, 4, 5, and 15. The least convergence over time

Table 4.3. Current Endangered Species Legislation across Provinces/Territories by Accord Criteria (1–15)

	1	2	3	4	5	6	7	8	9	10	11	12	13	14	15	Total criteria met
YU 2002	N	N	N	N	Y	N	N	N	N	N	N	N	N	N	N	1
BC 2004	Y	N	Y	N	Y	N	N	N	N	N	N	N	N	N	Y	4
QU 1997	Y	N	Y	Y	Y	N	N	N	N	N	N	N	N	N	Y	5
SK 1998	Y	N	Y	Y	N	N	Y	N	N	N	N	N	Y	N	Y	6
PEI 1998	Y	N	Y	Y	Y	N	N	N	N	Y	N	N	Y	Y	Y	8
AB 2000	Y	Y	Y	Y	Y	Y	N	N	N	N	Y	N	N	N	Y	8
MAN 2015	Y	Y	Y	Y	Y	N	N	N	N	N	N	Y	Y	Y	Y	9
NB 2013	Y	Y	Y	Y	N	N	N	Y	Y	Y	Y	N	N	Y	Y	10
NFLD 2001	Y	Y	Y	Y	Y	Y	Y	N	Y	Y	N	Y	N	N	Y	11
NU 2003	Y	Y	Y	Y	Y	N	Y	N	Y	Y	N	Y	Y	Y	Y	12
NWT 2010	Y	Y	Y	Y	Y	Y	Y	Y	Y	Y	N	N	Y	Y	Y	13
ON 2008	Y	Y	Y	Y	Y	Y	N	N	Y	Y	Y	Y	Y	Y	Y	14
NS 1998	Y	Y	Y	Y	Y	Y	Y	Y	Y	Y	Y	Y	Y	Y	Y	15
Totals	12	8	12	11	10	5	6	3	6	7	4	5	7	7	14	

is on criteria 9, 11, 6, and 12. Similarly, if we look only at current policies (those being enforced today), as illustrated in Table 4.3, we see the most convergence on criteria 1, 3, 4, and 15. There is the least convergence on 6, 8, 9, 10, and 11 – with less than 50 per cent of provinces adopting these criteria.

Policy Learning?

So whom did the provinces learn from? And what was the source of policy innovation? Table 4.4 illustrates who and what provincial legislators referenced in debates during the passage of their ESL. The rows represent each provincial policy while the columns illustrate whether or not a member of the Legislative Assembly referenced the 1996 Accord, the federal government's legislation (SARA and the attempts prior to it from 1996–2001), or any other prior provincial legislation. The table includes only policies passed between 1995 and 2013. Two of these provinces passed legislation in 1996 and prior to the signing of the Accord. However, since the draft of the Accord was available in 1995, we know that any province creating legislation from 1995 onward could use the Accord criteria as the source of policy inspiration. In cases where no transcripts were available, I have noted it in the table. More qualitative data are presented below, in the form of quotations from debates, to support and contextualize the data in Table 4.4.

Table 4.4. Provincial/Territorial Legislative Debates by Policy and Source of Possible Policy Learning

Province/ territory	Date & policy	Debates mention 1996 Accord?	Debates mention federal legislation?	Debates mention which prior provincial/ territorial legislation?
New Brunswick	1996 (April) Endangered Species Act	No transcripts available	No transcripts available	No transcripts available
British Columbia[a]	1996 Wildlife Act Amendment	No	No	None
Alberta	1996 (May) Wildlife Amendment Act	No	Yes	Manitoba
Saskatchewan	1998 Wildlife Act	No	No	None
Nova Scotia[b]	1998 Endangered Species Act	No	No	None
PEI	1998 Wildlife Conservation Act	No	No	None
Alberta	2000 Wildlife Act – Amendments	No transcripts available	No transcripts available	No transcripts available
NFLD	2001 Endangered Species Act	Yes	No	Nova Scotia
Yukon	2002 Wildlife Act	No	No	None
Nunavut	2003 Wildlife Act	No	No	None
British Columbia	2004 Wildlife Act Amendments	No	Yes	None
Ontario	2008 Endangered Species Act	Yes	Yes	None
Northwest Territories	2010 Species at Risk Act	Yes	No	None
New Brunswick	2012 Species at Risk Act	Yes	Yes	Nova Scotia, British Columbia, the Northwest Territories, and Ontario
Manitoba	2015 Endangered Species and Ecosystem Act	No	No	None

[a] The 1996 British Columbia Wildlife Act Amendment came through the budget speech. There was no debate – instead it was announced that the Wildlife Act is "amended to establish a new habitat conservation fund special account to allow for increased enhancement and habitat protection initiatives."

[b] There are only transcripts available for the first and second reading. The committee hearing transcripts are not available.

Overall, only five provinces mentioned the Accord when debating their own legislation. And in none of these cases did a member of a legislature mention any of the specific criteria contained in the Accord. Only four provinces mentioned the federal legislation in any capacity and only two discussed it in any detail. Finally, only three provinces mentioned ESL in other provinces during debate. These results will now be put in their political context and broken down by time periods.

Accord 1995–1996

Alberta was the first province to pass legislation within the Accord time frame. The province acted early and passed a bill in May of 1996 – five months before officially signing the Accord. When introducing the Wildlife Act, the bill sponsor suggested that the bill was both "complementary to the national approach to endangered species conservation by other jurisdictions across Canada, and it promotes co-operative approaches to solving problems" (Alberta 1996). This statement is far from true about the Wildlife Act, which provides almost no protection whatsoever to endangered species in Alberta (Fluker and Stacey 2012). Thus, it was not surprising that the opposition fired back by saying this bill in no way illustrates a government commitment to endangered species, "unlike Manitoba, which has now enacted endangered species legislation" (Alberta 1996). Manitoba passed its ESA in 1990, amended it in 1993, and was, at the time, the country's leader in protecting endangered species and habitat. The same minister also mentioned that other provinces had already "enacted endangered species legislation" but did not give any specifics. Aside from these brief references, there is no indication that Alberta tried to emulate or learn from Manitoba. And there is no indication that Alberta ever tried to meet the drafted Accord criteria. Nevertheless, just after passing the Wildlife Act, Alberta signed the Accord and agreed to collaborate on the creation of a policy that would meet the fifteen criteria. As of 2019, Alberta has not yet done so.

Post-Accord/Pre-SARA 1997–2000

In 1998, Nova Scotia debated and passed its first – and groundbreaking – Endangered Species Act. Legislative debates illustrate how the province was influenced by its commitments under the Accord as well as international treaties. The MLA who introduced the bill claimed the legislation "is modeled on exactly the kind of legislation that was contemplated by the federal government. This is a model that derives from international treaties where there has been consideration given to the kind of protection that is appropriate for endangered species" (Nova Scotia 1998). Another MLA supported the legislation by pointing out that "all of the provinces and, indeed, the federal government for some time have been working towards establishing legislation of this nature, so that we have a commonality across the country in dealing with the protection of endangered species" (Nova Scotia 1998). Nova Scotia did not use the template of any existing ESL in the country and was the first jurisdiction in Canada to meet Accord criteria 6, 9, 10, 11, 12, and 13. Moreover, the Nova Scotia ESL was dissimilar to Saskatchewan and Prince Edward Island's Wildlife Acts adopted in the same year, both of which barely met half the Accord criteria. In those provinces, legislative records gave no indication of any policy transfer from the Accord or other ESLs in Canada.

SARA 2000–2002

When Newfoundland passed its ESA in 2001, the bill sponsor began legislative debate by pointing out that Newfoundland was "the sixth province to do this now. This is modeled on other provinces across Canada" (Newfoundland and Labrador 2001). However, there was a divide among MLAs about whether to follow Nova Scotia's lead or go along with other provinces that opted to give politicians (normally cabinet) discretion over which species would be listed and what habitats would be protected. One MLA argued for the Nova Scotia model because a "Species at Risk Working Group, appointed by the minister, must have members who are recognized scientific experts in their field" (Newfoundland and Labrador 2001) to make listing decisions. He was suggesting that the Nova Scotia model met the Accord's criteria and, thus, should be followed. However, the government speakers responded by suggesting that nondiscretionary decision-making "hasn't worked in the United States and it will not work here. Conservation progress and lessons from years of experience working with private landowners and the farming community would go down the drain" (Newfoundland and Labrador 2001). Essentially there was a real debate about where to look for lessons and what lessons to draw. Nova Scotia wanted to follow the policy leader, while the other side wanted to learn from the American experience as well as past provincial experience. Ultimately, the Government of Newfoundland and Labrador passed its nondiscretionary ESL with the argument that it "is the same as in five other provinces. Basically, we are doing what the other provinces are doing" (Newfoundland and Labrador 2001).

The federal SARA was introduced in 2000 in the House of Commons and finally passed in 2002. During this time period, Yukon and Nunavut quickly passed their own Wildlife Acts. Yukon's law met only one of the Accord criteria, while Nunavut's law met twelve, which is interesting because the Yukon was a signatory to the Accord while Nunavut was not (since it did not exist in 1996). In both cases, the legislative proceedings contain no mention of the federal government, the Accord, or other jurisdictions in Canada. In the case of Yukon, the entire process lasted a little over a month with a first reading in October 2001, a second reading in early November, a committee hearing at the end of November, and a third reading (and passage) on 29 November 2001. It is unclear why the Yukon included a "specially protected species" category in its policy at all given that today the law only protects four species that are already protected by SARA.[5]

Post-SARA 2004

In 2004, British Columbia opted to amend its 1996 Wildlife Act. There is no indication that MLAs were looking to the Accord for inspiration. Indeed, if anything, the legislative debate suggests that British Columbia was actively trying to take its own approach to wildlife conservation – one that was set out in a number of overlapping policies, from forestry, to parks, to wildlife. The bill sponsor, MLA Barisoff, said, when introducing the 2004 amendments, "together with other legislation that addresses species at risk, such as the Forest and Range Practices Act, these amendments will provide the province with the necessary tools to address the protection and management of species in the manner that makes sense from the British Columbia perspective" (British Columbia 2004). Similar to Newfoundland in 2001, in British Columbia MLAs debated automatic versus discretionary listing of species. In this case, British Columbia's MLAs did not look to Nova Scotia but closely examined SARA, which also included automatic listings based on scientific evidence. After lengthy and in-depth discussion, about how SARA and COSEWIC work in terms of listing and making habitat decisions, British Columbia's Wildlife Act was made discretionary.

Ontario MPPs did not look to other provincial legislation in 2007, while debating their new ESA. However, the Liberal Party, which held a majority government at the time, did invoke the Accord on numerous occasions as both motivation and justification for policy innovation. When introducing the bill, the sponsor argued:

> When Ontario signed the 1996 accord for protection of species at risk in Canada, along with other provinces and territories, the government of the day made a commitment to put in place an effective legislative framework to protect our province's endangered and threatened species. This commitment remains unfulfilled in Ontario, while most other provinces have updated, or are updating, their legislation for species at risk today. We must act now to meet our commitment to the accord and our obligation to the people of Ontario. (Ontario 2007)

This rhetoric is used throughout debate to continually justify why the government was adopting new policy. The Ontario ESA had met fourteen of the Accord criteria and has become one of the strongest ESLs in North America.[6]

In 2009, the Northwest Territories passed their Species at Risk Act. While elaborating on the background behind this bill, one MLA explained that "all provincial, territorial and federal governments responsible for the management of wildlife agreed in principle to the National Accord for the Protection of Species at Risk" (Northwest Territories 2009). However, representatives from the territory did not discuss other jurisdictions' existing policies – not even the Yukon or Nunavut. In the end, the Northwest Territory SARA did include thirteen of the Accord criteria.

There is, however, evidence to suggest that the Accord and other provinces influenced New Brunswick in 2012. When introducing the second reading of the bill, the sponsoring MLA referenced that the Act "will allow us to meet the commitments set out in the national accord. This Act complements the national approach to the management of species at risk" (New Brunswick 2012). Moreover, he went on to suggest that New Brunswick was under pressure to "get up to the level of the other provinces and territories" (New Brunswick 2012). There is some recognition that the province was falling behind the others on this issue and was late to innovate. The government made specific reference to policy in other jurisdictions saying that, "the federal government has a federally incorporated Species at Risk Act. Nova Scotia, British Columbia, the Northwest Territories, and Ontario have their own provincial species at risk acts. They work in conjunction with each other, and they share information with each other" (New Brunswick 2012). It is not entirely clear why British Columbia was included on this list, but it might have been in reference to the British Columbia-Canada agreement on species at risk signed in 2005.

Finally, MLAs in Manitoba felt they were innovating with the passage of their 2014 Endangered Species and Ecosystem Act (ESEA). The bill sponsor told the House that "this is legislation that is unique in North America" and he trusts "that other jurisdictions will be looking at the implementation of this legislation here in Manitoba" (Manitoba 2013). He suggested that the only other places in the world that have endangered ecosystem legislation were Australia and New Zealand.[7] While Manitoba was reinventing its 1993 ESA, the 2014 law had a few caveats. For endangered species, listing was automatic and protection was to occur across all lands (private and Crown), but ecosystem listing was discretionary and protection was to occur only on Crown lands. Nevertheless, the ESEA is taking biodiversity conservation in a new direction in Canada.

Discussion

Policy innovation occurred at the federal level and in all subnational jurisdictions after the 1996 Accord. Similar to other authors in this volume, notably Besco (chapter 6) and Wesley (chapter 7), I argue that the diffusion mechanisms in this case were competition and coercion. All signatories to the Accord kept their commitment to create new ESL, thereby confirming expectation one. Policy instruments (new ESL) were adopted everywhere. But diffusion happened slowly and unevenly. With respect to time, it was only after the government introduced SARA into Parliament that we saw provinces/territories passing ESL that met the Accord criteria. In fact, prior to SARA, only Nova Scotia's law met more than eight Accord criteria, while after SARA, only two provinces' laws met fewer than eight criteria.

This suggests that while the 1996 Accord may have been the source, SARA was the inspiration for innovation.

Why would provinces adopt new ESL more quickly after the federal government had? There are a few possible explanations. First, the passage of SARA at the federal level created national momentum and lowered the political costs of adopting new legislation. Public opinion data from the time suggest that the public was in favour of endangered species protection laws nationally (Elgie 2009). Essentially, the window had opened for provinces and territories to act. And the political ideology of the governing party was not an obstacle to innovation. Of the thirteen existing pieces of ESL, four were passed under Conservative governments, seven under Liberal governments, and two under New Democratic Party (NDP) governments. This means that when the window opened after SARA, any government could act on the basis of national consensus about endangered species protection.

The post-SARA trend could also have been a result of perceived coercion from both the federal government and other provinces. British Columbia, Ontario, and New Brunswick MLAs all made reference to SARA during legislative debate around their own legislation. And one MLA in New Brunswick did mention that other provinces were enacting ESL and New Brunswick should "keep up" with the others. While not having ESL legislation could both lower the costs of business and attract industry to a province, the fact that so many provinces were passing legislation meant that the political costs of not enacting ESL had been raised.

One important thing to note about SARA has been the inclusion of an "emergency order" clause that empowers the federal government to protect a species inside provincial jurisdiction, if the federal environment minister determines that a province is failing to protect a species and/or habitat. This is arguably a form of coercion as the federal government is suggesting to provinces that if they do not protect endangered species, the federal government will do it for them. The emergency order has been used twice – once in 2013 to protect the sage grouse within Alberta and Saskatchewan (two provinces that have never created stand-alone ESL) and again in 2016 to protect the western chorus frog in Quebec. This could certainly be construed as coercion (direct force), providing an incentive for the provinces to create ESL in order to keep the federal government out of the province.

With regard to the uneven diffusion of Accord criteria, we see that convergence is happening for a handful of criteria while little to no convergence is happening with respect to other criteria. In Table 4.3 the total row along the bottom illustrates how many Accord criteria current ESL legislation meet. Less convergence could be expected with criteria 2, 3, 4, 5, 8, and 9 because these criteria place economic or regulatory burdens onto industry and/or landowners. Listing habitat and implementing recovery plans that protect habitat will indefinitely infringe on the activities associated with forestry, hydroelectricity, mining, farming and ranching, fisheries, and oil and gas extraction. Thus, as was the case with the federal bills C-65 and SARA, the existence of concentrated costs could motivate political action from the business community (Illical and Harrison 2007) in each province as they "would bear the costs of habitat protection measures" (Amos, Harrison, and Hoberg 2001, 148).

The data suggest that, by and large, we do see the least convergence over time on the former criteria. For criteria 2 and 3, there are nine existing policies that include an independent process for assessing the status of species at risk, and all twelve subnational policies and SARA legally designate species as threatened or endangered. That may look like significant convergence, but it is important to note that only SARA and the Province of Nova Scotia have a *mandatory* process for the listing of species based on scientific criteria. For all other jurisdictions, the jump from assessing species to legally protecting them is a discretionary leap.

Eleven provinces do protect the habitat of endangered species, but only five require recovery plans in an immediate time frame, and only six require that recovery plans be implemented at all. It is one thing to "protect" habitat (as eleven ESLs do), but it is another thing to actually create mechanisms that set that protection into motion. Similarly, only five provinces have aligned their environmental assessments laws with ESL such that land must be surveyed for endangered species prior to development permits. Overall, this suggests that the lack of convergence on these criteria signals the power of industry in the provinces (especially the Western provinces).

With regard to expectation three, there is little evidence to support policy learning. Provinces do not appear to be carefully examining each other's ESL. There are really only two exceptions: New Brunswick carefully examined Nova Scotia (and the United States ESA) and British Columbia carefully examined the federal SARA. In both cases the purpose was to understand different options for listing species: listen to science only or let politicians make decisions. Nova Scotia and SARA listened only to science, while British Columbia and New Brunswick went on to listen to politicians. This suggests that learning was about drawing "negative lessons," concerned with "what not to do."

The fact that so few provinces discussed the Accord, SARA, or each other during the legislative debate process is not to say that examination of policy had not happened behind closed doors. However, careful reading of each bill suggests that emulation was not at play since no two bills were similar in language or even style. One possible exception is that after SARA's preamble mandated the use of "precautionary principle" in listing decisions, Nova Scotia, Northwest Territories, and New Brunswick all enacted legislation with similar language. It is not clear if these provinces were drawing from SARA or from international conventions, such as the UN Convention on Biodiversity. But overall, there was little evidence for emulation in the diffusion process.

Finally, with regard to the last expectation about later adopters reinventing policy, we do see that Manitoba's 2013 legislation is an innovation in both name and substance – the instrument and the setting are part of the innovation. The ESEA allows for entire ecosystems to be designated as endangered or threatened. This is a move away from the "species-focus" of all existing prior legislation in Canada (and the United States). It is the first law in North America to innovate in this way. Manitoba is learning, but not from its domestic peers. The law is ambitious and, as Nova Scotia's ESL did in 1998, Manitoba's ESEA could set the bar for future Canadian legislation.

Before concluding, I highlight a number of shortcomings of this research, such that future research can expand in scope and depth. First, case studies involving interviews with policymakers should be conducted. Interviews would better gauge motivations for the passage of ESL and the degree to which policy learning happened behind closed doors. This is especially the case since MLAs do not themselves draft legislation personally. Members of the bureaucracy draft the legislation and, in doing so, learn (or not) from other jurisdictions. Thus, interviews with informants would better capture the degree and extent of policy learning. Second, more careful attention should be paid to the territories, as there is good reason to expect that policy in the North would deviate from policy in the South. The territories have unique ecosystems and are under immense pressure from climate change. The territories also have differing governance structures that include wildlife management boards (Olive 2014; White 2016). Third, and of critical importance, future research must examine the implementation of Accord criteria. This chapter has looked only at whether the ESLs as adopted include Accord criteria, but it has not examined the extent to which the provinces have *implemented* their ESL. This is important because we know that SARA includes timelines for recovery plans, but provinces are not keeping pace – this is similar in Ontario. Similarly, we know that provinces have been slow to designate and list species (Olive 2014; Wood and Flahr 2004). Thus, a logical next step would be to see which Accord criteria are most likely to be implemented compared to those least likely to be. This would give a better picture of how provinces handle the economic and political costs of endangered species protection and recovery. In essence, it would be a better test of conservation norms across the country and the degree to which coercion and competition impact policy transfer through implementation.

Conclusion

Through signing the 1996 National Accord for the Protection of Species at Risk, the governments of Canada committed themselves to creating consistent and collaborative endangered species legislation. In the 20-plus-years since the Accord was introduced, there has been much progress and a few pitfalls. While I was interested in the spread of ESL across Canada, broadly, in this chapter I paid close attention to nuanced variation, or settings, in existing policy. All provinces and territories (with the possible exception of Yukon) have policy that offers some recognition and protection of endangered wildlife. Prior to 1996, only five provinces had such legislation and none of it applied to all native species or provided independent scientific assessment for at risk species. Thus, in the past twenty years, the political environment has changed and policies have improved for species at risk. The changes indicate there has been significant innovation and diffusion of policy.

However, as of 2019, there remains great variation in the quality of ESL across the country. Four provinces and two territories have outright failed to create endangered species acts, and instead rely on wildlife acts that offer little in the way of habitat protection and recovery planning. Why have British Columbia, Alberta, Saskatchewan, Prince Edward Island, the Yukon and Northwest Territories never created ESL that would meet the Accord criteria and be consistent with the other provinces? These other provinces all acted early and passed legislation prior to SARA (with the exception of Nunavut in 2003). This may have been strategic and a way to avoid pressure from the federal government. Or it may reflect norm consensus in the West and North, or what Besco in chapter 6 describes as "geographical convergence," because wildlife played a central role in the settling and building of those regions. (Prince Edward Island would be an outlier in that hypothesis.) Future research should seek to explain this lack of diffusion and examine the geographical patterns present in the data.

Nevertheless, the fact that seven jurisdictions and the federal government have enacted legislation – and some very strong legislation – suggests that ESL is more than just symbolic politics in Canada. Most of the provinces that created policy after SARA went on to adopt the majority of Accord criteria – even against their own economic interest. This suggests that there is value consensus about the importance of endangered species protection. While there is no notable evidence of policy learning or emulation across the provinces, there is innovation that may be explained by competition and coercion. ESL in Canada offers a rich case study of transfer and diffusion that should be further explored.

NOTES

1 Except in Quebec.
2 "Species at risk" is an umbrella term that includes the categories endangered, threatened, and/or special concern, as defined by the Committee on the Status of Endangered Wildlife in Canada. However, "endangered species" is often used interchangeably with "species at risk" in the literature. The United States 1973 Endangered Species Act, for example, protects threatened and at risk species. Similarly, the Ontario Endangered Species Act protects the same categories. In this paper "endangered species legislation" refers to laws that protect species classified as endangered, threatened, and/or special concern.

3 Some authors see transfer as a type of diffusion (Newmark 2002) and others see it diffusion as a type of policy transfer (Busch and Jorgens 2005). This nuance lies outside the scope of this paper.

4 No data were available for New Brunswick 1980, Prince Edward Island 1988, Northwest Territories 1988, Nova Scotia 1989, Newfoundland 1990, and Ontario 1990. These laws have all been amended numerous times, leading to their present-day form.

5 Perhaps more interesting is Nunavut's Wildlife Act, which is the first in the country to include provisions for the collection and use of Aboriginal traditional knowledge (Olive 2014).

6 It must be acknowledged that the Ontario government exempted most industries from the regulatory provisions of the ESA, thereby significantly weakening the law.

7 Australia passed its Environmental Protection and Biodiversity Conservation Act in 1999 and New Zealand passed its 1991 National Resources Management Act. Both laws permit the listing and protection of entire ecosystems and not just single species.

WORKS CITED

Amos, William, Kathryn Harrison, and George Hoberg. 2001. "In Search of a Minimum Winning Coalition." In *Politics of the Wildlife: Canada and Endangered Species*, edited by Karen Beazley and Robert Boardman, 137–66. Toronto: Oxford University Press, 2001.

Baumgartner, Frank R., and Bryan D. Jones. 2009. *Agendas and Instability in American Politics*. Chicago: University of Chicago Press.

Berry, Frances Stokes, and William D. Berry. 2018. "Innovations and Diffusion Models in Policy Research." In *Theories of the Policy Process*, edited by Christopher M. Weible, and Paula A. Sabatier, 253–97. Boulder, CO: Westview Press.

Bocking, Stephen. 2001. "The Politics of Endangered Species: A Historical Perspective." In *Politics of the Wildlife: Canada and Endangered Species*, edited by Karen Beazley and Robert Boardman, 117–36. Toronto: Oxford University Press, 2001.

Busch, Per-Olof, and Helge Jörgens. (2005). "The International Sources of Policy Convergence: Explaining the Spread of Environmental Innovations." *Journal of European Public Policy* 12 (5): 860–84.

Dobbin, Frank, Beth Simmons, and Geoffry Garrett. 2007. "The Global Diffusion of Public Policies: Social Construction, Coercion, Competition, or Learning." *Annual Review of Sociology* 33: 449–72.

Dolowitz, David, and David Marsh. 1996. "Who Learns What from Whom: A Review of the Policy Transfer Literature." *Political Studies* 44 (2): 343–57.

– 2000. "Learning from Abroad: The Role of Policy Transfer in Contemporary Policy-making." *Governance* 13: 5–24.

Elgie, Stewart. 2009. "The Politics of Extinction: The Birth of Canada's Species at Risk Act." In *Canadian Environmental Policy and Politics*, edited by Debora L. VanNijnatten and Robert Boardman, 197–215. Toronto: University of Oxford Press.

Fluker, Shaun, and Jocelyn Stacey. 2012. "The Basics of Species at Risk Legislation in Alberta." *Alberta Law Review* 50 (1): 96–114.

Glick, Henry R., and Scott P. Hays. 1991. "Innovation and Reinvention in State Policymaking: Theory and the Evolution of Living Will Laws." *Journal of Politics* 53: 835–50.

Government of Canada. 1996. "National Accord for the Protection of Species at Risk." https://www.registrelep-sararegistry.gc.ca/6B319869-9388- 44D1-A8A4 -33A2F01CEF10/Accord-eng.pdf.

Hall, Peter A. 1993. "Policy Paradigms, Social Learning and the State: The Case of Economic Policy-Making in Britain." *Comparative Politics* 25 (3): 275–97.

Hays, Scott P. 1996. "Influences on Reinvention During the Diffusion of Innovations." *Political Research Quarterly* 49 (3): 631–50.

Hoberg, George. 1991. "Sleeping with an Elephant: The American Influence on Canadian Environmental Regulation." *Journal of Public Policy* 11 (1): 107–31.

Illical, Mary, and Kathryn Harrison. 2007. "Protecting Endangered Species in the US and Canada: The Role of Negative Lesson Drawing." *Canadian Journal of Political Science* 40 (2): 367–94.

Klingler-Vidra, Robyn, and Philip Schleifer. 2014. "Convergence More or Less: Why Do Practices Vary as They Diffuse?" *International Studies Review* 16: 264–74.

Knill, Christoph. 2005. "Introduction: Cross-National Policy Convergence: Concepts, Approaches and Explanatory Factors." *Journal of European Public Policy* 12: 764–74.

Marsh, David, and Jason Campbell Sherman. 2009. "Policy Diffusion and Policy Transfer." *Policy Studies* 30 (3): 269–88.

Mooers, Arne Ø., Laura R. Prugh, Marco Festa-Bianchet, and Jeffrey A. Hutchings. 2007. "Biases in Legal Listing under Canadian Endangered Species Legislation." *Conservation Biology* 21 (3): 572–5.

Newmark, Adam J. 2002. "An Integrated Approach to Policy Transfer and Diffusion." *Review of Policy Research* 19: 152–78.

Olive, Andrea. 2014. *Land, Stewardship, and Legitimacy.* Toronto: University of Toronto Press.

Ringquist, Evan J. 1994. "Policy Influence and Policy Responsiveness in State Pollution Control." *Policy Studies Journal* 22 (1): 25–43.

Shipan, Charles R., and Craig Volden. 2008. "The Mechanisms of Policy Diffusion." *American Journal of Political Science* 52 (4): 840–57.

Simmons, Beth A., and Zachary Elkins. 2004. "The Globalization of Liberalization: Policy Diffusion in the International Political Economy." *American Political Science Review* 90: 171–89.

Simmons, Beth A., Frank Dobbin, and Geoffrey Garrett. 2008. "Introduction: The Diffusion of Liberalization." In *The Global Diffusion of Markets and Democracy,* edited by Beth A. Simmon, Frank Dobbin, and Geoffrey Garrett, 1–63. Cambridge: Cambridge University Press.

Walker, Jack L. 1969. "The Diffusion of Innovation Among American States." *The American Political Science Review* 33: 880–99.

White, Graham. 2016. "Aboriginal Peoples and Environmental Regulation: Land Claims Co-Management Boards in the Territorial North." In *Canadian Environmental Policy and Politics*, edited by Debora L. VanNijnatten, 162–80. Toronto: Oxford University Press.

White, Linda, and Susan Prentice. 2016. "Early Childhood Education and Care Reform in Canadian Provinces." *Canadian Public Administration* 59 (1): 26–44.

Wood, Paul M., and Flahr, Laurie. 2004. "Taking Endangered Species Seriously? British Columbia's Species at Risk Policies." *Canadian Public Policy* 30: 381–99.

LEGISLATIVE DEBATES

Alberta. 1996. *Legislative Assembly Debates*. 14 May. Legislature 23. Bill 42.

British Columbia. 1999. *Debates of the Legislative Assembly*. 8 June. Legislature 36. Bill 63.

British Columbia. 2004. *Debates of the Legislative Assembly*. 13 May. Legislature 37. Bill 51.

Manitoba. 1990. *Legislative Assembly of Manitoba Legislative Debates*. 17 January. Legislature 34. Bill 8.

– 2013. *Legislative Assembly of Manitoba Legislative Debates*. 2 December. Legislature 40. Bill 24.

New Brunswick. 2012. *Journal of Debates Legislative Assembly Province of New Brunswick*. 10 April. Legislature 57, Bill 28.

Newfoundland and Labrador. 2001. *House of Assembly Proceedings*. 6 December. Legislature 44. Bill 33.

Northwest Territories. 2009. *Legislative Assembly Hansard*. 1 June. Legislature 16. Bill 6.

Nova Scotia. 1998. *Legislature Hansard*. 3 December. Legislature 57. Bill 65.

Nunavut. 2003. *Legislative Assembly of Nunavut Hansard*. 2 December. Legislature 1. Bill 35.

Ontario. 2007 *Legislative Assembly of Ontario Debates and Proceedings*. 16 May. Legislature 38. Bill 184.

5

Competing, Learning, or Emulating? Policy Transfer and Sales Tax Reform

MATTHEW LESCH

Introduction

Policy experimentation has long been touted as an advantage of policymaking in federal systems. Armed with lawmaking authority and fiscal capacity, subnational governments can serve as "laboratories of democracy" (Rabe and Borick 2012; Wallner 2010; Bernstein and Hoffmann 2018; Boyd 2017). Furthermore, successful policy ideas adopted in one jurisdiction can spread, either horizontally or vertically, to others. Scholars in the United States have long been sensitive to the interdependent nature of subnational policymaking. Charting the development and diffusion of public policies has been a core staple in the study of American politics (Walker 1969; Boushey 2010; Shipan and Volden 2008; Berry and Berry 1992; Matisoff 2008). While less pronounced in the Canadian political context, students of provincial policymaking have also looked to the drivers of policy experimentation and transfer (see Boyd, chapter 1 of this volume; Boyd 2017; Atkinson et al. 2013).

Researchers studying policy transfer and policy diffusion have focused on the specific mechanisms generating the spread of policies, including competition and learning (see chapter 1, Table 1.2). In its most classic setup, scholars have explored how shifting material interests within a federal context can induce policy transfer and/or convergence. According to this logic, the threat of exit by firms and/or voters to other jurisdictions generates powerful inducements for economic, environmental, and social policy alignment (Tiebout 1956; Massey 1999; Pierson 1995).

There are sound theoretical reasons to expect policy learning to take root in federal systems. When multiple governments operate in identical policy areas, the prospects for "lesson-drawing" between constituent units (Rose 1991) should also increase. At least in the Canadian context; however, the extent of cross-provincial policy learning is unclear (there are exceptions; see Millar, chapter 3 of this volume, for example). The specific configuration of Canadian political institutions might account for the apparent absence of policy learning. As Brown (2012,

14) suggests, Canadian federal and provincial governments have largely resisted "extensive collusive arrangements" and thus lack the formal mechanisms for policy coordination or information sharing. This account, however, may have overlooked other institutional forums in which policy learning can unfold. Snow (chapter 2 of this volume), for example, identifies the role of courts in initiating processes of policy learning. This is not to suggest that formal political institutions are necessary for policy learning. There are plenty of other vehicles, including the mass media, policy networks, and social media, which can fill this void. In the absence of formal institutions, these alternative informational channels can enable policymakers to track policy developments elsewhere.

At the same time, the relationship between learning, institutions, and information-sharing underscores a major gap in the literature on policy transfer and diffusion. Policymaking is commonly portrayed as a linear and "more-or-less rational" process. Decision-makers will identify policy problems and goals, engage in solution search by looking at peer jurisdictions, evaluate the efficacy of such solutions, and then select the best solution. As one recent critique suggests, it is often assumed that policymakers are (a) capable of recognizing policy failure, and (b) able to respond accordingly "through processes of evaluation and learning" (Stone 2017, 55). Theories that stress competition and learning assume that policymakers possess the cognitive and/or institutional capacity to attend to external policy developments. This highly stylized model of decision-making, however, sits uncomfortably with research findings in public policy (Lindblom 1959; Cohen, March, and Olsen 1972; Kingdon 1995; Jones and Baumgartner 2005; Cairney and Weible 2017), political psychology (Simon 1985; Taber 2003), cognitive psychology (Kahneman and Tversky 1979), and behavioural economics (Thaler and Sunstein 2008; Wilson 2011). At the core of these research traditions is a model of bounded rationality, where decision-makers' capabilities are tempered by a combination of external constraints (e.g., time) and cognitive limitations (e.g., limited attention and bottleneck memory) (Simon 1985; Jones 1999; Taber 2003; Millar, Lesch, and White 2019). A model of bounded rationality assumes the policy environment is replete with "incomplete information" and that actors are limited in their capacity to process such information (Cairney and Weible 2017, 622). This suggests that policymaking ought to be understood as a much more disjointed and fluid process than rational models would seem to indicate (Zahariadis 2003, 2008; Jones and Baumgartner 2005). These constraints limit the capacity of policymakers to fully attend to all relevant policy information, including the search for and identification of policy successes elsewhere. However, as other authors in this volume suggest (see, for example, Snow in chapter 2 and Millar in chapter 3), under certain conditions, policymakers will look to and learn from the experiences of their peers.

Thus, it is important for scholars to examine what policy transfer processes look like, and how these processes may be mediated by the micro-level forces described above. Recent work on policy diffusion has begun to do this. Some scholars have demonstrated the importance of geographic proximity, or closeness, in affecting the likelihood of policy transfer. When policymakers find themselves close to the site of an innovation, policy information is more cognitively accessible (Weyland 2005). Moreover, the speed of a policy innovation's spread is often linked to its level of complexity and salience. Policy solutions that are less cognitively complex and more politically salient will tend to spread faster than more complex and less salient ideas (Boushey 2010). Thus, cognitive insights into theories of policy change can yield more precise explanations about how micro-level dynamics, such as attention and information processing, are linked to causal mechanisms at the meso-level (Millar et al. 2018).

The purpose of this chapter is to demonstrate the fruitful relationship between the model of bounded rationality and mechanisms of policy transfer and diffusion. The analysis identifies numerous policy transfer mechanisms (see chapter 1 of this volume, Table 1.2) – rational learning (Gilardi 2003, 2010), bounded learning (Meseguer 2005, 2006), and competitive and social emulation (Brune and Garrett 2000) – and interrogates the micro-level assumptions underpinning them.

The core theoretical contribution of this chapter is that it proposes a novel mechanism of policy change in processes of policy transfer. *Bounded emulation* describes a change where policymakers mimic the policy solution – including instruments or settings – of a peer government because their ideas are cognitively accessible. Unlike with other variants of emulation, competitive and social (Brune and Garrett 2000), in this case the behaviour of policymakers stems more from endogenous considerations. That is, jurisdiction B's decision to emulate is driven less by its relationship to jurisdiction A; the decision is linked to forces or pressures that are more internal to jurisdiction B. Moreover, the micro-foundation underpinning each of these emulative mechanisms differs. Competitive emulation is underpinned by logics of consequence. It assumes, either explicitly or implicitly, actors are comprehensively rational and will respond to shifts in the environment, including policy changes made by peer governments (Brune and Garett 2000). Social emulation, in contrast, assumes that logics of appropriateness (March and Olson 1996) underlie human behaviour. Here policymakers will copy the policy decisions of their peers due to other-regarding preferences or other normative considerations (i.e., which policy decision is most appropriate). At the micro-level, bounded emulation shares more in common with competitive emulation. Bounded emulation assumes policymakers are "intendedly rational" (Jones 1999) but can be constrained in their capacity to recognize what their interests are and/or how to advance those aims. Facing these constraints, actors will turn to satisficing strategies (Simon 1985), including poaching policy solutions from other governments.

Actors engaged in bounded emulation should exhibit distinct and empirically observable behaviours in the policymaking process. First, since emulators are copying a policy decision, we would expect them to invest fewer cognitive and institutional resources into the study of a policy problem and the expected effects of a policy solution. Second, consistent with bounded rationality, we might expect policy decisions to be arrived at over a fairly limited time frame. In contrast, a more prolonged decision-making process would suggest systematic information-processing (Chaiken 1980; Jacobs 2011), whereby different courses of action are carefully contemplated. Finally, in the face of uncertainty, we should expect them to turn to satisficing strategies (Simon 1985). We should, for example, observe policymakers restricting the frames or dimensions that they use to analyse a policy problem (or solution). We might also see actors coping with complexity and/or uncertainty by using heuristic information-processing (Chaiken 1980) or taking cognitive shortcuts (Jacobs 2011).

The current chapter provides an empirical illustration of the mechanism described in the preceding discussion through an examination of British Columbia (BC) government's decision to restructure its sales tax system in 2009. Following Hall's typology of policy change (see chapter 1, Table 1.3), the explanatory focus of this chapter is on second-order change, or a shift in policy instruments. The analysis is also restricted to a specific point in the policy process; it examines the initial stages of policy transfer, or what Karch (2007) refers to as *agenda-setting* and *information-generation* processes (see Boyd, chapter 1 of this volume).

Given the design of Canadian provincial policymaking institutions, the focus of this chapter is on policymakers – elected officials, political staff, and civil servants – who are responsible for policy development. Thus, less attention is paid to the role of other policy actors, including the public and organized interests. In the specific case of sales tax reform in BC, one of the more noteworthy aspects of the case is what happened *after* the policy decision was announced. The success of a citizen-led referendum campaign (see below) to overturn the policy is worthy of analysis but is well beyond the scope of this chapter (for further discussion, see McArthur 2011; Abbott 2015; Lesch 2018).

Existing analysis suggests that BC's sales tax reform was driven by policy transfer from Ontario; however, the mechanisms linking the two policy decisions are less clearly understood. On the one hand, there were sound public policy reasons for BC to follow Ontario's lead. From an economic and fiscal policy perspective, eliminating the retail sales tax (RST) and replacing it with a federally harmonized value-added tax (VAT) was a sensible course of action. Yet a careful examination of the decision-making process shows that these dimensions configured very little in the actual decision.

The decision to adopt the harmonized sales tax (HST) was linked more to a combination of external pressures and internal constraints. On the one hand, the BC government found itself in the midst of a global economic crisis and, thus, was limited in its capacity to respond. On the other hand, policymakers made a number of strategic errors. The decision to follow Ontario's lead was the result of a highly insulated decision-making process, which left policymakers impervious to alternative constructions of the policy problem and potential solutions. This insular context led to and reinforced numerous satisficing strategies and cognitive biases. The chapter shows how the adoption of the HST in BC is thus analytically consistent with a micro-foundation of bounded rationality and a policy transfer mechanism of bounded emulation.

To demonstrate the argument, the chapter presents a detailed analysis of the decision-making context. This chapter uses qualitative methods and specifically *process tracing* to examine a single case study. Process tracing is particularly well suited for investigating the plausibility of causal theories and hypotheses. Process tracing enables analysts to draw inferences based on careful, thick description of case studies. The "within-in case" analysis (Jacobs 2011; George and Bennett 2005) provides a fruitful way for researchers to adjudicate between competing causal explanations, or mechanisms, of policy change. To generate these inferences, this chapter relies on a combination of qualitative sources, including nineteen interviews with key policy participants, secondary literature, primary documents, and media coverage between March and July 2009.

The chapter proceeds with the following sections. Section two provides an overview of research on policy diffusion and bounded rationality. Building from this, the analysis parses different types of diffusion mechanisms and links them to different micro-logics. In section three, using BC's HST case, the chapter provides an empirical illustration of the preceding discussion. The final section of the chapter concludes with some of the broader implications of the research findings.

Bounded Rationality and Bounded Emulation

At the root of policymaking theories are different assumptions about how actors interpret their environment and define their goals. Theories that stress rationality, including rational learning models, assume that actors are utility-maximizers but can be constrained by material and institutional conditions (North 1990; Shepsle 1989). Policy scholars have long been critical of rational actor models (Lindblom 1959). In particular, research has pointed to a variety of biases that inhibit rational calculation, prompt preference reversals, and lead to suboptimal choices (Druckman and Lupia 2000; Jones 1999; Tversky and Kahneman 1985; Wilson 2011).

As an alternative, scholars have developed a micro-theory of bounded rationality, proposing three fundamental ideas: first, actors are assumed to have relatively stable preferences; second, they are seen as "intendedly rational" (i.e., goal following); and third, they are assumed to be subjected to a host of cognitive limitations, including scarcity of attention, uncertainty, and framing effects (Jones 1999; Simon 1985; Weyland 2005; Jacobs 2011). In Simon's (1957) work on the subject, he describes how individuals rely on a strategy of satisficing, as opposed to optimizing.

These assumptions are particularly important for understanding the behaviour of policymakers. Limited time and attention, together with other cognitive biases, can influence what information actors attend to, determining how they conceptualize policy problems and policy solutions. According to Jones and Baumgartner (2005), policymakers will be drawn to information that is more salient or cognitively accessible. Thus, theories of policymaking, including studies of policy transfer and diffusion, need to consider the implications of bounded rationality and, specifically, what its theoretical assumptions imply for the movement and processing of policy information.

Policy diffusion studies emphasizing competition stress the importance of structure, incentives, and material interests in shaping policymaking (Dobbin, Simmons, and Garrett 2007). Other analysts, however, stress that a shift in ideas or beliefs is what underlies policy transfer. Within the policy diffusion and policy transfer literature, scholars have presented learning as a distinct causal process, marked by goal-oriented or problem-solving behaviours (Gilardi 2003). Under learning, governments accumulate new information about the effects of a policy (see, for example, chapters 2 and 3 of this volume). Rational learning describes a process whereby actors revise "the causal links between policies and outcomes [based on] observed experience" (Meseguer 2005, 73).

One common critique of this variant of learning studies is the failure to distinguish rational learning from other similar-looking diffusion processes. For Kahler (1992, 124), to be convincing, students of learning must show that "a particular behavioral change" results from a "clearly specified cognitive alteration at one level or another." This is distinct from what Dobbin, Simmons, and Garrett (2007) term "mindless emulation." Demonstrating the presence of rational learning, then, demands a rigorous examination and illustration of *how* beliefs have shifted. If rational learning is at the root of a policy transfer, then there should be clear behavioural manifestations of learning-like behaviour. The expertise of epistemic communities, for example, should be integral to belief change, rather than be used for political cover after the fact.

In contrast, bounded learning describes a process where actors use the experience of others "but use cognitive shortcuts rather than Bayes' rule to update their beliefs" (Gilardi 2003, 6). Thus, the key distinction between these variants of learning is about whether actors' core beliefs or causal ideas have shifted. Weyland's (2005) analysis offered a clear illustration of bounded learning, or what he terms a cognitive-heuristic approach. Drawing on a combination of interviews and document analysis, Weyland demonstrated how a reliance on heuristics – anchoring, representative bias, and availability bias – led decision-makers to mimic suboptimal policy designs.

In addition to their focus on learning, diffusion scholars have described how governments emulate or mimic their counterparts. Scholars have identified two primary types of emulative mechanisms. *Social* or *cultural emulation* refers to governments' "taking cues from other countries in a given social network" due to a cultural or social affinity (Brune and Garrett 2000, 7). In contrast, *competitive emulation* describes a material-based policy logic; governments try to "keep up with their competitors" by mimicking the latter's policy choices (Brune and Garrett 2000, 1). These two types of emulation share some conceptual overlap by stressing interdependence, or the relationship between jurisdiction A (the initiator) and jurisdiction B (the subsequent adopter). That is, jurisdiction B copies jurisdiction A due to the social and/or economic nature of their relationship.

The concept of bounded emulation captures how policymakers decide to mimic the decision of a peer because it is cognitively accessible and defined as consistent with their own perceived interests. This form of emulation is distinct from rational learning, since it does not involve a profound shift in the actors' core beliefs or the causal ideas of policymakers. The central innovation of this concept is that it specifies an alternative micro-foundation for emulation and identifies observable implications of this process (see below). While there is some conceptual overlap between bounded learning (Gilardi 2003) and bounded emulation, the core difference is that bounded emulators do not revise their core beliefs (i.e., they are not learning).

Both competitive and social emulation fail to capture emulative behaviour that is driven less by these relational considerations and more by endogenous, or internal, forces. A policy solution developed in jurisdiction A might serve as a template or inspiration for jurisdiction B. Yet the motivation(s) for policy uptake might also have little to do with the relationship between the governments. In fact, one way to analytically distinguish between these processes is to consider cases where policy transfer is followed by subsequent policy reversal. If social or economic pressures account for the initial transfer, then all else being equal, we would expect the same outcome (i.e., transfer), if one jurisdiction reverses itself. In contrast, since bounded emulation is driven more by endogenous factors, we would not necessarily expect a policy reversal in one jurisdiction to automatically lead to a corresponding policy shift in the other jurisdiction.

The preceding discussion implies a series of testable implications which are presented as the five hypotheses below (H1–H5). If bounded emulation is occurring, then, empirically we might observe several cognitive and/or institutional processes.

- In comparison to rational learners, policymakers should spend *less* time and use fewer resources examining the effects of existing policy reform. That is, the decision-making process should be characterized by limited deliberation and ought to be take place over a relatively short period of time (H1).
- Bounded emulators might also spend *less* time and fewer resources consulting with external experts or stakeholders about the expected effects of a policy (H2).

- Bounded emulators should be guided *more* by their initial construction of the policy problem and thus exhibit *less* attentiveness to dimensions of the policy that are inconsistent (or irrelevant) to that initial framing (H3).
- In comparison to rational learners, emulators should be *more* selective in terms of the sources of data and/or information they consult, illustrating heuristic information processing (Chaiken 1980; Jacobs 2011) (H4).
- In contrast to social or economic emulators, governments should spend *less* time and *fewer* resources exploring the implications of policy adoption for the social and/or economic relationship between the two jurisdictions (H5).

Bounded Emulation in British Columbia's Sales Tax Reform

Background: Sales Taxation

Sales taxes are among the most common revenue tools on which governments rely to raise revenue. In Canada, sales taxes are imposed at the federal and provincial levels. Unless exempted by legislation, all goods and services are subject to a sales tax. Traditionally, governments have levied retail sales taxes, such as provincial sales taxes (PSTs) (Eccleston 2007). Over time, however, RSTs have been replaced with VAT systems.

The main difference and disadvantage of an RST is in its failure to distinguish between consumption and capital investment. Under an RST system, businesses pay sales taxes on all purchases, including capital inputs. This has significant downstream consequences for businesses, as the cost of these taxes will cascade throughout the supply chain. At each stage of production, these costs are passed on to other businesses but eventually borne by the consumer in the form of higher prices. The purpose of a VAT system is to eliminate this problem, primarily through input-tax credits (ITCs). ITCs enable businesses to recoup any sales tax paid on their capital inputs. Economists, regardless of ideological predisposition, have long recognized the superiority of VAT systems. The consensus is that RST systems put jurisdictions at a competitive disadvantage; they impose an unnecessary tax burden on businesses and leave consumers worse off (Bird, Mintz, and Wilson 2006; Smart 2007). This widespread consensus is key to understanding why almost every member state of the Organisation of Economic and Co-operative Development (OECD)[1] has converted its sales tax system to a VAT.

The Canadian experience with VAT reform underscores the political challenges of sales tax reform. In 1991, the Canadian federal government faced considerable public backlash, following the introduction of the goods and services tax (GST). Although consumers had historically paid the cost of a federal sales tax, these were indirect costs, levied on businesses and embedded into the price of goods and services. The GST made these costs visible to the consumer for the first time. The introduction of the GST, however, was widely credited with contributing to the Progressive Conservatives' (PCs) historic defeat in the 1993 federal election (Hale 2002). Despite public opposition, many policy experts expected a VAT to be replicated at the provincial level (e.g., Quebec sales tax) or for federal and provincial sales tax bases to be harmonized (e.g., harmonized sales taxes). The belief was that as the fiscal and macroeconomic benefits of the federal GST grew apparent, provincial governments would embrace the VAT model.

One issue for provinces is that replacing an RST with a VAT almost invariably broadens the sales tax base. This means that goods and services – such as restaurant meals or gym memberships in BC's case – previously exempted from sales taxation would now be subject to the tax. From a public finance perspective, exemptions are suboptimal policy; they undermine the efficiency of the tax system and reduce public revenues, thus limiting capacity for redistribution. The political consequence of base broadening, however, can create a major dilemma for provincial governments looking to reform their sales taxes. The GST experience in Canada dissuaded many provinces from following the federal government's lead. Despite the expected macroeconomic benefits, provincial governments were unwilling to take the electoral gamble.

By the mid-1990s, this dynamic began to shift when new fiscal pressure forced the hands of several provinces. In 1996, three Atlantic provinces agreed to eliminate their RSTs and replace them with a federally harmonized VAT system (Hale 2002). In each instance, however, these governments were ultimately rebuked at the ballot box. Thus, for provinces with RST systems still intact – Ontario, British Columbia, Saskatchewan, Manitoba, and Newfoundland and Labrador – the political lesson was clear: "consumption tax reform is bad for the political lives of government."[2]

The 2008 global recession, however, shifted conventional wisdom about economic and fiscal policy. Facing a bleak economic outlook, the crisis enabled governments to re-evaluate different policy options, including VAT reform. During the fall of 2008, VAT reform was given renewed focus in Canada when Ontario Premier Dalton McGuinty began musing about switching the province's sales tax system. With declining exports and a battered manufacturing sector, Ontario was looking for a major structural change that would attract capital investment back into the province. In March 2009, the HST was included in the province's first post-recession budget. Just as had been the case elsewhere, the adoption of the HST attracted opposition from a variety of stakeholders.[3] Given Ontario's economic weight, however, the announcement also sent shockwaves beyond the province's boundaries. The decision by Ontario to adopt a VAT could not be ignored by finance ministers across the country.

Just a few months later, on 23 July 2009, the BC government announced it would follow Ontario's lead. Premier Gordon Campbell's announcement set in motion what would become one of the most contentious policy debates in the province's recent history. Even though Ontario's decision on HST was well known, the decision by the Campbell government to follow suit caught many observers by surprise. In May, the Campbell-led BC Liberals had secured a third consecutive mandate, yet plans to restructure the sales tax system were not included in the party's platform. Moreover, the announcement signalled a major departure from the BC government's long-standing position on sales tax harmonization. Since taking office in 2001, the premier had – both publicly and privately – expressed opposition to sales tax harmonization. It is clear that the Ontario government's decision played a key role here. Less clearly understood, however, is why or how this policy change mattered.

What led the Campbell government down the road of HST reform? Were the structural pressures associated with Ontario's decision so significant that it forced policy convergence? Alternatively, did the Ontario government's decision prompt a process of policy learning? Did Campbell and his advisers alter their beliefs about the efficacy of sales tax harmonization due to the actions of the McGuinty government?

The analysis below describes the decision-making context that led to the policy decision. The analysis confirms that this was indeed a case of policy transfer. Absent the Ontario government's decision, it is highly unlikely that the BC government would have pursued sales tax reform. At the same time, the analysis shows neither competition nor learning accounts are particularly helpful in explaining these dynamics. Instead, the chapter presents a much less comprehensively rational process, one reflecting the importance of cognition and other external pressures on the ultimate policy decision, namely a process of bounded emulation.

The Economic Context of the Policy Decision

In early 2009, as elsewhere in Canada, the effects of the financial crisis on the BC economy were becoming increasingly apparent. With a resource-based economy highly sensitive to external economic shocks, BC faced strong headwinds following the global recession (British Columbia Ministry of Finance [BCMoF] 2010). Between its 2008 and 2009 fiscal years, provincial revenues fell by almost $1 billion (BCMoF 2011). The province's labour market also suffered. By the end of 2009, BC's economy had lost 48,500 jobs. Only Ontario and Newfoundland and Labrador experienced higher job losses over that period (Usalcas 2010).[4]

Initially, the provincial government stated that, despite the downturn, it was committed to fiscal discipline. The economic news, however, only worsened over the course of the recession. At the close of its 2009 fiscal year, the province's economy had shrunk by 2.3 percentage points (BCMoF 2010), forcing the premier to announce deficit spending (Palmer 2009). The reversal was a symbolic blow for a government that had prided itself on its fiscal record. Following its election in

2001, the BC Liberals had enacted a balanced budget bill. To allow the government to run a two-year deficit, the premier was forced to revise his own legislation in 2009.

Similar to other Canadian provinces, the BC government's revenues derive primarily from personal income taxes, corporate income taxes, and sales and property taxes.[5] The province also relies on a consumption tax on goods and services as a major revenue tool (BCMoF 2007). The first sales tax in BC was introduced on 1 July 1948 under the Social Service Tax Act. Like many RSTs, the 3 per cent tax applied to most goods or services purchased within the province, unless subject to a legislated exemption. The PST was administered by the BC Ministry of Revenue; businesses were charged the PST on consumer purchases (including to other businesses) and then remitted those repayments to the ministry.

While the PST has been a pillar of public finance in BC, over the years it has been roundly criticized. Complaints about the arbitrary nature of tax exemptions were common. Policy experts routinely complained about the "antiquated" structure of the PST and its consequences for competitiveness.[6] Despite these criticisms, there was little appetite at the political level for policy change. Governments in Victoria, regardless of ideology, were unwilling "touch the tax with a ten-foot pole."[7] As noted in the previous section, one particular challenge was that harmonization with the federal GST would broaden the tax base, thus raising the costs of various goods and services.

The Influence of Ontario's Decision

As the governing BC Liberals began preparing for the May 2009 provincial election, the subject of sales tax reform unexpectedly entered BC politics. The Ontario government's decision to bring in its own HST attracted the attention of new media outlets across the country (Cowan 2009). To help offset concerns about the tax, the federal government offered Ontario a one-time compensation fund, which could be used however the province pleased. Policy experts began calling on the BC premier to see whether the federal government would be willing to cut BC a similar deal.[8] The decision to eliminate the PST in Ontario prompted concerns about BC's tax competitiveness. For some experts, the competitive disadvantages created by the Ontario move, coupled with the federal government's commitment to provide compensation, were too great for the premier and finance minister to ignore. In fact, some analysts predicted that, with Ontario's decision, harmonization in BC was "not a question of if but when" (Kesselman 2009).

Ontario's announcement garnered the attention of the BC Ministry of Finance.[9] Discussion about sales tax reform in BC followed news coverage about the Ontario-Ottawa sales tax agreement (CBC News 2010). This is not surprising; a key responsibility of bureaucratic officials is "to keep an eye on developments across the federation, particularly when it involves deals with Ottawa."[10] On 26

March 2009, an assistant deputy minister (ADM) at the Ministry of Finance prepared a briefing note for BC Finance Minister Colin Hansen. The note identified Ontario's HST decision and provided a brief overview of the fiscal and distributive impact of making a similar move in BC. Interviews with finance officials and political staff revealed that there had been no discussion or mention of sales tax reform, including any mention of federal assistance, prior to March 2009.[11] Thus, we can be reasonably confident that the Ontario government's policy decision was the impetus behind opening up the policy discussion on sales tax reform in BC.

Discussion about sales tax reform was not exclusive to the provincial bureaucracy. The Ontario HST was announced just as the 2009 provincial campaign was getting under way in BC. The two major parties in BC – the BC Liberals and BC NDP – were asked for their position on sales tax harmonization. Each stated that they had no plans to introduce HST if they were to form a government.[12] During the campaign, Premier Gordon Campbell was pressed on how his government planned to respond to a deteriorating economic situation. Here the premier restated his commitment to run a small deficit of $495 million (Palmer 2009). On Election Day, 12 May 2009, voters seemed to endorse the BC Liberal's incremental approach; Campbell and the Liberals were returned to Victoria with a third consecutive majority government.

One other reason the 2009 election was significant is because it was the first electoral test of BC's carbon tax. In 2008, the Campbell government had successfully, though not entirely without controversy, enacted a province-wide tax. The government managed to escape electoral punishment for the policy. According to Harrison's (2012) analysis, the 2008 economic crisis overshadowed discussion of the carbon tax. Growing public concern about the health of the economy worked to the electoral advantage of the incumbents.[13]

Inside the BC Decision-making Process

The BC government decided to adopt the HST following a handful of meetings between senior members of the government. On 7 May 2009, just days before the provincial election, the premier was briefed by top finance officials about the state of provincial finances. The initial news was concerning. In the first month of its fiscal year, revenues were off target by between $200 and $300 million. The premier chose, however, to keep this information from the public ahead of the election (Palmer 2009). Two days after the election, the premier met with the deputy minister of finance. The premier was told that the economic outlook and state of revenues "were much grimmer than previous forecasts had predicted."[14] Based on the projections, the deficit would be $1.1 to 1.3 billion, a much larger figure than Campbell had committed to on the campaign trail. The post-election meeting had put Campbell in a difficult political bind just days into his new mandate.[15] Finance officials were told by the premier to "go and figure something out."[16]

For Campbell, then, the initial policy problem the province was facing was a fiscal one, critically, not an economic (or structural) issue. This differed significantly from the approach, and the problem-definition, of his counterparts in Ontario. At Queen's Park, the 2008 economic crisis signalled broader problems with the medium- to long-term health of the province's economy. This realization in the fall of 2008 triggered an extensive exploration of different policy options, including numerous consultations with policy experts within and external to the Ontario Ministry of Finance (Lesch 2018). There was no indication of anything resembling consultation with experts or comprehensive study. At no point were the pillars of the BC economy under any kind of scrutiny. Instead, BC finance officials were instructed to find a quick fix to what the premier defined as a significant policy (or political) problem: the size of the provincial deficit.

On 15 May 2009, officials in Victoria asked the federal government if it would be willing to provide a similar level of compensation to the province as Ontario had received.[17] Discussions then shifted to senior levels of the government. At a meeting of finance ministers, BC Finance Minister Colin Hansen, told his federal counterpart that BC[18] was "considering changing [its] previous position on opposition to the HST" (Palmer 2009, A3). Based on these initial discussions, the federal government said it would be willing to provide $1.6 billion in compensation. At this point, it appeared that the deficit problem could be resolved by the federal government's timely offer. In June, however, the premier's hopes were dashed. New data from the federal Department of Finance showed that BC's tax revenues and transfers were in even worse shape than the earlier modelling had suggested.[19]

One of the central challenges that the premier and finance minister faced was that they had to make a decision about the federal offer in "a very short time window."[20] According to Hansen, when discussions began in May, the federal government made it clear that its compensation offer was time-sensitive; the province would need to finalize its decision by the middle of July.[21] The federal government wanted the policy change to correspond with "Ontario's timeline for sales tax harmonization."[22] The federal government "did [this] for their own political reasons," wanting to have the money "booked in that fiscal year."[23] But this meant that the analysis by the provincial finance department would be fairly limited. Replacing the sales tax system would have major consequences for stakeholders across the province, particularly retailers as sales tax collectors. These issues, however, were given very little consideration in decision-making. The government failed to consult with external experts or stakeholders, including the business community, which had historically been an important ally of the government. According to Hansen, the reason for this was time: "We were rushed by the feds ... [and so] there was a complete absence of a communications plan."[24] The failure to identify what the distributive and political consequences of the HST were, beyond the deficit as well as how these effects would be mitigated and communicated, contributed to the public and interest groups' mobilization against the tax.[25]

The pace of the policy decision as described by many interviewees was uncharacteristically rushed. As the former Official Leader of the Opposition described it, "Usually when governments talk about doing things, it's normally a year to change something, especially if it's something as significant as tax policy."[26] According to one journalist, "I think [Campbell] looked at that money, knew it was a generally good policy idea and said, 'Yeah, let's do it.' I mean, really that's the only way to make sense of the timing of the decision."[27] Others shared a similar sentiment but stressed the role of political expediency. It was well understood within the finance department that economic and revenue issues were a cyclical (i.e., temporary) problem. As one policy expert remarked, "As a general rule, governments do not overhaul the tax system in order to deal with a cyclical problem like a budgetary deficit."[28] Thus, it seems more likely that the decision reflected the premier's desire to find a quick and easy solution. Campbell could have used other means to reduce the deficit, including expenditure cuts. Instead, however, Campbell turned to the solution that was most salient at the time. As one NDP political strategist noted:

[The government] needed to find money; they looked around and went, "Oh, the HST" … This explains why there [were] no research papers, why there was no notice to the business community. There were no secret papers, there weren't any secret documents, in fact, there weren't any documents at all. They did not do the research, they did not do the studies, they did not do the polling or the focus groups. Nothing.[29]

The Political Fallout

The HST decision had significant electoral and political consequences for BC politics. Following the announcement of the policy, an anti-tax grassroots movement coalesced under the leadership of former premier Bill Vander Zalm, who spearheaded a "Fight HST" campaign. Despite this counter-mobilization, in March 2010, the BC government proceeded with the enabling legislation. In response, Vander Zalm and his allies turned to the province's Recall and Initiative Act, which provided citizens the capacity to launch voter initiatives. HST opponents were successful in garnering a high threshold of public support required by the initiative legislation. In the spring of 2010, during a ninety-day period, Fight HST convinced 10 per cent of registered voters in each provincial riding to sign a recall petition to force the HST back to the provincial legislature. Rather than reversing the controversial legislation, the government chose to put the matter to a public vote in spring 2011 through a provincial referendum. As the two sides geared up for the referendum, the premier's grip on power became untenable. Facing a caucus revolt, Premier Gordon Campbell announced his resignation in November 2010. The downfall of such a prominent figure helped absorb some of the public's anger, but the resignation was not enough to save the besieged policy. By a nearly ten-point margin, voters rebuked the HST in the referendum, with almost 55 per cent of voters favouring a return to the PST system.

The HST's defeat in BC is noteworthy when considering the policy's contrasting fate in Ontario. Unlike the BC government, the Ontario government faced relatively muted opposition to the HST. One plausible explanation for this is the varying institutional context: unlike in BC, Ontario voters do not have the capacity to challenge legislation via initiatives or referenda. On the other hand, the public in Ontario possessed several opportunities – including several by-elections and the 2011 provincial election – to render judgment on its government's HST decision. In each instance, though, the HST was left unscathed. This suggests that there is something qualitatively different about how the politics of the HST played out in these two contexts. Existing research shows that the Ontario government showed great political deftness in managing the HST. More specifically, by articulating the need for the policy *prior* to announcing it, the Ontario government mobilized key constituencies and neutralized arguments from potential opponents. These decisions, among other choices, helped the Ontario government manage public opposition to the HST (for further discussion, see Lesch 2018).

Discussion

Competition

One explanation for the HST decision in BC is that the Campbell government felt competitive pressure to follow the Ontario government. A competition-induced explanation would expect that Ontario's decision would shift the economic incentives of the BC government. Under this explanation, the status quo becomes too costly for the government, so policy transfer is the logical result.

On the surface, BC's decision reads like a classic case of competition. Ontario's policy decision left BC with "little choice" but to follow suit (Dobbin, Simmons, and Garrett 2007, 457). As previously described, however, there is little evidence that horizontal competitiveness factored into the decision-making process. For one, there is no indication that the economic consequences of Ontario's HST decision on the BC economy were ever systematically examined by the government.[30] If concerns about competitiveness were prominent, we would generally expect policymakers to seek out this type of vitally important policy information. In line with Hypothesis 5 stated above, the failure of the government to consider these dimensions of the tax reform suggests that competition was not a prominent concern.

While concerns about competitiveness did not play a decisive role, the case does reveal an interesting dynamic of coercion. Just as BC would not have adopted the new tax in the absence of Ontario's decision, it is also unlikely that the policy would be pursued without federal assistance. Furthermore, by imposing the time-sensitive offer, the federal government used its fiscal position to exert pressure on the BC government. This is not entirely consistent with the ways in which policy transfer scholars have conceptualized coercion (see chapter 1 of this volume, Table 1.2); BC was not forced by Ottawa to adopt the HST. At the same time, it is clear that this process of policy transfer was facilitated and shaped by the actions of the federal government.

Learning

A second potential explanation for the policy decision is that of rational learning. According to this theory, elected officials, aided by the expertise of policy experts, engaged in a highly systematic search and analysis of different policy options. This process results in a revision of causal beliefs about the efficacy of VAT reform or sales tax harmonization. Again, however, the evidence above provides little indication that learning was at play.

Overall, governing elites in the BC case spent limited time and resources studying the issue of VAT reform. The decision was characterized by remarkably little deliberation and seems to have been finalized over a handful of exchanges between the premier, the finance minister, and senior civil servants. Processes of rational learning involve the alteration of beliefs and ideas based on exposure to new policy-related information. There is little evidence here that decision-makers' beliefs changed in any meaningful way. Moreover, it is unclear how that process would have unfolded. There are no records or personal recollections of meetings or institutional processes that were dedicated to studying sales tax reform. Finance officials in Victoria were not afforded sufficient time or institutional resources to study the distributive impact of sales tax reform. Finally, at no point did the government seek out expert advice from outside the government. The latter is not necessarily a requirement of rational learning, but its absence is striking.

Bounded Emulation

Across primary documents and interview data, the weight of evidence in this case study leans in the direction of bounded emulation. Consistent with Hypothesis 2 stated above, the HST decision-making process was characterized by limited consultation with external experts or stakeholders. Had the government engaged more with external tax policy experts or business interests, then, we would expect to see some record(s) or recollection of these exchanges. Instead, the decision to enact the HST was made by a small group of individuals and was primarily driven by the premier's prevailing problem-definition. A failure to consult with external actors likely only reinforced the premier's narrow framing of the policy problem. Had external actors, including the business community or the news media, caught wind of what policy change was being contemplated, policymakers would likely have been more attentive to alternative dimensions or framings of the problem and policy solution.

Interviews and document analyses also suggest that the study of the HST policy instrument and its effects was quite limited (Hypothesis 1 stated above). There is no indication that the premier, the finance minister, or their respective staff members deliberated over the political and distributive implications of the tax policy shift. The absence of such deliberation makes it highly improbable that the actors' core beliefs (Jenkins-Smith et al. 2014) or causal ideas (Hall 1993) had undergone a profound shift. Moreover, we also know that the HST decision was made over a very short period of time, a further indication of bounded rationality. The limited timeframe also likely inhibited the ability of the civil service to provide a comprehensive analysis and evaluation for the premier and finance minister.

The evidence also suggests that the government was highly selective in terms of the information it consulted (Hypothesis 3 stated above). Part of the reason that its solution search was so limited is because of the specific framing or construction of the policy problem. Finance officials were provided with a specific goal (i.e., deficit reduction) and were tasked with finding an instrument that would address that goal. One of the key tasks given to finance officials was to study the Ontario-Ottawa HST agreement; this was to enable them to understand how much compensation they would be entitled to as well as how exemptions would be treated. Strikingly, however, there was limited time devoted to evaluating the implications of the policy shift for stakeholders (i.e., businesses, voters) in BC. By defining the problem as one of deficit reduction, the premier had circumscribed the lens through which the HST was viewed. Constructing the problem this way made some data points more salient (e.g., effect of compensation fund on the deficit) than others (e.g., effect of sales tax reform on voters' pocketbooks and for specific business sectors).

Finally, it is unclear why political or electoral calculations did not figure more prominently in the BC decision-making process. The HST created a major political problem for the government, enough so that Premier Campbell was forced to resign and his successor had to reverse the policy. One potential explanation for this miscalculation is the role of heuristic-information processing. The premier and his closest advisers were likely biased from their own recent experience with tax reform. It is worth noting, however, that the conditions surrounding both the carbon tax and HST were different. In the case of the former, the public and stakeholders were given ample warning that the tax was being contemplated.[31] Moreover, "[the civil service] was afforded much more time to study and analyze different carbon tax policy options" as well as given resources to help communicate those alternatives to the public.[32] The carbon tax reflected a genuine effort by the government to learn about the policy instrument.

One potential consequence of the BC carbon tax experience is that it may have coloured the premier's perceptions about the electoral risks. It also may be the case, however, that the wrong lesson was ultimately drawn. Rather than showing the government's capacity to competently manage tax reform, the carbon tax may have simply underscored the role of luck in politics. As Harrison (2012) notes, the recession helped the government avoid paying a penalty at the ballot box. That is, it succeeded electorally in 2009 in spite of the carbon tax, not because of it. The government's "successful" experience with the carbon tax left it with the wrong takeaway, leading the premier to believe tax policy changes could be politically managed.[33]

Relying on a cognitively accessible but an ultimately unrepresentative event to inform subsequent behaviour is a common mistake in human reasoning. Viewed this way, the premier's behaviour is broadly consistent with two types of decision-making heuristics (Hypothesis 4 stated above). First, the availability heuristic, when actors place "excessive importance on information that … is especially immediate and striking" and second, the representative heuristic, when actors "overestimate the extent to which patterns observed in a small sample are representative of the whole population" (Weyland 2005, 264). These concepts are particularly helpful in understanding how recent (i.e., availability) and similar-looking (i.e., representative) experiences, such as the adoption of the carbon tax, can lead to errors in strategic judgement. We might expect these types of cognitive errors to be correlated with specific institutional settings and conditions. Policy decision-making contexts where deliberations are limited both in time and membership (i.e., insulated) are likely to be more conducive to these types of systematic biases. Again, the BC HST case offers a helpful illustration of how cognitive biases and institutional failure intersect in policy decision-making.

Conclusion

The purpose of this chapter has been to demonstrate the role of bounded emulation in processes of policy transfer. Drawing on the case of sales tax reform in BC, the analysis shows how cognitive and institutional forces can contribute to suboptimal policy decisions. While there were compelling reasons for the adoption of this specific policy instrument (in principle), the analysis shows that these rational considerations did not figure prominently in the decision-making process. Rather, the BC case illustrates how sometimes policymakers choose a policy solution simply because the idea is "floating around" (Kingdon 1995).

To be analytically compelling, studies of policy change, including policy transfer, require researchers to specify the process by which policy ideas are taken up by decision-makers. Methodologically, the chapter illustrates how within-case analysis can capture these processes, illustrating the precise mechanisms that underlie policy change. The study shows how interview data and document analysis provide useful methodological tools to distinguish bounded emulation from rational learning and economic competition. More broadly, these findings suggest that charting and scrutinizing policymakers' assumptions, goals, and behaviour provide a fruitful way to distil causal mechanisms in the policymaking process.

NOTES

1 The United States is a notable exception here. The majority of state governments collect sales taxes, but all of these have retained RST systems. As of 2019, British Columbia, Saskatchewan, and Manitoba are the only provinces that still have an RST in place.
2 Political adviser, confidential interview with author, 1 December 2015.
3 Strikingly, however, the Ontario government managed to avoid electoral retribution (see Lesch 2018).
4 Political adviser (1 December), interview.
5 The province also collects fuel, carbon, tobacco, and property transfer taxes.
6 Jock Finlayson, interview with author, 8 July 2015, Vancouver, British Columbia.
7 Finlayson, interview.
8 Finance ministers in Ottawa had been keen to push for federal-provincial sales tax harmonization. In several of Jim Flaherty's budgets and economic updates between 2006 and 2009, the finance minister urged provincial governments to consider harmonizing their sales taxes, firmly committing federal assistance for the transition. His former political staff in Ottawa stressed the priority of provincial sales tax reform for the late finance minister. From a political and a policy perspective, the motivations of the federal government are clear. From a policy standpoint, and specifically an administrative and economic efficiency perspective, Ottawa was keen to see a streamlined tax system; these preferences were particularly strong among senior officials in the Canada Revenue Agency. Politically, the federal government faced less risk in partnering with the provinces on sales tax harmonization
9 Policy adviser, confidential phone interview with author, 2 March 2015.
10 Policy adviser (2 March), interview.
11 Political adviser, confidential interview with author, 3 March 2015.
12 Carole James, phone interview with author, 13 March 2015.
13 According to polling data cited in Harrison's (2012) study, taken over 2007 and 2008, the NDP led the BC Liberals in public opinion polls. By October 2008, as public attention shifted to the economy, there was an accompanying increase in support for the BC Liberals. For Harrison, this affirmed the government's advantage on economic issues. For a discussion of "issue ownership," see Petrocik, Benoit, and Hanson (2003).
14 Policy adviser (2 March), interview.
15 Political adviser (3 March), interview.
16 Political adviser (3 March), interview.
17 Colin Hansen, interview with author, 8 July 2015, Vancouver, British Columbia.

18 Federal political adviser, confidential telephone interview, 6 January 2016.
19 As part of an agreement with the federal government, the Canada Revenue Agency collects the provincial corporate income taxes.
20 Hansen, interview.
21 Hansen, interview.
22 Federal political adviser (6 January), interview.
23 Don Drummond, phone interview with author, 23 October 2015.
24 Hansen, interview.
25 Charles Lamann, interview with author, 3 March 2015, Vancouver, British Columbia.
26 James, interview.
27 Don Cayo, telephone interview with author, 14 July 2015.
28 Drummond, interview.
29 Bill Tieleman, phone interview with author, 24 November 2015.
30 Policy adviser (2 March), interview.
31 Vaughn Palmer, telephone interview with author, 16 July 2016.
32 Policy adviser, confidential interview with the author, 12 July 2015.
33 Hansen, interview.

WORKS CITED

Abbott, George Malcolm. 2015. "The Precarious Politics of Shifting Direction: The Introduction of the HST in BC and Ontario." *BC Studies: The British Columbian Quarterly* 186: 125–48.

Atkinson, Michael M., Gregory P. Marchildon, Peter W.B. Phillips, Daniel Béland, Kenneth A. Rasmussen, and Kathleen McNutt. 2013. *Governance and Public Policy in Canada: A View from the Provinces*. Toronto: University of Toronto Press.

Bernstein, Steven, and Matthew Hoffmann. 2018. "The Politics of Decarbonization and the Catalytic Impact of Subnational Climate Experiments." *Policy Sciences* 51 (2): 189–211. https://doi.org/10.1007/s11077-018-9314-8.

Berry, Frances Stokes, and William D. Berry. 1992. "Tax Innovation in the States: Capitalizing on Political Opportunity." *American Journal of Political Science* 36 (3): 715–42. https://doi.org/10.2307/2111588.

Bird, Richard M., Jack M. Mintz, and Thomas A. Wilson. 2006. "Coordinating Federal and Provincial Sales Taxes: Lessons from the Canadian Experience." *National Tax Journal* 59 (4): 889–903.

Boushey, Graeme. 2010. *Policy Diffusion Dynamics in America*. Cambridge: Cambridge University Press.

Boyd, Brendan. 2017. "Working Together on Climate Change: Policy Transfer and Convergence in Four Canadian Provinces." *Publius: The Journal of Federalism* 47 (4): 546–71. https://doi.org/10.1093/publius/pjx033.

British Columbia Ministry of Finance (BCMoF). 2007. "Budget and Fiscal Plan 2007/08 to 2009/10." Government of British Columbia. http://www.bcbudget.gov.bc.ca/2007 /pdf/2007_Budget_Fiscal_Plan.pdf.

– 2010. "2010 British Columbia Financial and Economic Review." Government of British Columbia. http://www.fin.gov.bc.ca/tbs/F&Ereview10.pdf.

– 2011. "Budget and Fiscal Plan 2011/12–2013/14." Government of British Columbia. http://www.bcbudget.gov.bc.ca/2011/bfp/2011_Budget_Fiscal_Plan.pdf.

Brown, Doug. 2012. "Cooperative versus Competitive Federalism." *Zeitschrift Für Kanada-Studien* 32 (1): 9–27.

Brune, Nancy, and Geoffrey Garrett. 2000. "The Diffusion of Privatization in the Developing World." Paper presented at the annual meeting of the American Political Science Association, 30 August–3 September, Washington, DC.

Cairney, Paul, and Christopher M. Weible. 2017. "The New Policy Sciences: Combining the Cognitive Science of Choice, Multiple Theories of Context, and Basic and Applied Analysis." *Policy Sciences* 50 (4): 619–27. https://doi.org/10.1007/s11077 -017-9304-2.

CBC News. 2010. "B.C. Minister Briefed on HST before Election." *CBC News*, 1 September. http://www.cbc.ca/news/canada/british-columbia/b-c-minister-briefed-on -hst-before-election-1.876371.

Chaiken, Shelly. 1980. "Heuristic versus Systematic Information Processing and the Use of Source versus Message Cues in Persuasion." *Journal of Personality and Social Psychology* 39 (5): 752–66. https://doi.org/10.1037/0022-3514.39.5.752.

Cohen, Michael D., James G. March, and Johan P. Olsen. 1972. "A Garbage Can Model of Organizational Choice." *Administrative Science Quarterly* 17 (1): 1–25. https://doi .org/10.2307/2392088.

Cowan, James. 2009. "Ottawa to Give $4.3B to Ease Tax Reform; Harmonized 13% Sales Tax Set for July 1, 2010." *National Post*, 27 March, sec. Canada.

Dobbin, Frank, Beth Simmons, and Geoffrey Garrett. 2007. "The Global Diffusion of Public Policies: Social Construction, Coercion, Competition, or Learning?" *Annual Review of Sociology* 33 (1): 449–72. https://doi.org/10.1146/annurev .soc.33.090106.142507.

Druckman, James N., and Arthur Lupia. 2000. "Preference Formation." *Annual Review of Political Science* 3 (1): 1–24. https://doi.org/10.1146/annurev.polisci.3.1.1.

Eccleston, Richard. 2007. *Taxing Reforms: The Comparative Political Economy of Consumption Tax Reform in the United States, Canada, Japan and Australia*. Cheltenham: Edward Elgar Publishing Limited.

George, Alexander L., and Andrew Bennett. 2005. *Case Studies and Theory Development in the Social Sciences*. Boston: MIT Press.

Gilardi, Fabrizio. 2003. "Spurious and Symbolic Diffusion of Independent Regulatory Agencies in Western Europe." Unpublished manuscript.

– 2010. "Who Learns from What in Policy Diffusion Processes?" *American Journal of Political Science* 54 (3): 650–66. https://doi.org/10.1111/j.1540-5907.2010.00452.x.

Hale, Geoffrey. 2002. *The Politics of Taxation in Canada*. Peterborough, ON: Broadview Press.

Hall, Peter. A. 1993. "Policy Paradigms, Social Learning, and the State: The Case of Economic Policymaking in Britain." *Comparative Politics* 25 (3): 275–96.

Harrison, Kathryn. 2012. "A Tale of Two Taxes: The Fate of Environmental Tax Reform in Canada." *Review of Policy Research* 29 (3): 383–407.

Jacobs, Alan M. 2011. *Governing for the Long Term: Democracy and the Politics of Investment*. Cambridge: Cambridge University Press.

Jenkins-Smith, Hank C., Daniel Nohrstedt, Christopher M. Weible, and Paul A. Sabatier. 2014. "The Advocacy Coalition Framework: Foundations, Evolutions, and Ongoing Research." In *Theories of the Policy Process*, 3rd ed., edited by Paul A. Sabatier and Christopher M. Weible, 183–224. Boulder, CO: Westview Press.

Jones, Bryan D. 1999. "Bounded Rationality." *Annual Review of Political Science* 2 (1): 297–321. https://doi.org/10.1146/annurev.polisci.2.1.297.

Jones, Bryan D., and Frank R. Baumgartner. 2005. *The Politics of Attention: How Government Prioritizes Problems*. Chicago: University of Chicago Press.

Kahler, Miles. 1992. "External Influence, Conditionality, and the Politics of Adjustment." In *The Politics of Economic Adjustment: International Constraints, Distributive Conflicts, and the State*, edited by Stephan Haggard and Robert R. Kaufman, 89–138. Princeton, NJ: Princeton University Press.

Kahneman, Daniel, and Amos Tversky. 1979. "Prospect Theory: An Analysis of Decision under Risk." *Econometrica* 47 (2): 263–91. https://doi.org/10.2307/1914185.

Karch, Andrew. 2007. *Democratic Laboratories: Policy Diffusion Among the American States*. Ann Arbour: University of Michigan Press.

Kesselman, Jon. 2009. "What Our Taxes Needs Is Harmonization; B.C. Should Follow Ontario's Lead and Merge Its Sales Tax with the Federal GST – Only Do It Better." *Vancouver Sun*, 2 April, sec. Special to the Sun.

Kingdon, John W. 1995. *Agendas, Alternatives, and Public Policies*. New York: HarperCollins College Publishers.

Lesch, Matthew. 2018. "Playing with Fiscal Fire: The Politics of Consumption Tax Reform." PhD diss., University of Toronto. https://tspace.library.utoronto.ca/bitstream /1807/87367/3/Lesch_Matthew_201803_PhD_thesis.pdf.

Lindblom, Charles E. 1959. "The Science of 'Muddling Through.'" *Public Administration Review* 19 (2): 79–88. https://doi.org/10.2307/973677.

March, James G., and Johan P. Olsen. 1996. "Institutional Perspectives on Political Institutions." *Governance* 9 (3): 247–64.

Massey, Rachel. 1999. "The Credibility of Exit Threats: Refining the 'race to the Bottom' Debate." *Journal of Public and International Affairs* 10: 47–62.

Matisoff, Daniel C. 2008. "The Adoption of State Climate Change Policies and Renewable Portfolio Standards: Regional Diffusion or Internal Determinants?" *Review of Policy Research* 25 (6): 527–46. https://doi.org/10.1111/j.1541-1338.2008 .00360.x.

McArthur, Doug. 2011. "The British Columbia HST Debacle." *Policy Options* 32 (10): 29–33.

Meseguer, Covadonga. 2005. "Policy Learning, Policy Diffusion, and the Making of a New Order." *The ANNALS of the American Academy of Political and Social Science* 598 (1): 67–82. https://doi.org/10.1177/0002716204272372.

– 2006. "Rational Learning and Bounded Learning in the Diffusion of Policy Innovations." *Rationality and Society* 18 (1): 35–66. https://doi.org/10.1177/1043463106060152.

Millar, Heather, Matthew Lesch, and Linda A. White. 2019. "Connecting Models of the Individual and Policy Change Processes: A Research Agenda." *Policy Sciences* 52: 57–118. https://doi.org/10.1007/s11077-018-9327-3.

North, Douglass C. 1990. *Institutions, Institutional Change and Economic Performance.* Cambridge: Cambridge University Press.

Palmer, Vaughn. 2009. "Most of Campbell's Roughest Spots Were of His Own Making." *Vancouver Sun*, 11 December, sec. West Coast News, A3.

Peterson, Paul E., and Mark C. Rom. 1990. *Welfare Magnets: A New Case for a National Standard.* Washington, DC: The Brookings Institution.

Petrocik, John R., William L. Benoit, and Glenn J. Hansen. 2003. "Issue Ownership and Presidential Campaigning, 1952–2000." *Political Science Quarterly* 118 (4): 599–626. https://doi.org/10.1002/j.1538-165X.2003.tb00407.x.

Pierson, Paul. 1995. "Fragmented Welfare States: Federal Institutions and the Development of Social Policy." *Governance* 8 (4): 449–78.

Rabe, Barry G., and Christopher P. Borick. 2012. "Carbon Taxation and Policy Labeling: Experience from American States and Canadian Provinces" 29 (3): 358–82.

Rose, Richard. 1991. "What Is Lesson-Drawing?" *Journal of Public Policy* 11 (1): 3–30. https://doi.org/10.1017/S0143814X00004918.

Shepsle, Kenneth A. 1989. "Studying Institutions: Some Lessons from the Rational Choice Approach." *Journal of Theoretical Politics* 1 (2): 131–47.

Shipan, Charles R., and Craig Volden. 2008. "The Mechanisms of Policy Diffusion." *American Journal of Political Science* 52 (4): 840–57. https://doi.org/10.1111/j.1540 -5907.2008.00346.x.

Simon, Herbert A. 1957. *Models of Man; Social and Rational.* Oxford: Wiley.

– 1985. "Human Nature in Politics: The Dialogue of Psychology with Political Science." *The American Political Science Review* 79 (2): 293–304. https://doi.org/10.2307/1956650.

Smart, Michael. 2007. "Lessons in Harmony: What Experience in the Atlantic Provinces Shows about the Benefits of a Harmonized Sales Tax." *C.D. Howe Institute Commentary* 253: 1–21.

Stone, Diane. 2017. "Understanding the Transfer of Policy Failure: Bricolage, Experimentalism and Translation." *Policy & Politics* 45 (1): 55–70. https://doi .org/info:doi/10.1332/030557316X14748914098041.

Taber, Charles. 2003. "Information Processing and Public Opinion." In *Oxford Handbook of Political Psychology*, edited by David Sears, Leonie Huddy, and Robert Jervis, 433–76. Oxford: Oxford University Press.

Thaler, Richard H., and Cass R. Sunstein. 2008. *Nudge: Improving Decisions about Health, Wealth, and Happiness*. New Haven: Yale University Press.

Tiebout, Charles. 1956. "A Pure Theory of Local Expenditures." *Journal of Political Economy*, 64 (5): 416–24.

Tversky, Amos, and Daniel Kahneman. 1985. "The Framing of Decisions and the Psychology of Choice." In *Environmental Impact Assessment, Technology Assessment, and Risk Analysis*, edited by Vincent T. Covello, Jeryl L. Mumpower, Pieter J. M. Stallen, and V. R. R. Uppuluri, 107–29. NATO ASI Series 4. Springer Berlin Heidelberg.

Usalcas, Jeannine. 2010. "Labour Market Review 2009." Catalogue no. 75-001-X. Ottawa: Statistics Canada. https://www150.statcan.gc.ca/n1/pub/75-001-x/2010104/charts-graphiques/11148/c-g000h-eng.htm.

Walker, Jack L. 1969. "The Diffusion of Innovations among the American States" *American Political Science Review* 63 (3): 880–99. https://doi.org/10.2307/1954434.

Wallner, Jennifer. 2010. "Beyond National Standards: Reconciling Tension between Federalism and the Welfare State." *Publius: The Journal of Federalism* 40 (4): 646–71. https://doi.org/10.1093/publius/pjp033.

Weyland, Kurt. 2005. "Theories of Policy Diffusion Lessons from Latin American Pension Reform." *World Politics* 57 (2): 262–95.

Wilson, Rick K. 2011. "The Contribution of Behavioral Economics to Political Science." *Annual Review of Political Science* 14 (1): 201–23. https://doi.org/10.1146/annurev-polisci-041309-114513.

Zahariadis, Nikolaos. 2003. *Ambiguity and Choice in Public Policy: Political Decision Making in Modern Democracies*. Washington, DC: Georgetown University Press.

– 2008. "Ambiguity and Choice in European Public Policy." *Journal of European Public Policy* 15 (4): 514–30. https://doi.org/10.1080/13501760801996717.

6

Carbon Pricing Policies and Emissions from Aviation: Patterns of Convergence and Divergence

LAUREL BESCO

Introduction

In Canada, air travel has become an integral, and in many cases, essential part of the fabric of the country. For example, travelling from Newfoundland to mainland Canada became much faster once regular flights were introduced, reducing reliance on a lengthy ferry ride. In addition, residents of Canada's North are now able to travel and get supplies more quickly (though not necessarily more economically) by making use of air transport instead of seasonal shipments. Furthermore, the journey from major business centres in Canada's east (Toronto, Montreal, Ottawa, for example) to western hubs such as Vancouver has been made easier by daily flights between these locations. In terms of ease of transport, then, it is clear that the increasing use of air travel has largely been of benefit to the nation. As this mode of transportation exploded on the scene, it became obvious that new regulations were needed. As is the case with most new areas of policy in Canada, the question became, Who has the jurisdiction to regulate the industry? Over the years it has become clear that the federal government has the authority to regulate the aeronautics industry, though provinces have retained the power to tax aviation fuel within their jurisdictions.

At present, one of the pressing issues as it relates to aviation is the mitigation of greenhouse gas (GHG) emissions. Until recently, addressing emissions from the aviation sector has been largely set aside in domestic and international conversations around climate change policy because of the complexities of the impact of these emissions and responsibility for mitigating them. The international community, through the International Civil Aviation Organization (ICAO), recently adopted an offsetting mechanism targeted at carbon emissions from international aviation (International Civil Aviation Organization 2016). At the same time, climate change policy is developing in Canada, sped up by the federal government's requirement that carbon pricing be in place in all jurisdictions by the start of 2019 (Environment and Climate Change Canada 2018). The implicit question in this requirement is, given that the ICAO mechanism only deals with international emissions, how are domestic aviation emissions being dealt with?

How provinces and the federal government include (or not) emissions from aviation within their climate policies is an excellent opportunity to study the presence (or not) of policy diffusion. The focus in this chapter is on first-order change as laid out by Hall (1993) (also see chapter 1 of this volume, Table 1.3). In this case, I investigate how provinces have approached aviation within their carbon pricing schemes. Second-order changes, such as the instrument used, are less relevant since the federal government decided the instrument had to be carbon pricing. Investigation of third-order change will also be set aside, since paradigm shifting changes in goals or ideas relating to climate change and carbon pricing likely occurred earlier (e.g., in 2008 when the Liberal Party's "green shift" was the first serious proposal for a carbon tax at the national level).

In investigating how aviation is covered (or not) within the various climate policies across Canada, we might expect to see evidence of policy learning occurring as it relates to emissions from aviation, especially given the complexity of this sector, the time pressure of having a plan in place in a relatively short time frame, and the fact that some provinces have had their own climate policies, including carbon pricing, in place for some time. On the other hand, the aviation sector is a notoriously competitive one; therefore, evidence of competition affecting policy diffusion may prove strong. Finally, it is also possible that there would be top-down coercion from the federal government, playing a factor in policy diffusion.

This chapter examines two research questions: How has aviation been included or excluded in carbon pricing schemes across Canada? What are the mechanisms and pathways for policy convergence or divergence across jurisdictions, as well as patterns in their development? The chapter proceeds in six sections, the first of which provides a general framework for thinking about policy convergence and divergence as well as the pathways and mechanisms leading to these end points. Section two provides background information on the aviation sector in Canada and ends with a brief discussion of addressing greenhouse gas emissions from aviation. Methods are briefly discussed in the third section followed by section four, which presents the case study that looks at the extent to which different jurisdictions in Canada include or exclude the aviation sector from carbon pricing schemes. Section five draws together the results of this case study with the expectations from previous research findings, as provided in section two. The final section, the conclusion to the chapter, provides some general insights on this area of policy as well as more general trends.

Policy Convergence and Divergence

How laws, policies, and political ideas move between and within jurisdictions has been the focus of research for decades (for a thorough overview, see Marsh and Sharman 2009). What causes policy convergence or divergence is a matter of debate, but policy diffusion[1] is one of the main pathways considered, and for this there are four mechanisms that are typically referenced: learning, mimicry (which is sometimes considered a form of learning), competition, and coercion (see chapter 1 of this volume, Table 1.2 for more detailed definitions of these concepts). Exploring the concepts of policy convergence and policy divergence, as well as the mechanisms just identified, is important to the discussion in this chapter.

The oft-referenced definition of policy convergence comes from Kerr's 1983 book, *The Future of Industrial Societies*, which reads, "[c]onvergence is the tendency for polices to grow more alike, in the form of increasing similarity in structures, processes, and performances" (3). While this is an excellent starting point, Knill (2005) revises the definition to be more specific and, as a consequence perhaps, more useful for pulling out distinctive features of policy convergence. Knill (2005, 768) states that policy convergence is "any increase in the similarity between one or more characteristics of a certain policy (e.g., policy objectives, policy instruments, policy setting[, policy context]) across a given set of political jurisdictions (supranational institutions, states, regions, local authorities) over a given period of time." This definition is broad enough to allow its use in studying the varied types of policy convergence (of policy goals, of policy content, of policy instruments, of policy outcomes, and/or of policy style) (Bennett 1991) and to look beyond the commonly studied cross-national policy convergence and at convergence of policy between jurisdictions in the same country. For the purposes of this work, the focus is on the convergence or divergence of policy content, what Bennett (1991) defines as the more formal aspects of policy, such as laws, regulations, and administrative rules.

Policy diffusion (or the lack thereof) is a process that generally leads to convergence or divergence of policies in different jurisdictions (Dolowitz and Marsh 2000). In this chapter, this convergence or divergence is the outcome or the end point of analysis. Leading to convergence or divergence are pathways that include policy diffusion/policy transfer or other similar but independent responses. Though *policy diffusion, transfer*, and *convergence* are sometimes used interchangeably (as noted by Marsh and Sharman 2009, among others), here they are perceived as distinct parts of a process. The mechanisms that lead to the pathways are those commonly discussed in the literature and include learning, competition, coercion, and mimicry (see Marsh and Sharman 2009, for an overview of these concepts). This chapter uses the same categories elaborated on in chapter 2 of this volume, but here the mechanisms of learning and mimicry are combined with the latter defined as an "extreme" version of the former. This follows Rose's (1993, 30) typology of learning, which ranges from mimicry or copying all the way to inspiration, where policies or programs are more a type of "intellectual stimulus" rather than being directly transferred to a new jurisdiction. In the middle are types of learning that include adaptive, hybrid, and synthesis learning (see Rose 1993 for an overview). The motivation behind each may be slightly different – for mimicry or imitation it may be more ideational and related to not wanting to be seen as a laggard and instead following exactly what the leaders are doing (Heichel, Pape, and Sommerer 2005). Some of the less rigid forms of learning may occur instead because decision-makers simplify the task of finding a solution by "choosing an alternative that has proven successful elsewhere" (Berry and Baybeck 2005, 505).

Based upon the mechanisms and pathways, we might expect to see a number of patterns emerge as to how emissions from aviation are addressed in climate pricing policies across Canada:

1. That provinces might learn from one another, especially as it relates to dealing with aviation emissions in carbon pricing schemes. This should result in policy convergence.
2. That provinces situated geographically near one another might be more likely to adopt the same policies due to concerns of economic competitiveness.
3. That coercion might be a mechanism in the diffusion of policy as it relates to aviation and carbon pricing, because of the federal government's requirement for carbon pricing and its clear jurisdiction over the aviation sector.

In this chapter, I am explicitly not considering the transfer of knowledge or policy adoption according to Karch's (2008) agenda setting phase, as this is already set by the federal requirement for including a minimum carbon price within climate policy plans. Instead, I look at the other phases, particularly information generation and customization.

Evolution of Aviation Policy in Canada

The history of aviation law and policy in Canada reaches back to the First World War, and more specifically to the end of the war when the Dominion Government attempted to introduce a regulatory structure that emphasized the social and economic benefits of air travel (passenger and cargo transport) while controlling the "destructive aspects" (Seyer 2015). The result was the first aviation law in Canada, the Air Board Act in 1919. In 1920, the air regulations pursuant to this law were passed. Then, the 1922 National Defence Act was passed that defined powers, duties, and functions vested in the Air Board – at the same time the Air Board Act became the Aeronautics Act. In 1936, the Department of Transport Act transferred control of the civil aviation branch of the Department of National Defence to the Ministry of Transport, classifying civil aviation as non-military. Gradually, federal control over the area of aeronautics and aviation was strengthened – the 1930 *Reference re legislative powers as to regulation and control of aeronautics in Canada (Aeronautics Reference)* clearly places the power to regulate aeronautics in the hands of the federal government. This control was reiterated in two more recent Supreme Court of Canada cases, both decided in 2010 – *Quebec (Attorney*

General) v. Canadian Owners and Pilots Association and *Quebec (Attorney General) v. Lacombe.*

Although initially the federal government regulated the aviation sector very strongly, beginning in the late 1980s, deregulation across the board began. In 1988, the National Transportation Act substantially deregulated the sector and, in the same year, Air Canada was privatized (Iacobucci, Trebilcock, and Winter 2006). In the 1990s Canada signed the Open Skies Agreement with the United States, which allowed competition for routes between the two countries. In 1994, the federal government designated most major airports in Canada to be National Airport System (NAS) airports and ultimately transferred the management and upkeep of these locations to local airport authorities, while still retaining ultimate ownership (Canadian Airports Council 2017). Further, in 1996, the government transferred air navigation services out of its internal jurisdiction to NAV Canada, a private non-share capital corporation developed through a partnership between major players in the aviation sector (see NAV Canada 2015 for more details). As these examples make clear, though the federal government does have jurisdiction over the aviation sector, its direct role in its operation and regulation has dramatically decreased over time.

While the federal government has constitutional power over the regulation of aviation, the provinces have been able to tax aviation and jet fuel as part of their fuel tax processes. The 1970s saw the first federal excise tax appear on fuel used in air transport (National Airlines Council of Canada 2015). Subsequently, provincial fuel taxes began to also include fuel used in aviation, and at present the federal government as well as all ten provinces and three territories have their own fuel tax which, by and large, is levied on fuel used in all intrajurisdictional (within province and within territory) flights. Fuel used for international flights is exempt from tax by the federal government and by some provinces, while others charge a tax on fuel for these flights. Terms such as "transborder" and "continental" are used by some provinces to further distinguish flights and the fuel that is taxed or not, making the landscape of fuel taxes for aviation (beyond intrajurisdictional flights) quite divergent.

Since the federal government's 2016 climate plan requires carbon pricing schemes to be implemented in all jurisdictions – but allows provinces to implement this in different ways – the question becomes how emissions from aviation are being dealt with in climate change plans across the country. Olive (see chapter 4 of this volume) and Wesley (see chapter 7 of this volume) also investigate policy choices made in the aftermath of federal action on an issue – endangered species and legalization of cannabis, respectively – and therefore provide particularly useful companions to this chapter. It should be noted, though, that the federally imposed carbon pricing requirement has yielded much more opposition from provincial and territorial governments than either the National Accord for the Protection of Species at Risk or the federal plan to legalize cannabis. The federally imposed requirement to price carbon, plus the fact that there are already jurisdictions in the Canadian federation which operate carbon pricing schemes, might lead us to believe policy learning would occur (from the federal government or one of these jurisdictions). The fact that aviation emissions are a small but complex part of the entire emissions equation might lead us to the same conclusion: Why reinvent the policy content if someone else has already figured it out and implemented it? On the other hand, the experience with how aviation is taxed in terms of fuel taxes might lead us to think there would be policy divergence in terms of how carbon prices will or will not apply to emissions from aviation, since provinces might prefer continuity with their existing fuel tax policy.

Methods

The methods employed in this chapter were a qualitative comparative study between ten provinces, three territories, and the federal government, similar to the approach undertaken by Olive (chapter 4) and Wesley (chapter 7), who look at the same jurisdictions in their analyses. Specifically, to evaluate policy diffusion and convergence or divergence in aviation climate policy, we need to compare the coverage and exemptions of carbon pricing on aviation fuel. Given that these are often recent policy decisions and continue to be politically contested, this is more difficult than referencing a single government policy. Policy documents, legislation, regulations, press releases, news sources, as well as any published research in the area were reviewed. Efforts were also made to speak with relevant policymakers, though this had limited success, in part due to ongoing public debates. Examining Hansards from the ten provinces aided in a better understanding of mechanisms for policy diffusion and ultimately reasons why convergence or divergence might have emerged. Of course, a lot of the discussion about design and choice of policy is done by employees of the civil service, but gaining access to such information is extremely difficult. The following search terms were used in the data collection in order to ensure a comprehensive search: aviation, flight, jet, emissions, climate change, carbon, tax, carbon tax, and fuel.

Results: Carbon Pricing and Emissions from Aviation in Canada

The inclusion of aviation in carbon pricing varies by jurisdiction in Canada. Some do not cover aviation emissions at all, while others cover emissions from certain types of flights and not others. This section of the chapter provides an overview of these differences and some insight into why these variances occur. Understanding where and how these policies vary is important in order to get a fuller understanding of what mechanisms are at play in climate change policy in Canada, as well as in determining whether further federal oversight is needed

Table 6.1. Aviation Inclusion in Carbon Pricing Policy in Canada

Jurisdiction	Coverage of Aviation Emissions		
	International	Interjurisdictional	Intrajurisdictional
Federal government (backstop levy)	No (but covered by CORSIA)	No	Yes
Nunavut	No	No	No
Northwest Territories	No	No	No
Yukon	No	No	No
British Columbia	No	No	Yes
Alberta (pre-2019 election)	No	No	Yes
Alberta (post-2019 election)*	No	No	Yes
Saskatchewan*	No	No	Yes
Manitoba*	No	No	Yes
Ontario (pre-2018 election)	No	No	No
Ontario (post-2018 election)*	No	No	Yes
Quebec	No	No	No
New Brunswick*	No	No	Yes
Nova Scotia	No	No	No
Prince Edward Island	No	No	Yes
Newfoundland and Labrador	No	No	No

Note: * indicates jurisdictions with the federal backstop levy applied.

to ensure coverage of aviation emissions. Importantly, the results of this data collection identified that different types of flights are subject to different levels of coverage/exceptions of aviation emissions across Canada, both due to constitutional jurisdiction and policy choices. The three categories are shown in Table 6.1: international, interjurisdictional within Canada (i.e., interprovincial or interterritorial), and intrajurisdictional (i.e., within province or within territory) aviation emissions.

International Emissions

Emissions from international air travel have traditionally been excluded from international climate change agreements (Kyoto Protocol 1997; Paris Agreement 2015), and instead delegated to ICAO. In the Canadian context, international emissions are those produced from flights that originate or terminate in Canada, where the other end of the flight is outside of Canadian borders. While we might expect that the federal backstop levy would be applied here, since its international nature falls clearly within federal jurisdiction, this is not the case – both the federal backstop levy and all provincial and territorial climate pricing schemes exempt emissions from international fuels.

The exemption of emissions from international aviation from domestic carbon pricing schemes, in all fourteen jurisdictions in Canada, is clear evidence of policy convergence. Even among provinces that implemented their own carbon pricing policies prior to the federal government's requirement (British Columbia, Alberta, Quebec, and Ontario), emissions from international flights were excluded. This is not an unexpected convergence, though, because a recent development in the international arena means that (many of) these emissions will be covered under an international offsetting scheme – the Carbon Offsetting and Reduction Scheme for International Aviation (CORSIA), which Canada has signed on to. This means that federal legislation or regulation will be developed to implement these requirements in Canadian law and, consequently, emissions from fuel burned in international aviation will be covered by a climate policy scheme. As such, it makes sense that the national federal carbon backstop levy would include exemptions for international flights as do all provincial and territorial carbon pricing schemes. It is certainly possible, though, that in the longer term the federal government will choose to apply its backstop levy to international emissions in addition to the CORSIA requirements, should it be determined that CORSIA is not stringent enough or does not cover all international emissions. But at present that is not the situation.

Interjurisdictional Emissions

Interjurisdictional emissions (those from flights originating in one Canadian province or territory and terminating in another) are also not covered in the Canadian context. In fact, Shannon Phillips, the Alberta minister of environment and parks (and the minister responsible for the climate change plan), stated that "the exemption for inter-jurisdictional flights is standard across jurisdictions in Canada" (Legislative Assembly of Alberta [LAA] 2016). Surprisingly, Manitoba at one point proposed to include interjurisdictional Canadian emissions under its carbon pricing plan (Crab 2018), though ultimately its plan was rejected by the federal government, and the federal backstop levy, which only included intrajurisdictional flights in its coverage, was implemented in April of 2019.

Though at present interjurisdictional emissions are excluded from most carbon pricing policies, the federal government has acknowledged the importance of including this emission source in a carbon price. Specifically, the government suggests that it "will engage with provincial and territorial governments and stakeholders to ensure that this emission source [interjurisdictional aviation emissions] is properly covered, through a consistent national approach, and to determine which role the backstop should play in this regard, including in jurisdictions that have a carbon pricing system in place" (Environment and Climate Change Canada 2017, 15). Further, it is acknowledged that interjurisdictional emissions may have been excluded because of concerns about competitiveness, and the federal government alludes to the role that the federal backstop might be able to play in eliminating this concern through a consistent approach to coverage (Environment and Climate Change Canada 2017).

Intrajurisdictional Emissions

Coverage of intrajurisdictional flight emissions are an especially interesting case of policy diffusion, initially leading to convergence among geographically proximate provinces, though convergence based upon partisanship of governing parties has facilitated some shifts in this overall coverage in the past two years. The emissions discussed here are from flights that originate and terminate within the same province/territory. One of the earliest adopters of carbon pricing, British Columbia, includes intrajurisdictional emissions under its carbon price. Its neighbour to the east, Alberta, followed suit when it introduced its climate change plan years later and also covered intraprovincial emissions from aviation. With the election of the United Conservative Party in the spring of 2019, the Alberta carbon pricing plan was scrapped, but is set to be replaced by the federal backstop levy in January 2020. Effectively, this will have little impact on aviation coverage as both the original Albertan policy and the federal backstop levy cover intrajurisdictional aviation emissions, but there are different mechanisms at play with how this convergence is occurring.

The initial source of convergence between Alberta and British Columbia appears to be direct learning. The debate in the Alberta legislature about whether the carbon price should apply to intrajurisdictional flights rested largely on undermining the travel of Albertans in Alberta as well as on the impacts of northern Alberta communities (LAA 2016). The ultimate decision to keep intrajurisdictional emissions covered by the carbon price was explicitly justified in part by a reference to the fact that British Columbia has the same measures in place and its aviation and tourism industries remain strong (LAA 2016).

The new form of convergence post-2018 appears to be some form of mimicry based on governing party partisanship. The Alberta United Conservative Government followed quite closely what the Ontario Conservative government did after its 2018 election, in scrapping the previous government's climate plan and, therefore, opened the door for the federal backstop levy to be implemented. Then Alberta continued to follow Ontario (and Saskatchewan) in filing a court case challenging the constitutionality of the federal approach.

Conversely, other provinces explicitly (or implicitly, through making no direct reference) exclude intrajurisdictional aviation emissions from their carbon pricing plans. Quebec does not include aviation emissions within its cap and trade system (Government of Quebec 2011), which is not surprising because Quebec has a linked trading system with California, a state that excludes aviation (California Air Resources Board 2014; Kwan 2015). California began its carbon pricing mechanism first, and as Quebec designed its own cap and trade, the province followed many of the same coverage rules, including the exclusion of the aviation sector, as did Ontario in its own development of the now repealed cap-and-trade system (Kroft and Sinclair 2016). Further, Nova Scotia's approach specifically excludes "GHG emissions from fuels used in aviation and marine applications" (Government of Nova Scotia 2019, 8). Newfoundland and Labrador's approach also specifically provides exemptions for aviation fuel and for a number of other types of fuel use as well (Government of Newfoundland and Labrador 2018).

The Northwest Territories have a "Made-in-the-North" carbon tax that explicitly excludes aviation emissions from carbon pricing (Government of Northwest Territories 2018). Though the Yukon and Nunavut have the federal backstop levy applied in their jurisdictions, they have negotiated with the federal government to be given relief from the levy for aviation, where this type of fuel would be taxed at $0 per litre (Government of Canada 2018b, 2018c). Both of these territories have requested or are supportive of the federal backstop levy being implemented in their jurisdictions, with the caveat that the exemptions and special conditions be applied (Harris 2018). Given all of this, we can confidently say that intrajurisdictional aviation in the Northwest Territories is excluded from carbon pricing.

All jurisdictions that currently have the federal backstop levy applied (unless they have negotiated exemptions) have intrajurisdictional aviation emissions covered. As of September 2019 this includes Ontario (as already mentioned), New Brunswick, Manitoba, and Saskatchewan, with Alberta due to be covered by the levy in January of 2020. As already mentioned, many of these jurisdictions are challenging the federal approach to climate change with the hope that it will ultimately mean the backstop levy will be removed. Ontario and Saskatchewan have already had their cases heard before their respective provincial Courts of Appeal (COA) and, in both cases, the ruling was in favour of the federal government (*Reference re Greenhouse Gas Pollution Pricing Act, 2019 SKCA 40; Reference re Greenhouse Gas Pollution Pricing Act, 2019 ONCA 544*). Both provinces have subsequently appealed to the Supreme Court of Canada, and it is widely expected that the cases will be heard together (Keller 2019). Manitoba and Alberta are waiting to have their cases heard.

Though both COA rulings provide some confidence that the federal backstop levy will remain in place, ultimately the decision of the Supreme Court of Canada will determine this and, with it, the ultimate coverage of intrajurisdictional emissions. At present, though, the policy landscape relating to coverage of intrajurisdictional emissions is a situation of geographic, legal, and political convergence with a few instances of divergence. Ultimately, we may see coverage of intrajurisdictional emissions remain a bit of a patchwork, but it is also possible that provinces that have a carbon pricing scheme that excludes intrajurisdictional aviation emissions (Quebec, Nova Scotia, and Newfoundland and Labrador, specifically) will have coverage via a partial application of the federal backstop levy. This is because the federal government has stated that "[a]t a minimum, carbon pricing should apply to substantively the same sources as British Columbia's carbon tax" (Government of Canada 2018a). As has already been shown, British Columbia's carbon tax includes coverage of intrajurisdictional emissions. It is hard to say whether the federal government would step in and apply its backstop levy on only one set of emissions in a jurisdiction that is otherwise compliant. It is probably safe to assume, though, that this is much more likely if the same levy is introduced for interprovincial emissions, which, as John Moffet has suggested, "may be the one area in which the federal backstop applies beyond just in provinces that don't have a pricing system" (House of Commons 2018). He further clarified by saying "[w]e may need the backstop to apply also in provinces that have a pricing system but that do not address inter-jurisdictional aviation" (House of Commons 2018).

Convergence or Divergence?

Different mechanisms of policy diffusion can help explain the patterns of convergence and divergence across different jurisdictions in Canada as it relates to coverage of aviation in carbon pricing policy. As summarized above, at present no international or interjurisdictional aviation flight emissions are covered by domestic carbon pricing schemes. Conversely, in one way or another, the majority of intrajurisdictional emissions are covered by carbon pricing schemes. In chapter 2 of this volume, it was discussed that competition and central coercion might be the most likely mechanisms of diffusion in Canada, with the caveat that learning may play a larger part in this process than previous research has suggested. In the case of the diffusion of policy related to the coverage of aviation emissions under different carbon pricing policies, coercion is certainly relevant, but competition does not seem to play as big a part as one might expect – particularly as it relates to intrajurisdictional emissions. Instead, learning and mimicry appear to be significant motivators of diffusion of policy in this area. Patterns of learning are geographical, and perhaps also related to the economic profiles of different jurisdictions. The strongest patterns are between Alberta and British Columbia (prior to the 2019 Alberta election), Ontario and Quebec (prior to the 2018 Ontario election), and the Northwest Territories. The mechanism of mimicry is particularly important to consider when we look at the changes in provincial governments that occurred between 2018 and 2019. Coercion as a mechanism is relevant with respect to how aviation is considered in carbon pricing plans, especially given the number of provinces that have had the federal levy imposed upon them and the convergence over exclusion of interjurisdictional and international emissions.

Though competition concerns seem to have limited resonance in terms of carbon pricing as it relates to intrajurisdictional aviation, with perhaps the exception of Alberta's concern over reduced tourism by residents of its own province, coverage of interjurisdictional and international aviation emissions may well be more a consequence of pressure from competition.

Policy Learning as a Consequence of Geographical Proximity and Similar Economic Profiles

There is strong evidence that policy diffusion through learning occurred between Alberta and British Columbia, between Ontario and Quebec, and between the three territories, especially during the times of limited political animosity or when a number of years had passed and experiences could be learned from. This is not surprising given the similarities of the economic profiles of these three groups of jurisdictions (note that Table 1.1 shows Ontario and Quebec as being number one and two in terms of population and GDP, followed by Alberta and British Columbia, which ranked third and fourth, with the territories by far the smallest of the Canadian jurisdictions). Further, these groups of provinces and territories are geographically close, which may well make it easier and more likely that policymakers met at events or had more frequent meetings. The analysis above shows clear similarities between the ways that the various groupings of jurisdictions have proceeded with addressing (or not) emissions from aviation in their respective climate change and carbon pricing plans, especially regarding intrajurisdictional flights.

Introduced in 2008 by the provincial Liberal Party (equivalent to a conservative party in other provinces), British Columbia's carbon tax has often been heralded as an exemplary approach to mitigating climate change (e.g., see the Government of Canada's [2018] use of its coverage as part of its benchmark carbon pricing policy, as well as work by Murray and Rivers 2015; Elgie and McClay 2013, among others). Nearly a decade later, the newly elected New Democrat Party (NDP) government in Alberta released its Climate Leadership Plan (CLP) and took a page out of the British Columbia legislation when it came to dealing with emissions from aviation – it included emissions from flights originating and terminating in their provincial borders (i.e., intrajurisdictional flights), but excluded interjurisdictional and international flight emissions. In following British Columbia's lead, Alberta took a quite different approach from the Province of Quebec (the other Canadian jurisdiction that at the time had a carbon pricing scheme), which was partnering with the state of California under the umbrella of the Western Climate Initiative and excluded all emissions from aviation from its cap-and-trade system. This is perhaps especially surprising given that the NDP was learning from a policy put in place by a much more conservative government.

Importantly, there is clear evidence that Alberta explicitly drew on the policy experience of British Columbia. The Hansard from the Alberta Legislature illustrated concern on the part of Members of the Legislative Assembly about the impact of imposing carbon prices on aviation as it relates to tourism and the aviation industry. The minister in charge of the CLP responded to this by pointing out that British Columbia does the same, saying that "[c]ertainly, they still have an aviation industry in British Columbia, within the province, and certainly a very robust tourism economy" (LAA 2016). Interestingly, there was no reference to Quebec's system and, though there was discussion of Ontario, it was in relation to fuel taxes and not the carbon tax. Here, it seemed, Alberta learned directly from British Columbia's experience, and its approach to dealing with intrajurisdictional flights was diffused into Alberta's carbon pricing policy.

Policy convergence between Alberta and British Columbia, as it relates to aviation, does not just go one way – that is, Alberta does not just follow British Columbia. When British Columbia was faced with pressure to eliminate its fuel tax on transborder and international flights, the evidence provided was about what Alberta (and to some extent the bordering American states) was doing about the same issue. A representative of the Vancouver Airport Authority gave a presentation to the British Columbia legislature saying that "[o]ur closest competitors – the states of Washington, California and Alaska and the province of Alberta – do not charge fuel tax on international flights" (Legislative Assembly of British Columbia [LABC] 2007). The representative continued (with reference to using reduced taxes to improve the competitiveness of airports) by stating that "Calgary has been particularly aggressive and has been quite successful" (LABC 2007). Ultimately, British Columbia did remove fuel tax on international and transborder flights. In this case, the policy diffusion seemed to be motivated by perhaps both a learning as well as a competition mechanism.

Quebec and Ontario also show geographic policy convergence as both exclude emissions from intrajurisdictional flights. Quebec implemented its cap-and-trade system in 2013 and connected auctioning of permits with California in 2014. Ontario's approach to carbon pricing followed Quebec in a number of ways, including the use of a cap-and-trade system and the connection with Quebec and California in terms of auctioning. In fact, transcripts of a legislative session indicate the recognition on behalf of Ontario's Members of Provincial Parliament of the success of Quebec's and California's cap-and-trade systems. For example, a petition presented read, in part, "Whereas cap-and-trade programs in other jurisdictions like Quebec and California have been proven to reduce emissions" (Legislative Assembly of Ontario [LAO] 2016). It is perhaps no surprise to find convergence between Ontario and Quebec in their general climate change plans and their more specific treatment of aviation emissions – Foucault and Montpetit (2014) also found convergence in these two provinces as it regards policy attention. What is less clear in this case are the mechanisms that led to the diffusion of the cap-and-trade approach (and its exclusion of aviation emissions) from Quebec to Ontario. Given the large amount of trade and business done between the two provinces, concerns about competitiveness certainly provide a plausible explanation. Further, as with British Columbia and Alberta, the proximity of the two jurisdictions likely means policymakers and politicians in the two provinces have numerous opportunities to meet and discuss approaches, and therefore learning, leading to diffusion and convergence, is likely another piece of the puzzle.

Finally, there is convergence in the three territories with respect to the exclusion of aviation emissions from carbon pricing, though the exact implementation differs, with the Northwest Territories creating its own carbon pricing scheme and Yukon and Nunavut adopting the federal carbon levy with exemptions for aviation fuel. Here, the economic profile of the jurisdictions and the shared reliance on air travel in their remote northern communities, which is both essential and already very expensive, is likely one of the main factors causing this convergence. Once one territory proceeded with the plan to limit coverage of aviation emissions, the others were quick to learn that this approach was acceptable to the federal government.

The mechanism involved in the federal government's inclusion of intrajurisdictional emissions in its backstop levy is less clear. It may well be related to its general jurisdiction over the aviation sector and perhaps a feeling of obligation towards coverage. It is also possible that the federal government learned from British Columbia and Alberta, since some commentators have noted that the federal backstop levy is in fact very similar to the Alberta climate plan (Forrest 2017) and that the governments themselves have stated they intended to build upon the British Columbia model in terms of coverage (Government of Canada 2018).

Together, learning has occurred between jurisdictions that are geographically close and with similar economic profiles. In addition, the federal government's choice to include intrajurisdictional aviation emissions is quite possibly additional evidence of policy learning. That is to say, the federal government learned from British Columbia and Alberta in that they included this source of emissions, while the territories learned from one another, as did Quebec and Ontario, and these five jurisdictions exclude intrajurisdictional emissions. There is limited information about how the remaining jurisdictions came to their decisions; therefore, we cannot say for sure whether they were influenced by policy diffusion mechanisms or if they simply had similar but independent responses to dealing with the task of developing a carbon pricing plan. In the situations shown above, different mechanisms seem to be at play – while competition has been cited as the motivating factor in other studies of geographical policy convergence (e.g., Berry and Baybeck 2005; Shipan and Volden 2008), the evidence here more strongly suggests (as does Boyd 2017) that geographical convergence can be due to the learning mechanism. For the three territories, a shared socio-economic context of reliance on air travel in remote communities is likely to have played a strong role. Further, the federal government appears to have leaned upon its constitutional jurisdiction over aviation as well as learning from previously enacted (and successful) climate policies in two provinces.

Political Alliances Resulting in Policy Mimicry

In the months surrounding the implementation of the federal requirement for carbon pricing, provincial elections occurred that changed the approaches taken towards climate change for two large and influential provinces in Canada – Ontario and Alberta. While before the election both provinces had their own carbon pricing plans in place, the winning party in both jurisdictions campaigned on removing the existing climate policy and challenging the federal requirements. While ultimately this resulted in the same coverage of intrajurisdictional aviation emissions in Alberta (as the previous plan covered them and so too does the federal backstop levy that will be in place as of January 2020), in Ontario this resulted in coverage of a source under the federal backstop that had previously been excluded. So, while the carbon pricing coverage in place in these two provinces was not chosen, the path that brought them to such a place was very much a choice and can reasonably be considered mimicry based upon similarities in political priorities. In fact, the approach taken first by Ontario and then by Alberta is much the same as what Saskatchewan initially did as well. These three provinces (in addition to New Brunswick) all currently have right-leaning provincial governments in office, who have met numerous times to discuss ways to combat the federal climate policy requirements (e.g., Wherry 2019). This is not a silent sort of mimicry, but appears to be strategic mimicry based upon political platforms.

Federalism Leading to Top-Down Policy Coercion

It should come as no surprise that top-down coercion emerges as a mechanism of policy diffusion in the case of aviation emissions in Canada. This type of mechanism, as Wallner (2014) notes, is assumed in most cases to be prominent in the diffusion of policies amongst subnational jurisdictions in federations. In the Canadian case, as it relates to aviation, this mechanism is arguably even more significant in that the federal government has clear constitutional jurisdiction over the area of aviation and aeronautics (*Quebec (Attorney General) v. Canadian Owners and Pilots Association*; *Quebec (Attorney General) v. Lacombe*). Of course, ultimately the need to have a carbon price at all is itself forceful coercion from the federal government, but here we take this as a starting point and are more interested in the ways which aviation emissions were dealt with by the various jurisdictions in Canada.

As it relates to emissions from aviation, we can see two different areas where coercion from the federal government is causing policy diffusion – the first relates to international and interjurisdictional emissions and the second relates to intrajurisdictional ones. International emissions are by their nature to be dealt with by the international community, which means the national government is responsible (even in a country where domestic emissions might not be under the jurisdiction of the central government). Therefore, the legal delineation of this issue causes a form of soft coercion where it is made clear to subnational jurisdictions that they are not to consider this source of emissions under their own carbon pricing policy. In Canada's case, a similar form of coercion is likely at work on interjurisdictional emissions, given the clear jurisdictional authority given to the federal government surrounding aviation generally.

Interestingly, despite this clear power, intrajurisdictional emissions do not seem to have been universally excluded from subnational carbon pricing plans, and it is here that we see the use of more forceful coercion by the federal government by way of implementing its carbon pricing policy – the federal backstop – on provinces which did not develop an acceptable solution themselves. Because the federal backstop's parameters include intrajurisdictional emissions within its coverage, so too do the jurisdictions that have had the backstop levied upon them. This is a form of forceful coercion as in these cases the jurisdictions are protesting the constitutionality of the entire federal policy and, therefore, are not choosing to cover intrajurisdictional emissions of their free will. The exceptions here are the Nunavut and Yukon territories, which requested the federal backstop in their jurisdictions but negotiated the exclusion of aviation emissions. Going forward, it is possible that we may see further evidence of forceful coercion leading to coverage of intrajurisdictional emissions in all subnational carbon pricing policies (even where approved provincial plans are in place), should the federal government decide to pursue this as an area where it has exclusive control, as was mentioned above.

Competition

While competition is often cited as a potential driver for policy diffusion and convergence, the evidence for it driving policy diffusion on carbon pricing policy coverage of aviation emissions is mixed, despite the fact that the aviation industry is often characterized as being driven by competition (e.g., Standing Senate Committee on Transportation and Communications 2013).

The suggestion is often that competition concerns would lead to policy convergence through a "race to the bottom" (Shipan and Volden 2008), which, in this case, would leave jurisdictions vying to reduce the coverage of carbon pricing and would result in standardized low coverage. However, the economic competition mechanism as an explanation appears to produce mixed results here. While there are exemptions across the board for both international flights and interjurisdictional flights, intrajurisdictional flights are covered in a growing number of provinces. Notably, Alberta (in its climate policy prior to the 2019 provincial election) did seriously consider competitiveness in deciding whether or not to cover emissions from intraprovincial flights in its carbon pricing scheme, and yet ultimately decided to extend carbon pricing regardless of these competitiveness concerns. Of course, other provinces may also have considered this and chosen to exclude aviation emissions from their climate plans, but no clear evidence of this connection was found.

That international flights are excluded from carbon pricing due to competitiveness concerns seems more plausible, since the market for global air travel is much larger and more competitive than within a single province or territory. Importantly, international flight emissions have until recently been excluded from carbon pricing plans around the world (though the European Union did attempt to include them). The introduction of CORSIA has changed this and the large number of countries participating in this mechanism may well be mitigating competitiveness concerns.

At the interjurisdictional level within Canada, emissions are excluded which is a somewhat puzzling anomaly but is likely due to both competitiveness concerns as well as jurisdictional issues. Should the federal government decide to use the backstop levy to include emissions from interjurisdictional flights, as it and others have suggested might make sense (e.g., Environment and Climate Change Canada 2017; Chalifour and Besco 2017), domestic competitiveness concerns should be mitigated.

Conclusion

In closing, I return to the three expectations laid out at the beginning of the chapter. First, the provinces would learn from one another in this policy area, especially given its complex nature and highly specific source of emissions, as well as the fact that some jurisdictions have had policies in place for some time. In this case, the answer is "yes," this clearly did happen – particularly for intrajurisdictional flights and, in many cases, this occurred prior to the federal government imposing a minimum carbon price requirement.

Second, there was an expectation that convergence would be driven by competition and we might also expect this to be strongly tied to geographical orientation. Interestingly enough, it seems the mechanism of competition did not play out as strongly, in relation to putting a carbon price on intrajurisdictional emissions, as might have been expected. In seems the geographical convergence of this type of emissions coverage was more a consequence of the learning mechanism (at least in the clearest cases of convergence on this type of emissions – between British Columbia/Alberta and Ontario/Quebec pre-provincial elections). That said, competition does emerge as an important mechanism in other areas of aviation policy (fuel taxes, for example), as well as likely being a driver of unanimous exclusion of interjurisdictional aviation from carbon pricing and previous restraint by the international community in its dealing with international aviation emissions.

Third, there was an expectation that coercion would be an important mechanism in how emissions from aviation are dealt with, especially given the federal government's carbon pricing mandate and its clear constitutional authority over aviation. This did play out, particularly as it related to the exclusion of international and interjurisdictional aviation emissions and the imposition of the federal backstop in jurisdictions which either did not propose their own carbon pricing policy or whose policy was deemed unacceptable.

In addition to the three expectations, it is noteworthy that mimicry as a mechanism has played out quite recently as a pathway to policy convergence, especially as provincial governments have changed – the mimicry has been clearly intentional, coordinated, and based upon similar political ideals and positions among these various jurisdictions. This outcome is in contrast to what Wesley found in chapter 7 and Olive found in chapter 4 because in this case the partisan considerations led to conflict with the federal government and an attempt to obstruct implementation, something not found by the other authors. This may well be because climate change, generally, has become an increasingly polarizing issue in politics, particularly in the United States, but also increasingly in Canada (see Brulle, Carmichael, and Jenkins 2012; Dunlap and McCright 2008; Rabe et al. 2011).

In the future, one important question is going to be whether emissions from this sector *should* actually be covered by individual provinces and territories, or whether the federal government should be the one implementing monitoring, reporting, and pricing on this entire sector of the economy, given its clear jurisdiction over the area. At present it seems the federal government is happy to let provinces and territories cover emissions from intrajurisdictional flights in their individual carbon pricing schemes, while the federal government takes on the responsibility for international emissions. It also appears likely that emissions from interjurisdictional aviation are a prime source for coverage by the federal backstop, though any definitive plans for this to occur have not been released. Still, this set-up will result in a fragmented policy environment, with the same type of fuel for different types of flights taxed by different levels of government, possibly at different rates, and maybe through entirely different systems (e.g., cap-and-trade versus carbon tax). Consolidation of aviation climate policy under the federal government seems both a natural and constitutionally valid solution, but whether this is the direction policy evolves towards is hardly certain.

NOTE

1 The distinction between policy diffusion and transfer has been the subject of much debate, the nuances of which are beyond the scope of this chapter; instead, the focus is on the mechanisms that both of these concepts have in common. Policy diffusion is used throughout for consistency.

WORKS CITED

Bennett, Colin J. 1991. "Review Article: What Is Policy Convergence and What Causes It?" *British Journal of Political Science* 21: 215–33.

Berry, William, and Baybeck, Brady. 2005. "Using Geographic Information Systems to Study Interstate Competition." *American Political Science Review* 99 (4): 505–19.

Boyd, Brendan. 2017. "Working Together on Climate Change: Policy Transfer and Convergence in Four Canadian Provinces." *Publius: The Journal of Federalism* 47 (4): 546–71.

Brulle, Robert J., Jason Carmichael, and J. Craig Jenkins. 2012. "Shifting Public Opinion on Climate Change: An Empirical Assessment of Factors Influencing Concern over Climate Change in the US, 2002–2010." *Climatic Change* 114 (2): 169–88.

California Air Resources Board. 2014. *Regulation for the Mandatory Reporting of Greenhouse Gas Emissions*. https://www.arb.ca.gov/cc/reporting/ghg-rep/regulation/mrr -2013-clean.pdf.

Canadian Airports Council. 2017. *Canada's Airports: Brief History*. http://hub.cacairports .ca.

Chalifour, Nathalie J., and Laurel Besco. 2017. "Taking Flight: Federal Action to Mitigate Canada's GHG Emissions from Aviation." *Ottawa Law Review* 48 (2): 577–625.

Crabb, Josh. 2018. "Winnipeg Airports Authority Concerned about Impact of Carbon Tax on Aviation Fuel." *CTV News Winnipeg*, 28 March. https://winnipeg.ctvnews.ca /winnipeg-airports-authority-concerned-about-impact-of-carbon-tax-on-aviation -fuel-1.3863470.

Dolowitz, David, and Marsh, David. 1996. "Who Learns What from Whom: A Review of the Policy Transfer Literature." *Political Studies* 44: 343–51.

– 2000. "Learning from Abroad: The Role of Policy Transfer in Contemporary Policy-Making." *Governance: An International Journal of Policy and Administration* 13 (1): 5–24.

Dunlap, Riley, and Aaron McCright. 2008. "A Widening Gap: Republican and Democratic Views on Climate Change." *Environment: Science and Policy for Sustainable Development* 50 (5): 26–35.

Elgie, Stewart, and Jessica McClay. 2013. "BC's Carbon Tax Shift Is Working Well after Four Years ('Attention Ottawa')." *Canadian Public Policy* 39 (Special Supplement on Environmental Policy in Canada): S1–S10.

Environment and Climate Change Canada. 2017. "Technical Paper on the Federal Carbon Pricing Backstop." Ottawa: Government of Canada. https://www.canada.ca /content/dam/eccc/documents/pdf/20170518-2-en.pdf.

– 2018. *Putting a Price on Carbon Pollution in Canada*. Ottawa: Government of Canada. https://www.canada.ca/en/environment-climate-change/news/2018/04/putting-a -price-on-carbon-pollution-in-canada.html.

Forrest, Maura. 2017. "What We Still Don't Know about the Federal Carbon-Pricing Plan." *National Post*, 18 May. https://nationalpost.com/news/politics/what-we-still -dont-know-about-the-federal-carbon-pricing-plan.

Foucault, Martial, and Éric Montpetit. 2014. "Diffusion of Policy Attention in Canada: Evidence from Speeches from the Throne: 1960–2008." In *Agenda-Setting from a Policy Theory to a Theory of Politics,* edited by Christoffer Green-Pedersen and Stefaan Walgrave, 201–19. Chicago: University of Chicago Press.

Government of Canada. 2018a. *Guidance on the Pan-Canadian Carbon Pollution Pricing Benchmark.* https://www.canada.ca/en/services/environment/weather/climatechange/pan-canadian-framework/guidance-carbon-pollution-pricing-benchmark.html.

– 2018b. *Nunavut and Pollution Pricing.* https://www.canada.ca/en/environment-climate-change/services/climate-change/pricing-pollution-how-it-will-work/nunavut.html.

– 2018c. *Yukon and Pollution Pricing.* https://www.canada.ca/en/environment-climate-change/services/climate-change/pricing-pollution-how-it-will-work/yukon.html.

Government of Manitoba. 2009. *Information Notice – Cargo Flights: Reduced Aviation Fuel Tax Rate.* https://www.gov.mb.ca/finance/taxation/pubs/bulletins/noticecargo.pdf.

Government of New Brunswick. 2017. *Bill 39 – Climate Change Act.* http://www.gnb.ca/legis/bill/FILE/58/4/Bill-39-e.htm.

Government of Newfoundland and Labrador Municipal Affairs and Environment, Finance, and Natural Resources. (2018, 23 October). "Provincial Government Releases Federally-Approved Made-in-Newfoundland and Labrador Approach to Carbon Pricing." News release, 23 October. https://www.releases.gov.nl.ca/releases/2018/mae/1023n01.aspx.

Government of Northwest Territories Finance. 2018. *Implementing Carbon Pricing in the NWT.* https://www.fin.gov.nt.ca/en/carbon-pricing.

Government of Nova Scotia. 2019. *Nova Scotia's Cap and Trade Program: Regulatory Framework.* https://climatechange.novascotia.ca/sites/default/files/Nova-Scotia-Cap-and-Trade-Regulatory-Framework.pdf.

Government of Prince Edward Island. 2018. *Taking Action: A climate change action plan for Prince Edward Island 2018–2023.* https://www.princeedwardisland.ca/sites/default/files/publications/climatechange2018_f8.pdf.

Government of Quebec. 2011. *Regulation Respecting a Cap-and-Trade System for Greenhouse Gas Emission Allowances.* http://legisquebec.gouv.qc.ca/en/ShowDoc/cr/Q-2,%20r.%2046.1.

Hall, Peter. 1993. "Policy Paradigms, Social Learning, and the State: The Case of Economic Policymaking in Britain." *Comparative Politics* 25 (3): 275–96.

Harris, Melissa. 2018. "Your Cheat Sheet to Carbon Pricing in Canada." Delphi Group. https://delphi.ca/2018/10/your-cheat-sheet-to-carbon-pricing-in-canada/.

Heichel, Stephan, Jessica Pape, and Thomas Sommerer. 2005. "Is There Convergence in Convergence Research? An Overview of Empirical Studies on Policy Convergence." *Journal of European Public Policy* 12 (5): 817–40.

House of Commons. 2018. January 05 Debate. (42nd Legislature, First Session). https://www.ourcommons.ca/Parliamentarians/en/PublicationSearch?targetLang=&Text

=aviation+fuel+carbon&PubType=37&ParlSes=&Topic=&Proc=&Per=&com=&oob
=&PubId=&Cauc=&Prov=&PartType=&Page=1&RPP=15#.

Iacobucci, Edward, Michael J. Trebilcock, and Ralph A. Winter. 2006. "The Canadian Experience with Deregulation." *University of Toronto Law Review* 56 (1): 1–74.

International Civil Aviation Organization. 2016. *Carbon Offsetting and Reduction Scheme for International Aviation.* https://www.icao.int/environmental-protection/CORSIA /Pages/default.aspx.

Karch, Andrew. 2007. *Democratic Laboratories: Policy Diffusion among the American States.* Ann Arbor: University of Michigan Press.

Keller, James. 2019. "Ontario Files Appeal with Supreme Court in Fight against Federal Carbon Tax." *Globe and Mail,* 28 August. https://www.theglobeandmail.com/canada /article-ontario-files-appeal-with-supreme-court-in-fight-against-federal/.

Kerr, Clark. 1983. *The Future of Industrial Societies: Convergence or Continuing Diversity?* Cambridge, MA: Harvard University Press.

Knill, Chritoph. 2005. "Introduction: Cross-National Policy Convergence: Concepts, Approaches and Explanatory Factors." *Journal of European Public Policy* 12 (5): 764–74.

Kroft, P. Jason, and Luke Sinclair. 2016. "Examining California, Quebec and Ontario's Cap-and-Trade Systems." Strikeman Elliott. https://www.stikeman.com/fr-ca/savoir /droit-canadien-energie/examining-california-quebec-and-ontario-cap-and-trade -systems.

Kwan, Irene. 2015. "Off the Radar: Aviation in California's Climate Policy." International Council on Clean Transportation Blog. https://www.theicct.org/blogs/staff/radar -aviation-california%E2%80%99s-climate-policy.

Kyoto Protocol to the United Nations Framework Convention on Climate Change, 1997, 2303 U.N.T.S. 162.

Legislative Assembly of Alberta. 2016. June 6 Debate (29th Legislature, Second Session). http://www.assembly.ab.ca/net/index.aspx?p=han&section=doc.

Legislative Assembly of British Columbia. 2007. September 21 Debate (38th Legislature, Third Session). https://www.leg.bc.ca/advanced-search.

Legislative Assembly of Ontario. 2016. June 8 Petitions (41st Legislature, First Session). http://hansardindex.ontla.on.ca/hansardeissue/41-1/l184.htm.

Marsh, D., and J. C. Sharman. 2009. "Policy Diffusion and Policy Transfer." *Policy Studies* 30 (3): 269–88.

Murray, B., and N. Rivers. 2015. "British Columbia's Revenue-Neutral Carbon Tax: A Review of the Latest 'Grand Experiment.'" Environmental Policy. Nicholas Institute Working Paper. https://nicholasinstitute.duke.edu/climate/publications /british-columbia%E2%80%99s-revenue-neutral-carbon-tax-review-latest -%E2%80%9Cgrand-experiment%E2%80%9D.

National Airlines Council of Canada. 2015. *National Airlines Council of Canada Submission to the Canada Transportation Act Review Panel.* https://tc.canada.ca/sites /default/files/migrated/national_20airline_20council_20of_20canada.pdf.

NAV Canada. 2015. *The Test of Time: How NAV Canada Really Works*. https://www
.navcanada.ca/EN/media/Publications/Test%20of%20Time-EN.pdf.

Paris Agreement. 2015. Registration Number 54113.

Quebec (Attorney General) v. Canadian Owners and Pilots Association, [2010] 2 SCR 536.

Quebec (Attorney General) v. Lacombe, [2010] 2 SCR 453.

Rabe, Barry G., Christopher P. Borick, and Erick Lachapelle. 2011. *Climate Compared:
Public Opinion on Climate Change in the United States & Canada*. Center for Local,
State, and Urban Policy (CLOSUP) Report. https://ssrn.com/abstract=2313303.

Rose, Richard. 1993. "What Is Lesson-Drawing?" *Journal of Public Policy* 20 (1): 3–30.

Seyer, Sean. 2015. "Walking the Line – The International Origins of Civil Aviation
Regulation in Canada." *Scientia Canadensis* 38 (2): 79–89.

Shipan, Charles R., and Craig Volden. 2008. "The Mechanisms of Policy Diffusion."
American Journal of Political Science 52 (4): 840–57.

Standing Senate Committee on Transportation and Communications. 2013. *One Size
Doesn't Fit All: The Future Growth and Competitiveness of Canadian Air Travel*. https://
sencanada.ca/Content/SEN/Committee/411/trcm/rep/rep08apr13-e.pdf.

Wallner, Jennifer. 2014. *Learning to School: Federalism and Public Schooling in Canada*.
Toronto: University of Toronto Press.

Wherry, Aaron. 2019. "Premiers Say They Want a 'Co-operative' Approach to Climate
Policy. Are They Serious?" *CBC News,* 10 July. https://www.cbc.ca/news/politics
/trudeau-kenney-ford-climate-change-carbon-tax-1.5205131.

7

Policy Replication: The Case of Canadian Cannabis Legalization

JARED J. WESLEY

In legalizing cannabis, governments across Canada have undertaken one of the most intense exercises in national policymaking in the country's history. Under tight timelines imposed by their federal counterparts, provincial and territorial (PT) governments had to decide how integrated the new regime should be, across provincial and territorial borders. Should governments work together to create a common approach to regulating the distribution or sale of cannabis, be it public or private? Should they set a coast-to-coast-to-coast minimum age of consumption? Should they tax marijuana at the same rate?

The federal government gave its provincial, territorial, and municipal partners eighteen months to answer these sorts of questions and to pass hundreds of legislative and regulatory changes, in order to set up the new pan-Canadian regime. Precisely how did PT policymakers address this challenge in the lead-up to legalization in the second half of 2018? And what explains their choice of policy mechanisms? With the presence of a federal framework and direction, we would expect to see diffusion of policy through coercion (see chapter 1 of this volume, Table 1.2). However, according to the results of this study, PT governments turned inward. Rather than seeking alignment with other governments in their strategic or operational policies, or seeking innovation within their own borders, PT governments have engaged in a process of internal *policy replication*. That is, they have chosen to convert or adapt their own existing approaches in analogous policy fields to address concerns with cannabis. In large measure, this has entailed applying alcohol and tobacco regulations to new ends. As used in this chapter, the term "replication" should not be confused with mechanisms like policy learning or imitation; the latter constitute forms of interjurisdictional policy diffusion (see chapter 1 of this volume). Replication means turning inward, not outward, for policy ideas and instruments to solve a new or evolving challenge. Provincial and territorial government decisions were driven by a host of ideological, partisan, cultural, and economic considerations, most of which had little to do with the tight timelines imposed by the federal government. In other words, even with more time to collaborate, PT governments were unlikely to opt for a more integrated pan-Canadian cannabis regulation regime.

Analytical Framework

Students of comparative public policy remain committed to understanding why, how, and when different governments develop similar approaches to common policy challenges (Cairney 2012, 244–63; Berry and Berry 2018; Evans and Davies 1999; Knill 2005). For the purposes of this chapter, this concept is defined as *policy alignment* – an umbrella term that captures both spatial and temporal notions of similarity. Aligned policy is similar across jurisdictions (as potential evidence of policy diffusion) and/or may become increasingly similar over time (through policy convergence). In short, alignment can be either a static descriptor (with its opposite being non-alignment) or a dynamic process (in contrast to de-alignment).[1] Table 1.2 in chapter 1 of this volume identifies the possible mechanisms that could lead to alignment, including coercion, competition, learning, and emulation. In this case, the federal presence makes coercion the most likely source of diffusion (see chapter 1). By comparison, our theoretical understanding of policy non-alignment and de-alignment is far less robust, particularly at the subnational level. Precisely why, and under what conditions, do provincial and territorial governments develop unique policy approaches instead of seeking alignment with other jurisdictions, even in the presence of federal frameworks, which would increase the chances of diffusion?

To understand these questions, it is useful to conceptualize policy as existing on three levels (see Table 7.1). *Directional policy* establishes a government's high-level objective as it pertains to a specific issue. This could involve preserving the status quo either through action or inaction, or it could entail a change in approach in any number of different directions. Directional policy aligns well with Hall's (1993) third-order category of policy calibration. The federal government was responsible for setting directional policy in the cannabis field, by dictating its legalization across Canada. This authority comes by virtue of federal jurisdiction over public health (including the Controlled Substances Act) and public safety (e.g., the Criminal Code of Canada).

Strategic policy establishes mid-level plans to achieve these directional objectives. Such actions respond to core questions about how to fund and organize the state's approach to meeting the directional policy, including the pace and sequencing of reform. This may or may not involve reforming policy instruments, which Hall (1993) labels second-order change. Strategic policy also sets the rules for enforcement and sets parameters for the delivery of related programs and services. Depending on the specific decision involved, strategic policy in the cannabis field may be set by either order of government unilaterally, or may require co-decision. In either instance, however, governments are often well-advised to share information when it comes to strategic policymaking, so as to avoid conflict, duplication, or unintended consequences.

Operational policy breaks strategic policy-objective outcomes into narrower, shorter-term activities and outputs. These correspond with what Hall (1993) labels first-order policy considerations. Operational decisions are often focused around which specific program or service to employ to achieve the strategy. This could involve establishing new bodies, regulatory regimes, or initiatives, or repurposing existing ones. Because the issue reaches into so many areas of public health and public safety, a wide range of government actors – from federal to PT to municipal to Indigenous – are engaged in operational policymaking as it relates to cannabis legalization. This complexity, and the sheer multitude of operational concerns involved, makes it incumbent upon governments to cooperate to ensure smooth implementation of directional and strategic policy.

As Boyd indicates in chapter 1 of this volume, diffusion or alignment on one order of policy does not necessarily lead to diffusion on the other. As this chapter demonstrates, there has been a much higher degree of alignment at the directional level than at the strategic or operational levels of cannabis policy in Canada. The decision of provinces to carve their own paths on strategic and operational aspects of policy may be a conscious one, with governments deliberately diverging from their counterparts for a host of reasons. Yet misalignment may also be less deliberate or intentional. What drives governments inward in their policy development processes?

The following chapter relies on four principal explanations for why subnational governments choose to develop their existing policies, often through internal replication, rather than align them with those of other jurisdictions:

- *Ideological* considerations drive governments to ensure their policies correspond with their governing ethos. This approach may be at odds with others across the federation, resulting in policy misalignment.
- Notwithstanding Canada's historically truncated party system (Dyck 1998), *partisanship* played a role in governments' policymaking calculus. As they sought paths that benefitted their allies and punished their opponents in other jurisdictions, this contributed to a proliferation of policy frameworks across the country.
- Certain elements of a jurisdiction's *political culture* also influence its government to act in a more parochial fashion. In the case of cannabis, this included considerations as to the openness of society to relaxing restrictions on drugs, or expectations of the role of government in protecting its own autonomy to make policy decisions on behalf of provincial/territorial residents.
- *Economic and fiscal* circumstances also induced governments to go their own way. The capacity of a jurisdiction to support cannabis production industries, the nature of the domestic market, and the government's budgetary situation all influence this decision.

Methodology

This chapter employs a mixed-method design involving the analysis of government documents and elite interviews with key government officials. Each provincial and territorial cannabis policy framework was compared, along with those of the federal government and the Council of the Federation. These were analysed for similarities in rhetoric and policy instruments, and compared with each jurisdiction's alcohol and tobacco regulatory regimes. To better understand the cannabis-policy development process, the author invited public servants from each federal, provincial, and territorial government to participate in the study. A total of seven interviews were conducted with provincial-territorial officials in the spring of 2018, a complete list of which is found in the Appendix. Off-the-record interviews were conducted in the spring of 2019 with an additional seven respondents, which, combined with freedom of information requests, ensured that first-hand information was obtained from each jurisdiction. Respondents included justice, finance, and intergovernmental-relations officials from six provinces and territories, located in all regions of Canada; repeated requests for interviews with federal government officials were declined. Questions focused on how governments organized themselves to address the policy challenge, how they set policy priorities and objectives, and how they interacted with other governments in the process. An earlier draft of this chapter was shared with all interviewees for their feedback.

It is worth noting that many government agencies were unwilling to participate in formal interviews related to this study. Reasons provided ranged from interpretations of provincial law or internal communications policies that prohibit public servants from speaking publicly about their policy work. These concerns appeared heightened in the case under study, given elevated public attention focused on cannabis legalization.

Findings

In choosing to go their own ways, PT governments engaged in policy replication, adapting or converting existing policy frameworks in areas such as alcohol and tobacco regulation in order to encompass cannabis. They chose this path very early in the policy development process, abandoning attempts to establish a single, universal pan-Canadian policy framework. This is not to say there was no policy alignment. PT officials candidly admitted to copying and pasting large portions of each other's documents, such as public engagement surveys and legislative text, whether out of a desire to harmonize their approaches or to meet internal deadlines. This is important evidence of policy transfer, albeit of early plans as opposed to fully implemented programs and services. Moreover, many PTs ended up with broadly similar regulatory regimes for the distribution and sale of cannabis, combining private and public models. This operational policy alignment appears to be

Table 7.1. Levels of Cannabis Policy in Canada

Level of policy	Description	Primary jurisdiction	Degree of alignment
Directional	Signals a high-level, long-term commitment to address a particular problem or issue; focuses on outcomes and overarching objectives; found in campaign platforms, speeches from the throne, and legislation	Federal	Highly aligned
Strategic	Outlines mid-level, medium-term plans to achieve directional objectives, including priority-setting and resource allocation (e.g., timing, funding); focuses on outcomes and outputs; found in legislation and regulations, policy frameworks, and strategic planning documents	Federal Provincial Territorial	Contested
Operational	Details precisely how and by whom plans will be implemented in the short-term; focuses on inputs and throughputs; found in regulations, guidelines, by-laws, and other lower-level policy directives	Federal Provincial Territorial Municipal	Nonaligned

Note: This three-level model is based on one developed by Michael Calopietro for the Copenhagen School of Global Health: http://betterthesis.dk/research-methods/lesson -3-policy-research. It aligns well with similar hierarchical models of policy transfer developed by Bennett (1991), Dolowitz and Marsh (1996, 349–50), which emphasize the importance of aligning goals, resources, and instruments.

due more to isomorphism than other modes of policy alignment; PTs replicated their own internal alcohol and tobacco policy frameworks, which were generally similar to other governments' in the first place (Giesbrecht et al. 2006).

Yet the overall structure of cannabis policy in Canada features a high level of alignment among governments over the public health and public policy objectives set by the federal government, and less alignment in terms of strategic goals and operational policy instruments required to implement them.

Directional Policy Alignment

The federal government set directional policy for the entire country through its decision to legalize the production, distribution, possession, and consumption of cannabis. The catalyst for legalization emerged during the 2015 federal election, when the Liberal Party of Canada pledged to "legalize, regulate, and restrict access to marijuana" (Liberal Party of Canada 2015, 55). The pledge included a promise to "keep marijuana out of the hands of children and profits out of the hands of criminals," establishing the incoming government's dual commitment to preserving public health and public safety (55).

According to interviews, PT governments were not consulted in the development of this directional policy, despite the Liberal Party's campaign promise to strike a joint federal/provincial-territorial (FPT) task force on legalization. Federal jurisdiction over criminal law and the regulation of drugs meant the decision was Ottawa's to make, and they decided to exclude PTs from organizing the task force.

Nonetheless, provincial and territorial governments were drawn into lower-level policymaking by virtue of their responsibility for the administration of justice, and shared accountability for public health and public safety. As a result of their policymaking powers in these areas, PT governments' decisions will affect the means by, and extent to which, the directional policy is achieved across Canada.

Strategic Policy Contestation

The federal government's strategic policy approach was contested on two main points, both related to resources. The first concerned the rapid pace of legalization. After taking a year to establish its directional policy framework, the federal government provided its provincial-territorial partners with eighteen months to piece together the operational frameworks necessary to implement legalization across the country. PT officials reported that doing so would require dozens of legislative, regulatory, and policy changes (as many as seventy-six in one instance).

Some PT governments pushed back against the aggressive pace of reform, leaving the federal government to weigh its own priority for timelines against PT readiness. Without allowing sufficient time for PTs to establish enabling legislation and regulation, to train regulators, and to set up fully functioning government-owned enterprises and services, and so on, the federal government risks not achieving its own strategic and directional policy objectives. Provinces like Quebec and Manitoba railed against the federal government's target date. Citing the fact that federal legislation – the core of the new pan-Canadian legalization regime – had yet to be passed, as well as uncertainties around road safety enforcement, costs and funding, public education, and supply, these provinces urged the federal government to extend its deadline.[2]

Opposition members of the Senate reiterated many of these concerns, delaying the passage of the federal government's two pieces of legislation in the process. In the end, the federal government gave PT governments three months, following passage of the federal bills, to enact enabling legislation and regulations and prepare for the distribution, sale, possession, and consumption of cannabis in their jurisdictions. The legalization date for recreational (non-edible) cannabis was set for 17 October 2018.

Funding was a second major sticking point between the federal government and its provincial-territorial counterparts. Initially, the federal government proposed to grant provinces and territories half of the revenues collected within their jurisdiction from a new 10 per cent excise tax on cannabis sales. Within weeks, the federal government relented to PT pressure, reducing its own share of the tax revenue to 25 per cent and providing provinces and territories with greater resources to cover the anticipated increased costs of policing and health care. The revenue-sharing deal covered the first two years of legalization, at which point governments will reassess the balance between costs and government revenues (generated from a host of taxes and, in some cases, retail proceeds).

Operational Policy Replication

In an attempt to mitigate PT concerns over having sufficient resources, the federal government offered to provide a backstop for PTs whose distribution and retail systems were not in place at the time of legalization (or for those jurisdictions who may choose to forego establishing such systems on their own). The backstop would allow PTs to use the existing federal system of medical cannabis distribution and sales to provide access to recreational cannabis within their borders. No PT governments have taken up this offer, although some officials indicated that, in hindsight, a deeper consideration of the option might have resulted in adoption of the federal model (at least as an interim measure).

Fortunately for the federal government, few PTs appear intent on thwarting the directional policy objective behind legalization. Some PT governments established operational policies that ran counter to federal guidelines. Manitoba and Quebec intend to prohibit growing cannabis plants in private dwellings, despite the federal framework's allowance of up to four plants.[3] Yet, overall, little PT strategic or operational policy work is intentionally at cross-purposes with federal priorities.

According to PT officials, if they had issues with federal strategies or instruments, these were taken up on over a dozen federal, provincial, and territorial (FPT) committees, including those devoted to drug-impaired driving, a national cannabis tracking system, public education, internal trade, finance, public education, and others. PT officials indicated that their federal counterparts were receptive to addressing their concerns in these low-level fora, which helped to align strategic and operational policies with the federal government's overarching direction and across jurisdictions.

This said, the development of operational policy across Canada has resulted in considerable diversity – a patchwork of regulatory systems for the production, distribution, sale, possession, and consumption of cannabis not unlike those related to alcohol and tobacco use (see Table 7.2). This analogy is far from accidental; most PTs replicated their existing alcohol and tobacco regimes as models for their approach to cannabis. The Federal Task Force discussion paper and final report

Table 7.2. Provincial and Territorial Approaches to Select Operational Policy Areas, ca. September 2019

	Home production	Retail	Age of possession	Consumption (i.e., smoking)
BC	Yes, if out of public sight	Public plus[a]	19	Not in cars, child spaces, or where tobacco prohibited
AB	Yes, with landlord restrictions	Hybrid[b]	18	Not in cars, child spaces, or where tobacco prohibited
SK	Yes, with landlord restrictions	Private	19	Only in private spaces where minors are not present
MB	Not permitted	Private	19[d]	Only in private spaces
ON	Yes	Hybrid[b]	19	Only in private spaces, plus landlord restrictions
QC	Not permitted	Public	18[e]	Only where tobacco smoking permitted, except CEGEP and post-secondary campuses
NB	Yes	Public	19	Only in private spaces
NS	Yes	Public	19	Only where tobacco smoking permitted, plus landlord restrictions
PE	Yes, if not accessible to minors	Public	19	Only in private residences, with some exceptions for public spaces
NL	Yes	Hybrid[b]	19	Only in private spaces
YT	Yes, if out of public sight	Public	19	Only in private spaces, plus landlord restrictions
NT	Yes	Hybrid[b]	19	Only in private spaces, with some exceptions for public spaces
NU	Yes	Public[c]	19	Only where tobacco smoking permitted

[a] Private storefronts, public stores, and online.
[b] Private stores, public online.
[c] No storefronts, only public online.
[d] Does not align with age of provincial liquor possession (eighteen).
[e] The Quebec government has promised to increase the age to twenty-one.

supported this replication approach. While no interviewees reported being influenced by the federal government's recommendation in this area, the mention of alcohol and tobacco regimes as possible models helped frame the policy development process (Wesley 2019).

On the ongoing issue of distribution, for example, the PT Working Group Report noted that most jurisdictions were "considering the use of their already existing entities that are currently charged with distribution and oversight of liquor, or exploring ways to otherwise leverage existing structures and experience in order to establish a functioning distribution and regulatory system in advance of implementation given the limited timeframe" (Council of the Federation 2017, 15).

Similarly, in replicating their protectionist approach to liquor sales within their respective jurisdictions, PTs have elected to create a system of thirteen cannabis markets across the country (fourteen, if one counts the federal medical cannabis regime). This choice was foreshadowed during the negotiations of the new Canadian Free Trade Agreement (CFTA) in 2016. Entered into force in July 2017, Article 1206 of the CFTA creates an exclusion for non-medical cannabis, with jurisdictions committing to negotiating its potential inclusion under free-trade rules once legalization is established. In the meantime, however, each provincial and territorial government has the same level of control over its cannabis market as it does over liquor – within federal guidelines, it has full authority to determine what products are sold, by whom, and for how much. While critics view this as an affront to Canada's economic union, the constitutionality of this protectionist regime was reinforced by the Supreme Court's decision in the *Comeau* case in April 2018.[4]

If PTs largely replicated their respective liquor policies to deal with cannabis sales, distribution, and possession, they turned to their tobacco regimes to regulate the consumption (namely, smoking). As with home grow rules, PTs granted landlords varying degrees of control over smoking on their properties. And as with tobacco and liquor, many of the public consumption rules will be refined by municipalities and special districts through bylaws; many local councils and post-secondary institutions are taking steps to establish themselves as cannabis-free zones, for instance.

There were exceptions to this policy replication approach, although none of them appeared motivated by a desire to align policies with other jurisdictions. While most PTs applied nearly identical "open carry" rules for alcohol to cannabis, for instance, New Brunswick opted for a much stricter regime that requires residents to keep cannabis in locked containers or locked rooms in their homes. The government cited concerns over the safety of children in making this operational policy decision (Keefe 2017). Citing similar issues, Manitoba was the only government to create a different age of possession for cannabis (nineteen) compared to liquor (eighteen); once Quebec changes its rules, this will leave Alberta as the only jurisdiction with a minimum age standard of eighteen years for possession of both cannabis and alcohol.

Other governments appeared motivated by ideology when opting not to replicate existing policy frameworks for the regulation of cannabis. Contrary to its fully privatized system for liquor sales, Alberta decided to adopt a public-enterprise model for the online sale of cannabis, creating a hybrid system whereby the government will compete with private storefronts. This choice aligned with the pro-public sector ethos of the left-leaning New Democratic Party government. Governed by a right-leaning Progressive Conservative Party, Manitoba did the opposite, establishing a fully private approach to cannabis sales in contrast to its publicly operated retail system for liquor.

While highlighting significant agreement with the federal government's directional policy objectives, and disagreements with its strategic approaches to timing and funding, these findings reveal that PT governments chose policy replication over policy alignment, at the operational level. The result has produced a disjointed regime consisting of thirteen different provincial-territorial regulatory frameworks for the distribution, sale, possession, consumption, and taxation of cannabis.

Overall, the lack of policy alignment at the strategic and operational levels is likely to have detrimental effects on Canadian governments' individual and collective ability to successfully implement their directional policy objectives. Consider the issue of licensing. It is not inconceivable that a province or territory could scuttle the federal legalization project by failing to license enough distributors or retailers (whether deliberately or unintentionally). Setting different regulatory systems from province-to-province could produce similar externalities for neighbouring jurisdictions, placing strains on supply and demand. By the same token, provincial and territorial governments rely on the federal government to license enough producers to create sufficient supply and prevent consumers from turning to the illicit market for product (thus endangering public safety and public health, not to mention PT government revenues). As discussed, this type of policy misalignment has been limited in Canada, with governments in broad agreement over high-level policy objectives. The same is not true in the United States, for example, where federal and state governments often disagree over the merits, objectives, and processes involved in cannabis legalization (Bulman-Pozen 2014).

The question remains: Why did PT governments opt for this route, and what are the implications for achieving the public health and public safety objectives set out by the federal government and endorsed by premiers?

Explaining Replication over Alignment

It is worth reiterating that – while taking the federal government to task over resources, and securing additional time and tax revenue in the process – there was general agreement among all PT governments over the Government of Canada's ability to legalize cannabis (no one contested its constitutional authority). It is equally noteworthy that no provincial or territorial government objected to the directional policy objectives of legalization, namely to enhance public health and public safety. According to PT officials, political consensus had developed around the popular mandate granted to the federal government in the 2015 federal election to pursue legalization. Conversely, no provincial or territorial government was prioritizing cannabis reform at the time the federal government announced its plans to legalize cannabis. Major PT parties made no mention of the issue in their own campaign platforms, and governments made no mention of it in speeches from the throne. Perhaps out of this lack of interest or investment, or perhaps out of a desire to cede the potential political liabilities to the federal government, provincial governments decided to focus their attention on securing more resources to implement the federal government's directional policy objectives rather than contest them. This low level of salience, plus the limited amount of time available, may have convinced provincial-territorial policymakers to get on with the business of operational policy development.

Whatever their motivations, this was a conscious move on the part of provincial and territorial governments. Intergovernmental consensus is by no means guaranteed on issues like cannabis legalization, nor is it permanent. Consider the federal government's commitment to impose a price on carbon as a means of meeting its climate change objectives – another policy pledge made during the 2015 federal election campaign. The Government of Saskatchewan contested the federal government's constitutional authority to establish a national carbon tax; while initially in support, government changes in Ontario and Alberta have seen them join Saskatchewan's court challenge. And governments across the rest of the country have chosen a host of different policy instruments – from carbon taxes to cap-and-trade systems – to meet the federal government's directional policy objectives.

Similarly, under tight timelines, PTs decided to pursue their own operational policy routes with regard to minimum age, distribution and retail, youth possession, drug-impaired driving, public consumption, and research and training.[5] This is understandable. As Cairney (2012, 255) put it, "the more an importing [jurisdiction] feels compelled to act quickly, then the more bounded its decision-making process." Yet it is unclear whether more time could have helped them overcome a series of deep ideological, partisan, cultural, or economic differences that appeared to push them apart on operational policy.

Different governments were motivated by different considerations in choosing their own paths. Consider Quebec. Otherwise unpersuaded by the merits of legalization (former Premier Phillippe Couillard is a physician, and according to interviewees had been cautious about the public-health benefits and harms of cannabis smoking), and despite the province's long-standing political cultural tradition of defending provincial autonomy, Quebec nonetheless supported the implementation of the federal government's directional policy. Quebec did join Manitoba, however, in most vocally opposing the stringent timelines and in contesting the necessity of allowing home production within their jurisdiction.

Political culture did play a role in British Columbia's approach to retail. For decades, BC has been known as Canada's cradle of cannabis culture, with sizeable black and grey market industries operating openly to satisfy demand. Despite its ideological proclivity toward public management, BC's New Democratic Party government opted to keep private dispensaries open, and to allow people with previous convictions for cannabis-related offenses to play a role in the distribution and retail systems. BC notwithstanding, as discussed above in reference to public versus private retail models, the governing party's ideological bent appeared to have an impact on its decision to implement its own brand of operational policy instead of aligning with a pan-Canadian approach.

Partisan considerations also played a role, particularly in terms of a government's level of support for the federal government's plans. Throughout 2016 and 2017, all but four provincial governments were controlled by the same party as that in power in Ottawa. Half of those outliers (New Democratic governments in Alberta and British Columbia) were governed by ideological allies, at least on the cannabis issue. Opposition from the Progressive Conservative government in Manitoba could be understood through this partisan lens, as could the relative indifference of the right-leaning Saskatchewan Party government (who was last among provinces to release its cannabis policy framework).[6] Neither one of these provincial governments had a partisan incentive to faithfully or efficiently implement one of the federal Liberal government's signature policies. In fact, siding with Conservatives in the federal Senate, there may have been a partisan disincentive for Manitoba and Saskatchewan to act quickly; foot-dragging and court challenges would push full legalization closer to the fall 2019 federal election date, allowing the Liberals' opponents to attribute any problems with the launch to the federal government on the campaign trail. The establishment of conservative governments in Ontario, Alberta, and Quebec between 2018 and 2019 helped turn the tide of intergovernmental relations against the federal government. This sort of cross-jurisdictional partisan conflict has given rise to claims of "uncooperative federalism" in the United States (Bulman-Pozen and Gerken 2009). In the case of Canadian cannabis legalization, however, partisan differences among FPT governments have not devolved into outright obstructionism of federal directional policy goals, at least as of the time of writing.

It is likewise non-coincidental that, outside Quebec, the least vocal premiers in terms of opposing federal strategic policy were in Ontario, New Brunswick, Nova Scotia, Newfoundland and Labrador, and Prince Edward Island, where provincial Liberals formed government. From a political culture standpoint, these provinces were also most receptive to a stronger role for the federal government in pan-Canadian policymaking, particularly compared to their counterparts in Quebec, Saskatchewan, and Alberta. The harmonization of strategic and operational policies among Atlantic Premiers is also likely attributable to this partisan affinity, at least in part.

The latter group of provinces is also the most highly motivated in terms of building a regional economic development plan around the cannabis industry. A month after the pan-Canadian PT Working Group released its report, the Council of Atlantic Premiers announced their collective intention to pursue consistent pricing and common minimum age rules, and to ensure the cannabis industry aligns with their regional economic growth strategy (Laroche 2017). Economic and fiscal concerns figured prominently in debates over Nunavut's cannabis framework, although the government decided not to make use of the federal backstop for the distribution and sale of cannabis in the territory.

Thus, even with the benefit of time, it remains unclear whether PT governments would have put aside their ideological, partisan, cultural, and economic proclivities to forge a more aligned policy framework for cannabis legalization in Canada. These are foundational elements of the DNA of each jurisdiction and governing party, and building consensus on operational policy is difficult for this reason. Certainly, time constrains the ability of governments to engage in policy transfer. But they must be motivated to do so, and there is little evidence to suggest Canadian governments would have opted for a more integrated regime of cannabis legalization even with the benefit of more months or years to collaborate on one. Moreover, if carbon pricing is any indication, adding more time to the implementation calendar could have provided partisan opponents time to mobilize support against the strategic (and possibly directional) policy consensus that had developed in the two years following the Liberal government's election.

Conclusion

In legalizing cannabis, federal and provincial governments have undertaken one of the most complex and time-constrained national policymaking processes in Canadian history. The task is akin to setting up an entire system of alcohol production, sale, regulation, and taxation in less than two years. Yet there were only a handful of legal producers, questionable levels of supply, no agreed-upon safe consumption guidelines, no reliable tests for impairment, no international agreements in force, and no consensus on a host of other fundamental policy questions.

Rather than reaching out to align their policy with other jurisdictions at the strategic and operational level, PTs have primarily turned to familiar policy terrain. Through a process of internal policy replication they have converted existing regulatory frameworks for tobacco and alcohol to new ends.

The lack of diffusion is important, as smooth transition to the new legal framework will require extensive collaboration across sectors and jurisdictions. While the federal government could legislate changes to permit possession of small amounts for recreational use and make provisions to ensure the safety of the country's cannabis supply, provinces and territories would be required to establish new guidelines around the distribution, sale, and consumption of cannabis. Fortunately, most governments share common goals in this endeavour – namely the preservation, if not enhancement, of public health and public safety. The means through which they seek to achieve these ends has varied considerably, however.

Appendix: Interviews

The following is a list of confidential phone and in-person interviews performed for this chapter, arranged in chronological order. As many of the interviewees continue to work in the field, their names, precise positions, and jurisdictions have been withheld at their request and per the ethics protocol approved by the University of Alberta Research Ethics Board. Roles listed reflect those most pertinent to the research at hand. Dates of interview are included in year-month-day format.

A: Senior provincial government justice official from Western Canada (2018-02-23).

B: Provincial government justice official from Western Canada (2018-03-06).

C: Senior territorial government justice official from Northern Canada (2018-03-12).

D: Senior provincial government justice official from Western Canada (2018-03-12).

E: Senior territorial government finance official from Northern Canada (2018-03-27).

F: Senior provincial government justice official from Central Canada (2018-03-27).

G: Senior provincial government justice official from Atlantic Canada (2018-04-17).

NOTES

1 The present focus examines the level of policy alignment across Canadian jurisdictions and does not consider the prevalence or effects of policy contagions, learning, or adaptation from other countries. Lessons from several American states – particularly Washington, Colorado, and California – featured prominently in PT officials' policy research; nonetheless, many officials reported challenges in adapting these lessons from the American to Canadian context.

2 Two jurisdictions placed cannabis legalization on the policy backburner throughout the latter half of 2017, with outgoing premiers preferring to leave major decisions to their successors. Nunavut held a territorial election on 30 October, and incumbent Premier Peter Taptuna chose not to run. It took several months for the legislature to reconvene and weeks more for the consensus-based government system to elect a cabinet and new premier. On 10 August 2017, Saskatchewan Premier Brad Wall announced he would be stepping down. His Saskatchewan Party took five months to select his successor, Scott Moe, who assumed office in January 2018. In both instances, PT officials did as much background preparation as possible in anticipation of direction from their newly elected political leaders.

3 The issue is expected to be adjudicated in the courts.

4 *R v. Comeau* (2018).

5 Three areas of future PT collaboration were identified: "1. Continued Sharing of Information and Best Practices – through regular officials level discussions, jurisdictional scanning, and other mechanisms; 2. Aligning Approaches to Public Education and Awareness – which may include collaborative development of education materials and training resources, and considering alignment of research priorities and projects; and, 3. Interprovincial Movement of Cannabis – including seeking alignment of regulations and policies where feasible to avoid unintended trade barriers or complications" (Council of the Federation 2017, 7).

6 It is worth noting that the governing Saskatchewan Party was undertaking a leadership race from August 2017 to January 2018. All the same, sitting Premier Brad Wall chose not to advance a cannabis policy framework while his successor was being chosen.

WORKS CITED

Bennett, Colin J. 1991. "What Is Policy Convergence and What Causes It?" *British Journal of Political Science* 21 (2): 215–33. https://doi.org/10.1017/S0007123400006116.

Berry, Frances Stokes, and William D. Berry. 2018. "Innovation and Diffusion Models in Policy Research." In *Theories of the Policy Process*, edited by Christopher M. Weible and Paul A. Sabatier, 253–97. Boulder, CO: Westview Press.

Bulman-Pozen, Jessica. 2014. "Unbundling Federalism: Colorado's Legalization of Marijuana and Federalism's Many Forms." *University of Colorado Law Review* 85 (4): 1067–86.

Bulman-Pozen, Jessica, and Heather K. Gerken. 2009. "Uncooperative Federalism." *Yale Law Journal* 118 (7): 1256–311.

Cairney, Paul. 2012. *Understanding Public Policy: Theories and Issues*. New York: Palgrave Macmillan.

Calopietro, Michael. n.d. "Lesson 4: Policy Research." Better Thesis. Accessed 10 March 2020. http://betterthesis.dk/research-methods/lesson-3-policy-research.

Council of the Federation. 2017. *Report on Cannabis Legalization and Regulation*, edited by Working Group on Cannabis Legalization and Regulation. Ottawa: Council of the Federation Secretariat.

Dolowitz, David, and David Marsh. 1996. "Who Learns What from Whom: A Review of the Policy Transfer Literature." *Political Studies* 44 (2): 343–57. https://doi.org/10.1111/j.1467-9248.1996.tb00334.x.

Dyck, Rand. 1998. "Federalism and Canadian Political Parties." In *Challenges to Canadian Federalism*, edited by Martin Westmacott and Hugh Mellon, 55–62. Scarborough, ON: Prentice-Hall.

Evans, Mark, and Jonathan Davies. 1999. "Understanding Policy Transfer: A Multi-Level, Multi-Disciplinary Perspective." *Public Administration* 77 (2): 361–85.

Giesbrecht, Norman, Andree Demers, Alan Ogborne, Robin Room, Gina Stoduto, and Evert Anthony Lindquist, eds. 2006. *Sober Reflections: Commerce, Public Health, and the Evolution of Alcohol Policy in Canada, 1980–2000*. Montreal: McGill-Queen's University Press.

Hall, Peter. 1993. "Policy Paradigms, Social Learning, and the State: The Case of Economic Policymaking in Britain." *Comparative Politics* 25 (3): 275–96.

Keefe, Jeremy. 2017. "New Brunswick's Lock and Key Cannabis Legislation Receives Criticism." *Global News*, 8 November. https://globalnews.ca/news/3850851/lock-and -key-cannabis-legislation/.

Knill, Christoph. 2005. "Introduction: Cross-National Policy Convergence: Concepts, Approaches and Explanatory Factors." *Journal of European Public Policy* 12 (5): 764–74.

Laroche, Jean. 2017. "Atlantic Premiers Ponder Common Pot Price, Reach New Tax Deal with Feds." *CBC News*, 11 December. https://www.cbc.ca/news/canada/nova -scotia/pot-marijuana-cannabis-weed-premiers-politics-nova-scotia-new-brunswick -pei-1.4443346.

Liberal Party of Canada. 2015. *Real Change: A New Plan for a Strong Middle Class*. Ottawa: Liberal Party of Canada.

R v. Comeau. 2018. SCC 15.

Wesley, Jared J. 2019. "The Legalization of Recreational Cannabis." In *Assessing the Policy Performance of Justin Trudeau's Liberal Government 2015–2019*, edited by Lisa Birch and François Pétry, 137–48. Quebec City: Presses de l'Université Laval.

8

Conclusion: (Re)Theorizing Diffusion and Transfer in Canada's Federal System

ANDREA OLIVE AND BRENDAN BOYD

Where new policy goals and instrument ideas come from, and how they spread from one government to another, is an area of study that has puzzled and challenged policy scholars for decades. In Canada, anecdotal evidence, such as the story of Tommy Douglas and the country's health care system presented at the start of the book, and a handful of studies in various policy areas suggest that diffusion does occur and influence policymaking. But this topic has not received substantial academic study in the country, despite a well-developed body of research in the United States and at the international level. As a federal system, with thirteen subnational governments and a single federal government, Canada represents a useful case to study and learn more about diffusion and transfer dynamics.

This volume was created as a response to the lack of empirical case studies of diffusion and transfer in the Canadian provinces. All chapters explored the cross-jurisdictional movement of policies among governments in Canada's federal system. The cases were wide-ranging and included social, economic, and environmental policies. Three chapters included policy innovation in all thirteen provinces and territories: endangered species regulation, greenhouse gas emission policy in the aviation sector, and cannabis legislation. One chapter included all ten provincial parentage policies and two chapters focused on two provinces at a time – hydraulic fracturing regulations in Alberta and New Brunswick and sales tax in British Columbia and Ontario. Authors examined not just diffusion or the cross-jurisdictional spread of policies, but also policy transfer where knowledge in one political system is used to develop policy in another political system. The chapters that included multiple jurisdictions, namely the ten provinces, also allowed for consideration of policy convergence. Essentially, the six case studies presented new empirical research that allows scholars to (re)theorize policy diffusion and transfer in Canada. This volume will, hopefully, serve as a launching pad for more work in the field.

In chapter 1, Brendan Boyd posed four questions that will shape this concluding chapter: To what extent is policy diffusion occurring among jurisdictions in

Canada's federal system? What does it look like? How well does the literature explain diffusion in Canada? How can a better understanding of diffusion inform and contribute to policymaking in the country? Beyond these questions, the chapter will reflect on where future research is needed and where scholars should go from here.

Extent of Diffusion/Transfer and Convergence

In most of the chapters, diffusion and transfer of policy was extensive across subnational jurisdictions. In chapter 2, Dave Snow illustrated a gradual policy diffusion of parentage policy across Canadian provinces (his analysis did not include the territories). Moreover, these policies have diffused in a gradually more permissive direction. Quebec was the earlier innovator in 2002 when it became the first province to legislate a legal presumption of paternity to same-sex spouses. Manitoba, Ontario, Saskatchewan, and Prince Edward Island then followed suit. However, it was Alberta, Nova Scotia, and Newfoundland that led the way on surrogacy and parentage issues. Then two court cases in British Columbia led to new legislation in 2011 for paternity – legislation with the "fewest legal barriers for intended parents using assisted reproduction and surrogacy." After this, other provinces started to "loosen" their parentage policies. What the story of parentage policy in the provinces between 2002 and 2016 suggests is extensive diffusion. Only New Brunswick failed to amend or create policy. It also demonstrates that convergence was initiated following British Columbia's 2011 legislation. Since that time, policy has become more similar in the sense that it is more permissive.

In chapter 3, Heather Millar examined fracking policy in Alberta and New Brunswick. She demonstrated how New Brunswick incorporated Alberta's directives into its own regulatory framework and that Alberta looked to British Columbia's water management practices. In both cases, provincial policy – particularly knowledge – did transfer across provinces, even at large geographical range. Inspiration for policy amendments and innovation also came from American states. This came by way of "formal membership in US state organizations, regional forums, and informal networks." While the chapter focused on policy in only two provinces, it does demonstrate knowledge transfer between Canadian jurisdictions by showing how it affected decision-making.

Andrea Olive's cross-provincial and territorial analysis of endangered species legislation (ESL), in chapter 4, uncovered extensive policy diffusion across the country. Olive argues that policy developed at the federal level and within all subnational governments after the 1996 National Accord for the Protection of Species at Risk had been introduced. However, policy did not transfer evenly. The Western provinces, Yukon Territory, and Prince Edward Island lag behind other provinces and territories in terms of depth and scope in policy. Manitoba stands out as the only province to deviate and innovate on policy by including ecosystems as a unit for protection under its 2013 Endangered Species and Eco-systems Act (ESEA). Policy convergence also started to emerge after the federal government passed its legislation in 2002. Suffice it to say, diffusion of ESL is extensive in Canada and continues today with British Columbia's recent efforts to enact new legislation (2018) that is in line with Ontario and other Eastern provinces.

In chapter 5, Matthew Lesch uses the literature on decision-making to bol-ster our understanding of imitation processes. He suggests that internal politi-cal requirements could drive a bounded, rather than a rational, search for policy examples to copy. Lesch uses the example of the harmonized sales tax in British Columbia, which was influenced by the example of Ontario. The Liberal govern-ment in British Columbia did not adopt the policy from Ontario based on its technical merits, and it miscalculated the political opposition it would receive. This demonstrates the potential for suboptimal policy outcomes when the capac-ity for learning is limited and jurisdictions adopt policies based on expediency or visibility. The chapter provides the empirical means to distinguish between policy diffusion based on imitation and learning. This is an important contribution as the mechanisms are often confused and used interchangeably in diffusion and transfer studies (Stone 1999).

Laurel Besco, in chapter 6, examined Canada's subnational jurisdictions' avia-tion emission policies. She found evidence of extensive policy transfer. Specifically, there is "policy divergence over intraprovincial emissions, and almost unanimous policy convergence on how international and interjurisdictional emissions are addressed." And the convergence occurs in a geographical pattern with the West-ern provinces of British Columbia, Alberta, and Manitoba (prior to 2018), includ-ing intrajurisdictional emissions in their carbon pricing schemes.

Finally, Jared Wesley's cross-national study of cannabis legislation demon-strated policy diffusion, but only on limited aspects of policy. While the federal government's actions advanced the common goal of cannabis legalization across the country, Wesley found that provinces and territories "have primarily turned to familiar policy terrain" to meet this objective. Wesley asserted that "through a process of policy replication, they have converted existing regulatory frame-works for tobacco and alcohol to new ends." Provinces did not look to each other but did learn from, or perhaps imitate, their own policy in similar areas. Thus, cannabis is the only case where diffusion did not play a crucial role in policy decisions. This is an important counter-example where the conditions appeared favourable for collaboration and learning, yet policymakers opted to expand domestic policy regimes for tobacco and alcohol, which satisfied local ideological, partisan, and economic goals. The chapter serves as a reminder that just because there is an opportunity for collaboration, and information sharing is possible, this does not necessarily mean policies will diffuse and be adopted in multiple jurisdictions.

What Does Diffusion and Transfer Look Like?

While the empirical case studies illustrate policy diffusion among provinces and territories, what does that look like? How is diffusion occurring? As Boyd pointed out in the introduction, "similar policies in two or more jurisdictions does not necessarily mean that diffusion mechanisms are responsible." Thus, it is necessary to demonstrate an awareness of an external policy and that it played a role in the decision-making that led to policy adoption (Bennett 1991). In all chapters in this volume there was evidence of policy diffusion by way of competition, coercion, as well as policy transfer, through learning and emulation, and/or normative pressure. See Table 8.1 for a summary of diffusion in the empirical case studies presented in this volume.

In prior considerations of policy diffusion in Canada, economic competition was often determined or assumed to be a leading explanation of transfer (Atkinson et al. 2013; Galeotti, Salmon, and Wintrobe 2000; Harrison 2006). However, this was not borne out in Canadian case studies presented in this volume. While Olive and Besco cited competition as a possible explanation for policy diffusion, it was not the main motivation for policy innovation in a province. In the case of ESL, Olive showed that competition can also work against the diffusion of innovation, as provinces fear that enacting a new policy that increases costs for business or individuals could result in the loss of economic activity to other jurisdictions that have not yet adopted it. Moreover, diffusion of ESL across provinces was really a result of coercion from the federal government and other provinces.

In the introductory chapter, Boyd hypothesized that the presence of the federal government could mean that coercion was a common mechanism of diffusion. While coercion did not play a role in every case, it was salient in three cases: ESL, aviation, and cannabis. Wesley and Olive found coercion to be a source of diffusion at the level of policy objectives or goals in the cases of cannabis and ESL. But in neither case did it extend down to lower levels of policy as variation remained in the instruments and details. Besco found coercion was likely to have occurred in the area of interjurisdictional flights to ensure a coordinated national approach. Whether the federal government would extend this coercion to flights within a province remains to be seen. Finally, norms were only found to be a salient feature of parentage policy as court decisions and the examples of other provinces created pressure on governments to adopt new policies that went beyond what would meet basic legal requirements.

In the six case studies, policy transfer was also salient, as the exchange of information and ideas about a policy drove its diffusion. Besco, Millar, and Snow detected evidence of actual learning in the areas of aviation, hydraulic fracturing, and parentage policy. Besco suggested that provinces learned from each other on greenhouse gas (GHG) policy related to interjurisdictional flights, before the federal government adopted a national pricing scheme that could have potentially

Table 8.1. Case Studies and Diffusion Mechanisms

| | | Policy Transfer | | |
Competition	Coercion	Learning	Emulation	Norms
Endangered species legislation	Endangered species legislation	Fracking	Sales tax	Parentage
Aviation	Aviation	Aviation		
	Cannabis	Parentage		

led to a more coercive form of diffusion. Millar noted that, despite the potential for competition to drive provincial energy policy, New Brunswick learned from Alberta, which it viewed as a policy leader. Lesch observed that British Columbia emulated or mimicked Ontario's deal with the federal government on a harmonized sales tax but did not engage in learning that could have led it to anticipate the political backlash it would face. Finally, the evidence presented in this volume confirms Wallner's (2014) suggestion that horizontal policy transfer and vertical coercion are likely to be mutually exclusive, as both mechanisms occurred in only one instance: the case study of aviation policy.

Olive, Besco, and Wesley examined all fourteen subnational and national jurisdictions in Canada. They found some geographical patterns emerging – namely that Western provinces tend to have similar policies. This could be further evidence to support existing research about "the presence of regional and provincial political culture in Canada" (Lawlor and Lewis 2014, 605; see also Simeon and Elkins 1974; Wesley 2012). However, this regional pattern did not hold true in Snow's analysis of parentage policy (which excluded territories) where there was significant variation among British Columbia, Alberta, and Saskatchewan in terms of policy scope. Millar found that New Brunswick learned from Alberta because of its status as a leader on oil and gas regulation. Thus, while it is tempting to hypothesize regional or geographic diffusion and convergence in Canada, more work is needed to unpack the pattern. One question is whether technological changes that have increased information sharing and communication in the last forty years have disrupted regional patterns and allowed provinces to look anywhere within, or even outside, the country.

A Note on Methods

Examining what diffusion and transfer looks like across Canadian jurisdictions is also an opportunity to think more carefully about how we *measure* diffusion and transfer. As noted by Boyd in the introductory chapter, methodology in transfer studies is often determined by case study size. In American studies, the N can be as large as fifty – and sometimes larger when looking at policy in fifty states over long periods of time. With only fourteen national and subnational jurisdictions to examine in Canada, it is difficult to conduct large-N studies. In addition, large statistical studies of policy transfer are often criticized because they fail to explore the process of policy development and distinguish between different levels on which policy can diffuse (Gow 1992, 431; Howlett and Rayner 2008). The case studies in this volume confirmed the value of a qualitative approach in offering detailed examinations of diffusion mechanisms and the levels or components on which policy can change. Of course, there are some limitations. Several chapters relied exclusively on publicly available legislation and policy documents. This may provide only a partial picture, as much of the transfer of knowledge and learning is likely to occur behind the scenes among public servants, political staff, and technical experts. The reasons given publicly about why and how a policy was adopted could even be inaccurate, as policymakers seek to frame their choices in the best possible light. Thus, in several chapters, personal and sometimes confidential interviews were used to corroborate and expand on the documentary evidence. Other authors used multiple documentary sources in an attempt to triangulate and increase the reliability of findings.

Matching Theory to Canadian Experience

As noted by Boyd as well as other contributors in this volume, most diffusion and transfer literature focuses on American states or at the international level. Most theory, then, comes from case studies of a presidential system or from international relations literature. Do we need new theory to explain Canada – a federal parliamentary system with strong provinces that vary in population, wealth, and administrative capacity? How well does existing theory explain the Canadian experience of policy diffusion and transfer? As a start, all authors mentioned the common explanations of diffusion stemming from the American literature: competition, learning, emulation, coercion, and normative pressures. Without being instructed or guided to do so, every author in this volume applied or borrowed aspects of this framework. But there is good reason to suspect that, within this framework, differences between federal systems in Canada and those of the United States affected which mechanisms appeared most frequently.

In the introduction, Boyd considered different aspects of the Canadian system and hypothesized that coercion could be a common mechanism within federal systems where a centralized government can cause diffusion by setting benchmarks, providing incentives, or otherwise compelling policy adoption in the provinces. Overall, there was some, but not overwhelming, evidence of coercion as it was identified as salient in half of the cases. But it was mentioned in more cases than any other mechanism, tied with learning. The presence of coercion will depend greatly on the specific legal and political realities of individual policy areas, and this book covers only six. While not identified as the most important mechanism, the chapters by Wesley, Besco, and Olive also suggested that the federal government plays a role in provincial diffusion through normative pressures, as once a national benchmark is set, provinces often do not want to be viewed as laggards. This confirms Wallner's (2014, 106) suggestion "that diffusion processes are not always easily isolated, and that more than one process can be at work at any given time." Further case studies and empirical work is required to reach more definitive conclusions in this area.

Another hypothesis outlined in the introductory chapter is that learning might occur frequently in the exclusive and tightly knit networks of intergovernmental officials created by Canada's tradition of executive federalism, where there is less input and competition from domestic interests. Again, there is some, but not overwhelming, evidence of learning as a mechanism of diffusion. The mechanism was found to play a role in half of the case studies, more than any other mechanism apart from coercion. As mentioned above, it is more difficult to access information about the learning that goes on among public servants in provincial bureaucracies or by experts outside of government, operating across provinces. Thus, it is possible this mechanism could be present to a greater extent than was shown in these case studies. The addition of case studies in policy areas that differ from the six covered in this book will provide more evidence to further confirm or cast doubt on this hypothesis. In terms of methods, elite interviews and surveys of provincial policy officials would help uncover information about the role of learning that occurs outside the political realm by non-partisan actors.

The case studies in this book point to a few potential pathways to compare diffusion in the Canadian and American federal systems. Millar distinguished between technical learning (is it a good policy?) and political learning (is the policy feasible in a given political climate/context?). This could provide a useful way to examine the diffusion and transfer in interjurisdictional forums in Canada and the United States. Is it likely that technical learning is more common in Canada's tradition of executive federalism, while political learning is more frequent in the American system where, as Karch (2007) notes, interest groups play an important role in the diffusion process? Snow identified the courts as an important contributor to diffusion. Does this look different in Canada and the United States given the different structure and role the courts play in policymaking in each country? These are, of course, just two of many possible ways that diffusion may be different in Canada's federal system compared to that in the United States, leaving room for a fruitful avenue of new research.

Lastly, the concept of policy convergence is undertheorized and largely unexamined in this volume; however, Besco and Olive did offer some insights based on the Canadian experience. Both of their chapters demonstrated that convergence is occurring, at least regionally, over time. This is a result of competition to some extent, but more a result of coercion by the federal government. In the case of ESL and aviation policy, the federal government is a key player. But the extent to which we should expect convergence of policy among Canadian provinces and territories in the presence or absence of federal leadership is unclear. Convergence is a temporal process and not a simple snapshot in time. Aviation policy for greenhouse gas emissions is a relatively new policy area and is very much in flux today. ESL policy has a longer time frame, with the National Accord already twenty years old, but it remains a policy area under considerable change, especially in an era of increased international attention. Given how different the provinces and territories are in terms of resources (population, civil service, GDP), we might not expect total policy convergence in any given area. More research is needed in this area to generate theory and empirical evidence for convergence and divergence in Canada's federal system.

Opportunities to Impact Policymaking

Perhaps the most important insight is that, despite the prominence it is given in the academic literature, policymakers do not solely respond to competition. Only in the cases of ESL and emissions in the aviation sector did competition play a role, and, in both cases, it was not the only diffusion mechanism. One explanation is that arguments about competitiveness pressures are often overdrawn, as the costs of policies and regulations are relatively low compared to other input costs and of moving to another province (Olewiler 2006). Of course, policymakers may make decisions based on the perception or threat of losses in economic activity, but our research suggests they also respond to domestic pressures to address challenges and adopt innovative policies, which opens the door to diffusion mechanisms like learning, emulation, coercion, and normative pressures.

The opportunity to learn does not necessarily lead to better policy development. A tacit assumption underlying diffusion studies is that learning from each other leads to better policy. But, as Boyd mentions in chapter 1, this is not a simple or easy process, and there is the potential for failed transfer if there is not enough information about the policy itself and the differences and similarities of the contexts in which it would operate (Mossberger and Wolman 2003). Another way to phrase this is, the chances of a transferred policy being effective and appropriate will be higher if diffusion occurs through learning rather than imitation. Lesch provides a roadmap for moving from emulation to learning by suggesting policymakers ensure proper time and resources to conduct a comprehensive study of a new policy and understand its context, including engaging with relevant experts. Millar's chapter reminds policymakers that even when a policy is transferred with little learning about its effectiveness or appropriateness, the adopters may admire the policy because of the political benefits it created elsewhere. Thus, what may appear like emulation, with little learning about the technical aspects of the policy, may be a case of political learning.

In attempting to satisfy Mossberger and Wolman's two requirements, policy-makers may face a decision about whether they will look to jurisdictions with similar contexts, whether it is in regional, institutional, ideological, or political terms, or whether they will examine jurisdictions with policies that are considered leaders. The notion of best-practice research and evidence-based policy suggests that jurisdictions should look to policy leaders, who have the most innovative and effective policy solution. But our evidence highlights the importance of consider-ing whether a jurisdiction has similar contexts, or how a policy template could be adapted in new circumstances, as this could increase the chances that a success-ful policy will reproduce its effects in a new jurisdiction (Dolowitz and Marsh 2000). Lesch and Millar's chapters confirmed that context matters. In both their analyses, where jurisdictions looked to leaders, they found a lack of learning about the political aspects of policy that contributed to public opposition. Policymak-ers seem to be more likely to miss or overlook political lessons when focused on finding leading jurisdictions. In particular, Millar's work showed that institutional context matters. Indeed, there is "value in considering the influence of adminis-trative features such as the division of responsibility across departments, ad-hoc working groups, public consultations, and independent agencies on processes of policy transfer."

Canada's tradition of executive federalism and intergovernmental relations likely creates a tendency to look to the executive branch of government as the primary forum for policy diffusion. Policymakers should be aware that there are multiple institutional venues across governments that can contribute to policy diffusion. Snow's contribution to this volume suggests the courts will engage in policy dif-fusion as judges are aware of and learn from the rulings of their colleagues across the country. Even if diffusion is largely driven by decisions at the executive level, other institutional venues can play a role by creating opportunities or constraints for policy diffusion. In British Columbia, Alberta, and Ontario a judicial decision contributed to parentage policy change, and in all cases the province ultimately overhauled its entire parentage policy based on normative pressures, borrowing ideas and models from each other (Snow, chapter 2 of this volume). It is also important to be aware of the work done in legislatures, through their committees and agents, as they may also contribute to the sharing of policy knowledge. The composition of the legislative branch, as well, may also play a role in the likelihood that a policy from another jurisdiction would be adopted at home. The interac-tion and relative influence between different institutional venues will vary by case. However, the key lessons for policymakers is that there are different places they can look for policy models or inspiration within a jurisdiction, and that it is important to be aware of the opportunities and constraints that one's own institutional con-text plays in successfully bringing the policy home.

Future Studies

The authors who contributed to this volume presented six rich empirical cases across economic, social, and environmental policy realms. Hopefully, this is just the beginning, providing a foundation on which further work on diffusion and transfer in Canada's federal system can build.

More theoretical (and empirical) work is needed on the role of other actors, especially the federal government, interest groups, and the courts in provincial diffusion and transfer. Authors in this volume produced evidence that the federal government and the courts act to coerce and normatively pressure provinces. In Gow's 1992 study of fifteen administrative innovations in Canadian provinces, he found that in seven cases the federal government was the innovator. This is to say, the policy originated at the federal level and then other provinces, often Ontario was second, adopted a version of that original federal policy. The chapters in this volume revealed a similar pattern. In the case of endangered species legislation, aviation policy, and cannabis regulation, the federal government set the policy agenda. But a lot remains unknown about vertical diffusion in Canada. More work – theoretical and empirical – is required.

We need more studies that examine cases without federal leadership and cases with federal leadership to see how diffusion occurs when Ottawa plays an important role. As well, in the introduction, Boyd described a case wherein a single province created a national health care system. How common is that in Canada? It is common to hear that American states are "policy laboratories" but how often is that true for Canadian provinces? Addressing this question requires studies of policy areas that have been around since the middle of the twentieth century or longer, such as health, education, or social services. Vertical diffusion and transfer could also include municipal (including regional municipalities), provincial, and federal transfer of policy. We could also ask, How often does a single city create a provincial policy? We know that provinces grant municipal governments the authority to create legislation and regulations in areas pertaining to their communities (Nykiforuk, Eyles, and Campbell 2008). While provinces often set standards, municipal governments can then create policy to extend or exceed those standards. In their study of local tobacco policy, Nykiforuk, Eyles, and Campbell (2008) do find evidence of geographical diffusion in Alberta, from large cities to small cities. However, Gore (2010) argues that cities' influence on national climate change policy is weak and that such governments are not central players, despite their policy innovations, when it comes to vertical diffusion.

The role of other actors, such as interest groups, is under-theorized in transfer scholarship. As Yu, Jennings, and Butler (2018, 2) point out, "interest groups can change legislator's incentives to learn by making political contributions or providing policy-relevant information." Indeed, their study shows that Mothers Against Drunk Drivers, a large lobby group across the United States, successfully lobbied for more stringent DUI (driving under the influence) regulations. This is not surprising since interest groups are expected to provide knowledge (technical learning) to governments and shape public opinion. However, drawing from American studies is not necessarily going to be productive here because interest groups have a different relationship to politics and policy in Canada. While interest groups in Canada do provide technical information to politicians and policymakers, a parliamentary system (especially one with a strong party whip) requires that parties vote as blocks. This provides fewer avenues for lobbying efforts. An interest group needs to lobby an entire political party, as opposed to powerful individual House Representatives or Senators. There are no recent studies of influential interest groups in a Canadian context.

One approach that could allow for the study of multiple actors, such as interest groups, policy entrepreneurs, and politicians, is network scholarship. Networks are "collaborative, non-hierarchical, flexible, and potentially inclusive insofar as they connect participants who otherwise may not interact" (Gore 2010, 35; see also Leitner and Sheppard 2002). At the provincial level, we know that a multitude of informal networks exist where politicians and civil servants across the country would have opportunities to interact and, potentially, learn from each other. What role do these informal networks play? If politicians and policymakers learn – and our authors suggest they do – where are they learning? Who are they spending time with? Nykiforuk, Eyles, and Campbell (2008, 6) point out that "communication between players and opinion leaders within a network drives the diffusion process and influences the rate of adoption." Wallner (2014) goes further to suggest that, in education policy, networks facilitated cooperation and collective action. In this volume, Millar suggests that informal networks are important for both technical and political learning, but none of the authors in this volume examine informal network relationships.

On the more formal side, we know that provinces often meet amongst themselves at premiers' meetings and conferences. Wallner (2014) points to several formal institutions in education policy that facilitate common policy frameworks. But, as Lesch (chapter 5 of this volume) reminded us, "Canada has largely avoided establishing robust intergovernmental institutions that could facilitate collaboration, and there are few formal opportunities for provinces to learn about policy innovations elsewhere in the federation." Why does Canada have few formal networks? Are the ones that exist, such as premiers' meetings, opportunities for policy transfer? Again, no authors in this volume examine formal network relationships. This is an important and under-studied avenue of research for Canadian policy transfer scholars.

Finally, what is less examined in the scholarship writ large, as well as by authors in this volume, is the extent to which Canadian provinces and territories are influenced by the United States and, potentially, European jurisdictions. Often Canadian diffusion studies make mention of the American influence on Canada.

Hoberg (1991) famously suggested that Canada is sleeping with an elephant when it comes to environmental policymaking and its relationship with the United States, and there is plenty of literature to suggest that the US federal government and individual states have influence on Canadian climate, energy, and wildlife policy (Illical and Harrison 2007; Olive 2014; Boyd 2019; Boychuk and VanNijnatten 2004). In his study of administrative innovations, Gow (1992, 448) found "by far the greatest number of outside ideas came from the United States." White and Prentice (2016) found provinces "relied on evidence from small-scale longitudinal studies from the USA" when contemplating full-day kindergarten policy. In her chapter on fracking in this volume, Millar argued that the United States can also be an inspiration for policy, and she presents some empirical evidence for learning from American states. Does the Canadian tendency to look south for inspiration inhibit transfer and diffusion among provinces? In the example of vehicle GHG emissions standards, British Columbia and Quebec worked with California and others to simultaneously place pressure on their federal governments to adopt common national standards. How often do like-minded states and provinces work together to push for or facilitate parallel vertical diffusion? There is also evidence that Quebec has looked to the EU on issues like climate change (Boyd 2017). Does the province's unique status in the Canadian federation lead to distinct diffusion patterns and different transfer tendencies when compared to the other Canadian provinces and territories? These are areas in need of rich theoretical and empirical work.

Final Thoughts

The purpose of this book is to increase knowledge about policy diffusion and transfer and contribute to the understanding of policymaking and interjurisdictional dynamics in the Canadian federation. It represents a starting point much more than a final word on the topic. The six empirical chapters provided here highlight the fact that, indeed, policy diffusion is occurring and many different mechanisms of diffusion and transfer are present. However, there is ample opportunity for more empirical work in different policy areas during different periods of time, including different constellations of governmental and non-governmental actors and using different methodologies to gather and assess evidence. We found that, while insights from the literature on American states and at the international level are useful, more conceptual and theoretical work is needed on diffusion and transfer in a Canadian setting.

Finally, we assert that, regardless of debates about the effectiveness or appropriateness of any particular policy, a better understanding of policy transfer and learning will contribute to the practice of policymaking as well. This volume begins to identify lessons and insights that might be useful to practitioners, but we encourage future scholars in this area to also consider how their work might be relevant to those people who are looking beyond their provincial borders, in an effort to develop effective and politically acceptable solutions to the current challenges that Canadian governments face.

WORKS CITED

Atkinson, Michael M., Daniel Béland, Gregory P. Marchildon, Kathleen McNutt, Peter W.B. Phillips, and Ken Rasmussen. 2013. *Governance and Public Policy in Canada: A View from the Provinces*. Toronto: University of Toronto Press.

Bennett, Colin J. 1991. "What Is Policy Convergence and What Causes It?" *British Journal of Political Science* 21: 215–33. https://www.jstor.org/stable/193876.

Boychuk, Gerald W., and Debora L. VanNijnatten. 2004. "Economic Integration and Cross-Border Policy Convergence." *Horizons* 7 (1): 55–60.

Boyd, Brendan. 2017. "Working Together on Climate Change: Policy Transfer and Convergence in Four Canadian Provinces." *Publius: Journal of Federalism* 47 (4): 546–71.

– 2019. "A Province Under Pressure: Alberta Climate Change Policy and the Influence of the United States." *Canadian Journal of Political Science* 52 (1): 183–99.

Dolowitz, David P., and David Marsh. 2000. "Learning from Abroad: The Role of Policy Transfer in Contemporary Policy-Making." *Governance* 13 (1): 5–23. http://doi.wiley.com/10.1111/0952-1895.00121.

Galeotti, Gianluigi, Pierre Salmon, and Ronald Wintrobe. 2000. *Competition and Structure: The Political Economy of Collective Decisions: Essays in Honor of Albert Breton*. Cambridge: Cambridge University Press.

Gore, Christopher D. 2010. "The Limits of Opportunities of Networks: Municipalities and Canadian Climate Change Policy." *Review of Policy Research* 27 (1): 27–46.

Gow, James Iain. 1992. "Diffusion of Administrative Innovations in Canadian Public Administrations." *Administration & Society* 23 (4): 430–54.

Harrison, Kathryn. 2006. *Racing to the Bottom? Provincial Interdependence in the Canadian Federation*. Vancouver: UBC Press.

Hoberg, George. 1991. "Sleeping with an Elephant: The American Influence on Canadian Environmental Regulation." *Journal of Public Policy* 11 (1): 107–31.

Howlett, Michael, and Jeremy Rayner. 2008. "Third Generation Policy Diffusion Studies and the Analysis of Policy Mixes: Two Steps Forward and One Step Back?" *Journal of Comparative Policy Analysis: Research and Practice* 10 (4): 385–402. https://doi.org/10.1080/13876980802468816.

Illical, Mary, and Kathryn Harrison. 2007. "Protecting Endangered Species in the US and Canada: The Role of Negative Lesson Drawing." *Canadian Journal of Political Science* 40 (2): 367–94.

Karch, Andrew. 2007. *Democratic Laboratories: Policy Diffusion among the American States*. Ann Arbor: University of Michigan Press.

Lawlor, Andrea, and J.P. Lewis. 2014. "Evolving Structure of Governments: Portfolio Adoption across the Canadian Provinces from 1867–2012." *Canadian Public Administration* 57 (4): 589–608. http://doi.wiley.com/10.1111/capa.12088.

Leitner, Helga, and Eric Sheppard. 2002. "'The City Is Dead, Long Live the Net': Harnessing European Interurban Networks for a Neoliberal Agenda." *Antipode* 34 (3): 495–518.

Mossberger, Karen, and Harold Wolman. 2003. "Policy Transfer as a Form of Prospective Policy Evaluation: Challenges and Recommendations." *Public Administration Review* 63 (4): 428–40.

Nykiforuk, Candace I. J., John Eyles, and H. Sharon Campbell. 2008. "Smoke-Free Spaces over Time: A Policy Diffusion Study of Bylaw Development in Alberta and Ontario, Canada." *Health & Social Care in the Community* 16 (1): 64–74. http://www .ncbi.nlm.nih.gov/pubmed/18181816.

Olewiler, Nancy. 2006. "Environmental Policy in Canada: Harmonized at the bottom?" In *Racing to the Bottom: Provincial Interdependence in the Canadian Federation*, edited by Kathryn Harrison, 113–56. Vancouver: UBC Press.

Olive, Andrea. 2014. *Land, Stewardship, and Legitimacy: Endangered Species Policy in Canada and the United States.* Toronto: University of Toronto Press.

Simeon, Richard, and David Elkins. 1974. "Regional Political Cultures in Canada." *Canadian Journal of Political Science* 7 (3): 397–437.

Stone, Diane. 1999. "Learning Lessons and Transferring Policy across Time, Space and Disciplines." *Politics* 19 (1): 51–9.

Wallner, Jennifer. 2014. *Learning to School: Federalism and Public Schooling in Canada.* Toronto: University of Toronto Press.

Wesley, Jared. 2012. *Code Politics: Campaign and Cultures on the Canadian Prairies.* Vancouver: UBC Press.

White, Linda, and Susan Prentice. 2016. "Early Childhood Education and Care Reform in Canadian Provinces: Understanding the Role of Experts and Evidence in Policy Change." *Canadian Public Administration* 59 (1): 26–44. http://doi.wiley.com/10.1111 /capa.12156.

Yu, Jinhai, Edward Jennings, and J.S. Butler. 2018. "Lobbying, Learning and Policy Reinvention: An Examination of the American States' Drunk Driving Laws." *Journal of Public Policy* 40 (2): 259–79. https://doi.org/10.1017/S0143814X18000363.

Contributors

Laurel Besco is an assistant professor in the Department of Geography, Geomatics and Environment and the Institute for Management and Innovation at the University of Toronto Mississauga. Her area of expertise is environmental law and policy, specifically focusing on policy tools and regulatory instruments, aviation and climate change, and corporate sustainability.

Brendan Boyd is an assistant professor in the Department of Anthropology, Economics and Political Science at MacEwan University. His areas of expertise include public policy, the role of public servants, Canadian federalism, and climate policy. His research has been published in *Publius: The Journal of Federalism*, *Canadian Journal of Political Science*, and *Canadian Public Administration*.

Matthew Lesch is a postdoctoral research fellow in the Department of Health Sciences at the University of York. His research explores how cognitive and institutional factors influence the uptake and spread of evidence-based policy solutions. His research has been published in *Addiction*, *American Journal of Public Health*, *Policy Sciences*, and *Regional & Federal Studies*.

Heather Millar is an assistant professor in the Department of Political Science at the University of New Brunswick. Her research examines Canadian provincial energy and climate politics; policy learning and policy change; and social acceptance of new technologies. She has published research articles in *Review of Policy Research*, *Environmental Politics*, *Policy Sciences*, *Public Policy and Administration*, *Canadian Public Administration*, and the *Canadian Journal of Political Science*.

Andrea Olive is an associate professor in the Department of Political Science and the Department of Geography, Geomatics and Environment at the University of Toronto Mississauga. Her area of expertise is environmental policy, especially wildlife and species at risk conservation. She is the author of *Land, Stewardship,* *and Legitimacy* as well as *The Canadian Environmental in Political Context*. Her current research examines the transformative politics of the wild in Canada.

Dave Snow is an associate professor in the Department of Political Science at the University of Guelph. He is the author of *Assisted Reproduction Policy in Canada: Framing, Federalism, and Failure*, and the co-author (with F.L. Morton) of *Law, Politics, and the Judicial Process in Canada* (4th edition). His current research examines the governance of naturopathic medicine in the Canadian provinces.

Jared J. Wesley is an associate professor in the Department of Political Science at the University of Alberta. He studies the politics of bureaucracy and the bureaucracy of politics. He is co-author of *Inside Canadian Politics* and *The Public Servant's Guide to Government in Canada*.

Index

132–3; fuel tax, 116, 120, 121, 128, 129; geographical convergence, 126, 127–9, 131, 132; and learning, 124, 126, 128–9; northern territories, 129, 131; patterns of convergence/divergence, 123–4, 126–33; and political partisanship, 124, 126, 130, 133; provincial/territorial overview, *122*

aviation industry: background history, 119–21; deregulation and privatization, 120; fuel tax, 116, 120, 121, 128, 132; regulatory authority, 116, 119–20, 130–1, 133. *See also* aviation emission policies

Bakken shale (Saskatchewan), 53
Barisoff, Bill (MLA British Columbia), 83
Baumgartner, Frank R., 70, 97
benchmarks, federal: general, 9, 10, *13*, 127, 159; *Pan-Canadian Framework on Clean Growth and Climate Change*, 3, 10
Bennett, Colin J., 11, 118, 142
Benoit, William L., 110n13
Berry, Francis Stokes, 32, 34, 43
Berry, William D., 32, 34, 43
best-practice research, 162
Bill C-65 (ESL federal), 74, 75, 86
Bocking, Stephen, 74
"bottom-up" approaches, 19, 22
bounded emulation: vs bounded learning, 12, 97, 98, 108, 109; cognitive biases, 96, 108, 109; vs competition, 109; definition of, 18, 24, 94; vs rational learning, 98–9, 104, 107–9
bounded (limited) rationality, 93–4, 95, 96, 108, 156
Boushey, Graeme T., 8
Brandeis, Justice Louis, 26n1
British Columbia: cannabis policy, 145, 148–9; carbon pricing and aviation emissions, 122, 124, 126, 127–9; endangered species legislation, *77–9*, 80, 83, 85, 86, 88; "fracking" regulations, 59;

hydraulic fracturing development, 53; parentage policy, 40–1, 42, 43, 44, 45. *See also* British Columbia sales tax reform
British Columbia Family Law Act, 40, 41
British Columbia Ministry of Finance, 102, 103
British Columbia Ministry of Revenue, 102
British Columbia sales tax reform: background, 95, 99–101; vs carbon tax, 103, 108, 109; decision-making, 107–9; economic context, 101–2, 103–4; and federal compensation, 102, 104, 106–7; influence of Ontario, 95, 102–3; political consequences, 105, 108–9; problem-definition, 104, 105, 107, 108; public opposition, 104, 105, 106. *See also* bounded emulation
British Columbia Wildlife Act, 77, 80, 83
Brown, Doug, 92
Butler, J.S., 163

Cairney, Paul, 148
Calgary (airport), 128
California, 124–5, 127, 128, 151n1, 165
Calopietro, Michael, 142
Campbell, Gordon, 100, 103–4, 105, 108
Campbell, H. Sharon, 163, 164
Canada Health Act, 10
Canada Health Transfer, 7, 10
Canada Revenue Agency, 110n8, 111n19
Canada Social Transfer, 7
Canada's federal system: decentralization, 5, 6–7, 20–2, 32; executive federalism, 17–18, 160, 162; provincial jurisdiction, 5; provincial/territorial differences, 5–6; public sector overview, *6*
Canadian Charter of Rights and Freedoms, 33, 36, 37; Charter challenges, LGBTQ, 37, 38, 41, 45
Canadian Endangered Species Conservation Council, 72

endangered species legislation (ESL): Bill
C-65, 74, 75, 86; Crown lands, 72,
84; definition of, 69, 88n2; ecosystem
legislation, 73, 84, 86–7, 89n7, 156;
environmentalism, 71–4; "geographical
convergence," 88; on habitat
protection, 72–3, 74, 80–6, 87, 88; vs
hunting and fishing regulations, 74,
76, 77; industry exemptions, Ontario,
89n6; innovation, 81–7; language,
significance of, 75, 76–7; learning
(sources), *79, 80*; provincial overview,
16–17, 76–9. *See also* National Accord
for the Protection of Species at Risk;
SARA (Species at Risk Act)
Energy Institute (New Brunswick), 54,
61, 62n11
Environmental Impact Assessment (EIA),
New Brunswick, 55
Environmental Protection and Biodiversity
Conservation Act (Australia), 89n7
Environmental Resources Conservation
Board (ERCB), Alberta, 56, 57, 58, 59
environmentalism, 71–4. *See also*
endangered species legislation; wildlife
conservation
equality rights. *See* LGBTQ rights
Equalization: federal program, 7
European Union (EU), 22, 132, 165
Evans, Mark, 15
evidence-based policy, 162
executive federalism, 17–18, 160, 162
externalities, 70, 147
Eyles, John, 163, 164

family law. *See individual acts*
federal backstop levy: cannabis policy,
144, 150; carbon pricing schemes,
122–3, 124–6, 129, 130–1, 132–3;
provincial models, 3. *See also* aviation
emission policies
Federal Task Force (cannabis), 144

"Fight HST" (campaign), 105
First World War, 119
first-order change/settings, 15, 16–17, 45,
75, 117, 140
Flaherty, Jim, 110n8
Forest and Range Practices Act (British
Columbia), 83
Foucault, Martial, 128
Fox, Josh, 59
Fox Creek (Alberta), 57, 60
Fracfocus.ca (registry), 58, 59. *See also*
chemical disclosure
"fracking." *See* hydraulic fracturing
Fraess v. Alberta, 40, 43

Garrett, Geoffrey, 34, 97
Gasland (film), 59
gender-neutral and trans-inclusive
language, 35, 38–9, 42, 43, 45
Glick, Henry R., 71
goods and services tax (GST), 99–100
Gore, Christopher D., 163
Government of Canada: constitutional
authority, 147, 148
Government of Newfoundland and
Labrador, 82
Government of Saskatchewan, 148
Gow, James Iain, 163, 165
"green shift" (federal), 117
greenhouse gas (GHG) emissions, 15,
19, 116–17, 157, 165. *See also* aviation
emission policies; carbon pricing;
carbon tax
groundwater safety, 53, 55, 58, 59. *See also*
chemical disclosure

Hall, Peter, 11; orders of change framework/
typology of policy change, 15, 16, 45,
75, 95, 117, 139–40. *See also individual
orders*
Hansard, 121, 127
Hanson, Colin, 103, 104